# The Currency of Justice

D0238007

Fines and monetary damages account for the majority of legal sanctions across the whole spectrum of legal governance. Money is, in key respects, the primary tool law has to achieve compliance. Yet, money has largely been ignored by social analyses of law, and especially by criminology.

*The Currency of Justice* examines the differing rationalities, aims and assumptions built into money's deployment in diverse legal fields and sanctions. This raises major questions about the extent to which money appears as an abstract universal or whether it takes on more particular meanings when deployed in various areas of law. Indeed, money may be unique in that it can take on the meanings of punishment, compensation, denunciation or regulation.

*The Currency of Justice* examines the implications of the 'monetization of justice' as life is increasingly regulated through this single medium. Money not only links diverse domains of law, but also links legal sanctions to other monetary techniques which govern everyday life. Like prices or fees, the concern with monetary sanctions is not who pays, but that money is paid. Money is perhaps the only form of legal sanction where the burden need not be borne by the wrongdoer. In this respect, this book explores the view that contemporary governance is less concerned with disciplining individuals and more concerned with regulating distributions and flows of behaviours and the harms and costs linked with these.

**Pat O'Malley** is University Professorial Research Fellow in the Faculty of Law at the University of Sydney.

# The Currency of Justice

## Fines and damages
## in consumer societies

## Pat O'Malley

Routledge·Cavendish
Taylor & Francis Group

a GlassHouse book

First published 2009
by Routledge-Cavendish
2 Park Square, Milton Park, Abingdon, Oxon, OX14 4RN

Simultaneously published in the USA and Canada
by Routledge-Cavendish
270 Madison Avenue, New York, NY 10016

A GlassHouse book

*Routledge-Cavendish is an imprint of the Taylor & Francis Group,
an informa business*

© 2009 Pat O'Malley

Typeset in Times New Roman by Keyword Group Ltd
Printed and bound in Great Britain by CPI Antony Rowe,
Chippenham, Wiltshire.

*British Library cataloguing in Publication Data*
A catalog record for this book is available
from the British Library

*Library of Congress Cataloguing in Publication Data*
A catalogue record for this book has been requested

ISBN10: 0-415-42567-0 (hbk)
ISBN13: 978-0-415-42567-4 (hbk)

ISBN10: 1-84568-112-6 (pbk)
ISBN13: 978-1-84568-112-8 (pbk)

ISBN10: 020-3-88181-8 (ebk)
ISBN13: 978-020-3-88181-1 (ebk)

'A man is no longer a man confined
but a man in debt'

(Gilles Deleuze, 1995: 181)

# Contents

# Preface

I have been meaning to write this book for many years, particularly because money is so little discussed in criminology and the sociology of law despite being the most generally used legal sanction. Unlike, say, imprisonment or specific performance, money is a tool of justice that spans the civil–criminal divide. Moreover, it is usually the principal sanction in both domains. Money thus leads us to theorize across the civil–criminal divide. Surprisingly, this is something few social theorists do, despite Durkheim's pioneering example.

However, I should stress that fines were the starting point of the analysis and remain its principal concern. Damages are, in a sense, included more for what they can tell us about the broader contexts of monetized justice, and for what thereby they can add to our understanding of fines. For this reason, and in order to keep this as a relatively concise book, my analysis of damages is rather less developed than that of the fine. Even so, the analysis of money as a sanction or tool of justice threatened to be swamped by questions I sought to exclude. These include such issues as: whether fines and damages are effective sanctions; whether they bear harder on minorities, the poor and women; whether larger fines and awards of damages will deter corporations and whether other sanctions such as shaming or imprisonment of executives would be 'better'; whether tort law is less or more less 'efficient' than insurance; whether there really was an insurance crisis brought on by excessive damages in the 1980s, and so on. Such empirical and normative questions are all crucial, but they are not part of the intended analysis. Where they appear in my analysis, it is in their role as a part in the discourses and rationales of struggles over money sanctions. As this indicates, the questions this brief book seeks to raise have more to do with money as a tool or technology of government—with how money is imagined and intended to be used rather than with questions of actual impact on the subjects of government.

The key questions concern: what functions money is intended to perform; how is money imagined to 'work' as a tool of justice; how do these things vary across types of justice or diverse political rationalities; how does money articulate with other ways of governing; and how do trends in the use of the 'currency of justice' reflect or express other trends in governance such as neoliberal politics?

In trying to stick to this problematic, whole chapters have been written and deleted. One of these focused on the complex debates between those seeking to displace torts with third-party insurance, those seeking the opposite, and those seeking to displace both with first-party insurance. Of course, some of this material has been included, for this is an historic struggle over how money is to be used in justice—to punish, deter, compensate, discipline, increase social efficiency, spread risks—and thus it is also a struggle over what meanings money takes on in different political visions. But many of the detailed arguments and empirical demonstrations of the relative merits of various techniques, of their historical variations, of the development of lines of legal reasoning and so on, were jettisoned. In following these fascinating debates, I found that the analysis began to lose sight of money as a tool of governance and justice and to get too wrapped up in the arguments themselves. As a result, some readers will gnash their teeth at glaring omissions, gross oversimplifications, the apparently arbitrary selection of certain trends and so on. All of these complaints are going to be justifiable in some respects. But the aim was not to write the definitive book about fines and damages. Such a book would be huge, and this book is meant to be short. It is an attempt to pick out certain patterns in governmental thought and practice in order to understand how money makes it possible to govern in certain ways, how these ways of governing have changed in the past, and how new configurations of money sanctions may be changing what we imagine to be 'justice'.

Last, but not least, I have to draw attention to an important autocriticism of this book. It claims to be about 'consumer societies', but in practice, it is overwhelmingly about a handful of common law countries. Claims at the greater level of generality are intended to be provocative, to stimulate research and theory across other jurisdictions. I have myself criticized scholars who generalized about a global 'punitive turn' in criminal justice from similarly limited common law jurisdictions. Therefore, my own stance could be seen as hypocritical in the extreme. As few reviewers read prefatory remarks, I expect—even hope—to see this complaint levelled at my exploratory essay. It's a strange thing to say in a consumer society, but it is high time criminologists and theorists of law stopped ignoring money, and if this book provokes developments by its glaring inadequacies, well and good.

Many people have helped with this book and I can mention only a few. Chris Peters at Carleton University did a huge amount of work gathering material on official discourses relating to the fine. I would like to thank him for his efforts and good humour in this sometimes tedious task. In the middle of the project, my wife Margaret was dealt a devastating blow by viral encephalitis. Over the next eight months she bravely clawed her way back into life. I am deeply grateful to Sydney Law School for the patience and understanding I was afforded when forced to relocate to Ottawa at short notice to be at her side. And I wish to thank my colleagues in Sydney—especially Mark Findlay, Thalia Anthony and Shae McCrystal who provided advice, humour and a virtual lifeline to 'home'. Gary Wickham at Murdoch University and Mick Palmer at Lancaster provided much needed and appreciated commentaries on the work and its relationship to theories of money. In Ottawa, Alan Hunt of Carleton University and Steven Hutchinson at the University of Ottawa deserve a special mention for friendship as well as academic support. Thanks too to Colin Perrin at Routledge Cavendish for waiting so patiently and uncomplainingly. As ever, my dear friends Mariana Valverde, Nikolas Rose and Kit Carson contributed immeasurably in countless ways, including some morale boosting and invaluable comments of the manuscript. I can't thank them enough. As this all implies, the book was written under very adverse circumstances. Naturally, this explains any and all of the defects my colleagues in criminology and sociology are bound to discover.

Ottawa and Sydney, June 2008

# Chapter 1

# Money sanctions

Money is probably the most frequently used means of punishing, deterring, compensating and regulating throughout the legal system. This should come as no surprise. Most of us pay fines several times a year, perhaps for a parking infraction or speeding on the highway, some of us for being drunk in public, others for running afoul of health and safety regulations, still others for assault and more serious offences. If corporations cannot be imprisoned, at least like the rest of us they can be fined and made to pay monetary damages to those they have harmed, even inadvertently. If we are defamed, the law may compensate us in money, even if we may have lost nothing but our pride. If we are maimed, hurt or even just traumatized, this may be made up to us in the form of money damages. With respect to automobile accidents, monetary compensation is paid by insurance companies on our behalf often in lieu of court awarded damages. With the purchase of very many commodities we contribute to the cost of damages paid to those who fall victim to exploding soft drink bottles, industrial accidents or drugs that have unexpected side effects. The cost of liability insurance against such losses to the manufacturers is built into the purchase price. Not only that, but of course these monies often include not only damages but also the associated legal costs. Restorative justice issues, small claims courts and neighbourhood justice disputes are often settled by relatively small payments in restitution. Restitution orders are also adjuncts or alternatives to fines in many jurisdictions, as are punitive damages, especially with respect to corporations and government offices. Monetary penalties and compensations are ubiquitous. They outnumber other sanctions delivered by criminal justice in many jurisdictions. Monetary damages long ago became the default remedy in civil law. Therefore, it is a surprise how little criminologists and sociolegal scholars talk about the nature of money and of its specific characteristics as a legal sanction. Indeed, with respect to criminology and criminal justice policy, it is amazing how little theoretically guided work has been devoted to monetary penalties at all.

At first, things do not look this way, for there is a vast literature on monetized sanctions. On the fine, for example, there has been endless research and discussion on such matters as: how best to enable or to make people pay their fines; what constitutes an appropriate level of fine for certain offences; whether the same level of fine should be levied against the rich as against the poor; whether it is fair to imprison the poor for nonpayment of fines – and if so, then what term of imprisonment equates with what amount of money fined. Numerous experiments have been tried in relation to these problems and numerous evaluations carried out, all in the name of making fines more 'just', more 'affordable' or more 'effective'. These are important issues we will revisit, for they tell us much about what money can mean to those determining its role in justice. But theoretical and critical criminologists rarely talk about fines in terms of social theory – even though Georg Simmel, for example, provides a prominent and firm base from which they could have started. Overwhelmingly, criminologists much prefer to talk about prisons as if fines did not exist. For example, in the 1970s, a huge literature theorized about 'decarceration'. Depending on your theory, this alleged emptying of incarcerating institutions occurred as a cost-cutting response to a fiscal crisis of the state, or as part of a strategy to widen the scope of discipline through much cheaper and less visible community based sanctions. For some analysts, it was both. Others took decarceration at face value as a sign that we were becoming more humane, and still others thought that it was simply more effective to treat offenders in the community than in carceral institutions. While you could take your pick of these theorizations, you would be lucky to find the fine even being mentioned in the analytical discussions. This is despite the fact that in official discourse throughout much of the twentieth century the fine is prominent as an alternative to imprisonment, and especially is viewed as a way of relieving pressure on institutions and reducing the costs of justice. Perhaps this peculiar criminological oversight tells us something important about monetized justice.

Ironically, the 'decarceration' literature was published just before almost unprecedented increases appeared in rates and volumes of imprisonment. This 'punitive turn' in penality has become the subject of endless theorizations in terms of 'de-civilizing' processes, a 'culture of control' and neoliberal politics. Yet, since the early 1980s, virtually nothing theoretically new has been written about the fine, and nothing at all written about how it relates to the processes of the so-called 'punitive turn'.

David Garland's (2001) magisterial review of the emerging 'culture of control' associated with this question mentions the fine just once, and then only in passing. Indeed, we find only two generally recognized criminological attempts to think about fines in terms of social theory – that is if we discount the work of Jeremy Bentham and the specifically economic theorizations of the Chicago School spearheaded by Gary Becker. One of these theorizations, from the 1930s, was Rusche and Kirchheimer's (1939) brief attempt to analyse the fine in terms of Marxist theory. They concluded that the fine's form and function was an effect of relations of production. However, a harsh judge would say that they achieved little more than to say that fines would only develop into a major sanction when poor people could afford to pay them. Even this observation is dubious at best. Rusche and Kirchheimer paid no attention to the widespread use of fines in the seventeenth and eighteenth centuries. Moreover, they paid little attention to the reasons given in official discourse for preferring the fine to other sanctions, especially in preference to short periods of imprisonment. Perhaps this was because, in their view, these official discourses were to be regarded merely as an ideological window dressing to changes that had their true origins in the productive order. However, I will suggest that official discourse is rather revealing about the development of fines and about their place in a penal system that simultaneously decried them as nonreformative yet promoted them to a principal role.

Half a century after Rusche and Kirchheimer wrote their chapter in the 1930s, Anthony Bottoms (1983) wrote a brilliant but equally brief essay theorizing fines. He linked the growth of the fine to changes in forms of discipline in the factory, to the rise of automobiles, to electronic surveillance technologies and to the distinction between disciplinary and regulatory techniques for governing problems. He also suggested that the fine was linked to increasingly bureaucratic and administrative changes in the form of justice. We will visit these theorizations in depth in the next chapters, together with Richard Fox's (1995, 1996) rich and sustained – but almost totally ignored – application of Bottoms' insights in the Australian context.

This is a stunningly sparse theoretical literature for such an important sanction in criminal justice. Is there something about fines that makes them so obvious or uninteresting that people can't even see the point of analysing the topic theoretically? Why is this the case even though most of us recognize that money means very different things in different places and times? We distinguish between 'clean' and 'dirty' money, between money for buying 'necessities' and money that we spend on 'treats'. We give special meaning to people's 'lifetime savings', to 'hard earned' and 'easy' money. We may get outraged if a corporation is fined only a small amount for causing the death of a child, even though at the same time we might cheerfully suggest that money has no meaning. In this light, money paid in fines seems to have a magical property of meaning nothing but at the same time being a measure of pain, cruelty, death, shame, nuisance, outrage, wrongfulness and so on. Yet we virtually ignore fines in criminology, even though far more people pay fines than go to prison and many of those in prison are there because they did not pay fines! And we ignore fines even though, for the most part, they have the amazing characteristic of being virtually the only criminal penalty that legally can be borne by someone other than the offender. Is not this a striking peculiarity that is worthy of attention?

If we turn to the other great modern legal sanction, monetary damages, the story appears to be different. There is a considerable literature analysing fields such as tort law and contract law in terms of various social theories. For example, the rise of contract law is frequently linked to the rise of entrepreneurial ideologies and class interests (Atiyah 1979; Horwitz 1977). However, for the most part this takes for granted the specificity of the money form that is its principal sanction, even though money was not always the principal civil law remedy. Before the modern era, this honour more often went to 'specific performance', which required that a broken contract should be carried out as originally agreed, not 'compensated' for in dollars and cents. Why did money become the default remedy in civil law in the nineteenth century, and why did 'compensation' nearly always come to be defined as an amount of money? Or again, if I publicly ridiculed my neighbour I may have been required to pay money, but I may alternatively have been required to deny the insult in public, or to repeat defamatory words under humiliating circumstances. At some point in time, money began to appear as a better sanction. But how did jurists and legislators come to the conclusion that money 'compensates' better for a ridicule, injury or a trauma that has done me no economic harm?

Again, as with the fine, we find a vast jurisprudential and administrative literature examining questions of how damages should be calculated; about the conditions under which money should be justly awarded rather than some form of specific remedy such as delivery of goods; about the justice and efficiency of compensatory payments in tort law as opposed to insurance schemes; about the strange and wonderful innovative practices that emerge whereby judges allocate damages in the name of 'the most efficient tortfeasor' or 'deep pockets'. However, little of this refers to social theory. Again, there are a few exceptions, notably in Marxist or

Marxian theory. Richard Abel (1982), for example, has briefly analysed money damages as commodifying worker injury, putting a price on harm in a way consistent with capitalism's commodification of labour power. More centrally, there was a considerably flurry of interest about the same time – the late 1970s and early 1980s – over Horwitz's (1977) pungent thesis that the rise of negligence, privity of contract and related doctrines at the time of industrialization reduced workers' access to compensation and thereby reflected naked capitalist class interests. But, even in such work, where changes in access to remedies are at least subject to theoretical interpretation, there has been comparatively little interest with respect to the monetary form taken by compensation. If the fine seems to have been ignored, the monetary form of the major civil remedies has been taken for granted.

Nor is this a characteristic only of recent work. Consider Emile Durkheim, who raised the place of compensation in his evolutionary theory of legal sanctions. In his analysis, the increasing complexity of the division of labour was linked to changes in the forms of social cohesion. As the division of labour becomes more complex and diverse, shared experience of life diminishes. Correspondingly, fewer actions appear to be outrageous transgressions, simply because societies have become more diverse. Also, the violence of reactions to deviance dissipates for the same reason. While criminal law continues to be a domain that express moral condemnation, the social reactions and punishments become milder overall. More significantly, contract and restitutive sanctioning become the critical legal means that expresses the diverse yet interdependent nature of social relations. In place of outrage, individuals are seen to be unified into society through self-interest. Society, through the civil law (contract, tort, nuisance, etc.), will compensate any person harmed by another.

Of course, this theory has been extensively, if often mistakenly, criticized, significantly for its supposedly erroneous predictions of the course of criminal law.[1] My point is not whether this thesis is defensible, but rather that the rise of specifically compensatory law occupied a prominent place in fin de siecle social theory. It could have been expected that theoretical analysis of compensation would become a major issue in the sociology of law. Instead, Durkheim's work on physical and 'repressive' sanctions has been by far the main focus. Even so, it has to be recognized that Durkheim scarcely mentioned the money form of compensation as such, despite the fact that by the time he wrote, money damages had long become the default remedy in contract and tort law. Once again, money fell below the threshold of theoretical visibility, even though this form of sanction could be seen as best fitting a nonrepressive, complex and compensatory legal order. Indeed, as with the fine, and with almost as few exceptions, the invisibility of money itself to sociolegal theory's analysis of civil law is remarkable.

Perhaps again, this is because money is obvious: it buys things and we use it all the time. However, if money is so obvious how could Georg Simmel (1990), for example, make us struggle through nearly five hundred pages of dense reasoning on its nature? And, why is it that the law itself gets in such a knot over money as a sanction and what it means? One of the standard texts, *MacGregor on Damages*, poses the rhetorical question of why money is provided for nonpecuniary harms. It answers rather lamely that 'money is not awarded as a replacement for other money, but as a substitute for that which is generally more important than money: it is the best that the court can do'. (McGregor 1997: 9). Just why this is 'the best the court can do' and why money is used even when clearly regarded as inadequate, are questions explored when we turn to money damages in Chapter Four. But, what are the ramifications of this for justice and social order? In some cases, the answer seems obvious, where money makes up for lost wages, profits or other lost opportunities for financial gain. However, we will see that even this is less obvious than we suppose. For example, how on earth could we work out the money value of a lost chance to race a horse, when we do not know if it would have won races it never ran, for bets of unknown value at odds never offered? Courts have decided that this can be resolved in terms of the value of the opportunity to win. But, what is this 'value' of money if it includes the intangible pleasure of winning? Moreover, what about situations where damages are awarded for pain and suffering, mental anguish, ridicule and contempt?

The answer that will emerge is that money is meant to buy pleasure that offsets pain and trauma. It is a source of solace. But how is this calculated? If this seems plausible in a consumer society, can we really imagine the court calculating how many BMWs buy off the trauma of seeing your child die? Indeed, one insight into the importance of the money form of sanction can be gained here. Imagine if, instead of awarding so many millions of dollars, the court awarded the successful plaintiff in an action for wrongful death a Florida mansion, two Jaguars, a luxury cruise and free first-class air travel. Probably the reaction would be outrage, but an award of money sufficient to buy these things passes without comment. Money appears to work its own meaningful effects, perhaps by distancing and abstracting sanctions from the grubby world of commodities – for the courts will not tell successful plaintiffs how to spend their damages. Alternatively, is the money meant to signify something else? Under some conditions, money expresses the amount of outrage, sympathy or even contempt felt by the court, so that arguably money means the whole gamut of emotional states as well as pleasure. So, after all, perhaps it is not that money means nothing, but that money may mean almost anything, especially in a commodity-focused society such as ours. And if money *can* mean something other than – or as well as – the power to purchase, what might this tell us about damages and fines? As a way of thinking through this, we can do worse than start with a social theorist who did spend a lot of time thinking about the meaning of money: Georg Simmel.

## Simmel: money, meaning and freedom

For Simmel, money and money alone 'is free from any quality and is exclusively determined by quantity'. It is characterized by 'unconditional interchangeability': money is 'infinitely divisible and infinitely convertible' (1990: 292). It is thus abstract and expresses no value of its own, it is 'nothing but the representation of *other* objects', that is, the objects that it connects in a relationship. Probably the most familiar reading of this view is profoundly negative, for money depersonalizes, equates any person with any thing. Money makes us thing-like, turns the most precious things into commodities to be bought and sold and thus debases us. In this view, it is a vehicle for alienation. This certainly is one theoretical and political reading of money and, for Simmel, money can be seen this way, because it erodes the 'unique personality' that is so central at least to modern liberal visions of the self. For example,

> Such a personality is almost completely destroyed under the conditions of a money economy. The delivery-man, the money-lender, the worker, upon whom we are dependent, do not operate as personalities because they enter into a relationship only by virtue of a single activity such as the delivery of goods, the lending of money, and because their other qualities, which alone would give them a personality, are missing.
>
> (1990: 292)

In this way, money can be seen as consistent with legal penalties that are levied anonymously, not necessarily against specific individuals *per se* so much as against them in their roles, positions of ownership or employment, such as 'the licensee', 'the driver' or 'the proprietor'. Such 'modern

regulatory fines' will be the subject of Chapter Three. However, note that
Simmel is not suggesting that this transformation in relationships occurs
just because money makes it happen. Rather, money makes it possible.
Money is a condition of existence of a certain kind of anonymous or
secondary sociality that may arise for other reasons. In this way, money,
or more precisely the monetization of sanctions, is the foundation of a
certain kind of governance or regulation. It is a form in which the target
of governance may not be unique individuals at all but rather the distributions or collectivities, say drivers or owners, of which they are part.

However, while this depersonalizing property of meaningless money
may be alienating, Simmel was acutely aware of its other side. To the
extent that money depersonalizes and facilitates anonymity, it also is a
condition of existence of a certain kind of freedom. For Marx, the wage
was a vehicle that disguises the extraction of surplus value – the workers
cannot see that they are being paid less in value than the value they create.
At the same time, because in this view money buys commodities, not the
means to produce life's necessities, the worker cannot achieve independence from wage slavery itself. For Marx the money economy is critical,
because it is critical to the exploitation of workers. For Simmel, on the
other hand, while it is true that the workers still remain tied to employers
in general, they are no longer individually tied to a particular employer.
The money wage makes possible exchangeability of employers as well
as employees. In this way, regardless of changes in workers' material
conditions, which may or may not improve, they are 'already on the way
to personal freedom'. Independence from the will of a specific individual
is a step toward the 'independence from the will of others' – something
that Simmel regards as liberty. (1990: 300–301).

Simmel then connects this specific point to his previous argument
concerning the erosion of the unique personality. With monetization, the
form of sociability changes. This is so particularly for the urban dweller
who increasingly does not depend on other individuals qua individuals
'but only upon their objective services which have a money value and
therefore may be carried out by any interchangeable person'. In Simmel's
view, this does not simply liberate individuals through loosening personal
dependencies, but creates a vision of mutual dependence at the level
of the social that is quite redolent of Durkheim's 'organic solidarity'.
However, unlike Durkheim, Simmel is centring the money form itself.
For Simmel

> Only through the growth of the (money) economy to its full capacity,
> complexity and internal interaction does the mutual dependence of

people emerge The elimination of the personal element directs the individual toward his own resources and makes him more positively aware of his liberty than would be possible with the total lack of relationships. Money is the ideal representative of such a condition since it makes possible relationships between people but leaves them personally undisturbed; it is the exact measure of material achievements, but is very inadequate for the particular and the personal.

(1990: 303)

Moving ahead of the argument in many ways, it could now be sensed that monetary sanctions may have a place as the form of sanction appropriate to a particular governmental vision of freedom. If the world is increasingly a society of strangers, then it is in that measure also a society in which relations of contract come to predominate. In such settings, the imagery of 'normal' relationships is of the 'free and equal' bargaining parties, and in contract law the default remedy for wrongs arising in the relationships between such parties comes to be that of money. We could say that money is the form of exchange befitting a society of abstract strangers, and the form of justice likewise reflects this imagery. This is deceptively simple. While we will examine the genealogy of contractual remedies in a later chapter, one of the characteristics of the rise of modern contract law is money's displacement of specific remedies, remedies that required the specific performance of a bargain struck. If the original contract had called for the delivery of iron, and the price had been paid, then the legal remedy would be the delivery of the iron. By the nineteenth century, however, this had largely given way to remedy in an amount of money, one reason for which was precisely that to require specific performance was regarded as unduly coercive. It would compromise relationships between free people, because it would require the court to 'stand over' the defendant in order to ensure an action were properly performed, rather than simply requiring that compensation could be provided in the abstract and impersonal form of a money payment.

At a personal level, we may of course dispute this evaluation of relative kinds and degrees of coercion implied in the different remedies. However, for our purposes what counts is the official discourse, the formal or governmental declaration of this rationale for money damages in terms of freedom and coercion. Simmel's account of money makes some sense of how it could be that money both allows the depersonalization and contractualization of relationships, while at the same time takes its place in a vision of freedom that swings precisely around money's supposed impersonal and politically neutral character. The nexus between freedom and money that Simmel has begun to untangle for us will prove central to understanding the operation of money sanctions.

Simmel's argument in many ways swings around the 'meaningless-ness' of money. But, he is careful not to render this into an ahistorical truth. He argues that money has not always had the same meaning (or lack of meaning), and it has not always borne the same relationship to human lives that it now takes on. This comes to the fore in his analysis of the fine – for Simmel is one of those rare theorists who ever analyses the money *form* of legal sanctions. In his discussion of punishment by fine, Sim-mel draws attention to the Anglo Saxon sanction of *wergild*, a monetary payment required as expiation for serious offences such as the wound-ing or killing of a man. To the modern eye, *wergild* put a money value of a person's life, reducing the individual life merely to an object. All the more so because the higher the status of the victim, the higher the money value demanded. Simmel suggests, however, that this interpreta-tion would be anachronistic, for it overlays feudal meanings of money and persons with more modern meanings. In the feudal economy, which was extensively nonmonetary, money could be the bearer of meaning, because it was unusual and thereby, in degree, distanced from everyday life. For example, money could signal contrition in religious contexts, as in the payment of monetary penances, and could be used to purchase indulgences without this appearing to debase religion – at least to the Church hierarchy.

Conversely, Simmel suggests, the feudal order did not imagine human life in the ways of the post Enlightenment era. The uniqueness of individ-ual life was not the paramount issue – and for this reason the individual's ascribed social standing, not how much he or she was loved or admired as a personality, determined *wergild*. Likewise, the vision of the abstract and equal individual associated with 'human rights' and 'human dignity' was not part of a society that rigidly assigned people to statuses ranging from slave to serf, vassal to lord. Consequently, setting a money price could not violate an assumption that all individuals' lives are somehow intrinsically of equal value for there was no such assumption. A money price thus did not confront a vision of the unique individual life as price-less, in the modern sense, but was a measure of the stature of a status. Money and human life bore a different relationship to each other than is now the case.

Simmel suggests that as individual human life has become more impor-tant both in terms of its uniqueness and its universal abstraction as 'human', so it has passed money coming the other way. Money has *become* more colourless and indifferent and thus cannot be used to express those things that are valued most such as the 'innermost and most basic aspects of the person'.

> Money first attains the quality of cool indifference and complete abstractness in relation to all specific values to the extent that it becomes the equivalent of increasingly diverse objects. As long as the objects that may be acquired by money are limited in number, and as long as an essential part of economic values is excluded from being purchasable (as was the case, for example, with landed property over very long periods), money itself retains a more specific character and is not yet indifferent to either side. Under primitive circumstances, money may even possess the exact opposite of its real nature, namely, sacred dignity, the quality of exceptional value. The progressive differentiation of people and the equally progressive indifference of money combine to make expiation for murder and other serious crimes by money completely impossible.
>
> (Simmel 1983: 365–366)

The *monetization* of a society, in which money becomes more available, and in which all objects become exchangeable for money, creates this supposed 'meaninglessness' of money itself, and the apparent paradox of *wergild* provides the summation of this change. Thus Simmel (1990: 336) concludes that as long as money has restricted use, and is not available in such quantities as 'to slip through one's fingers' on a daily basis, then it is 'more apt to serve as a satisfactory equivalent for extraordinary objects such as human life'.

With this process in mind, Simmel argues that today fines can become an inappropriate sanction for serious crimes, consigning *wergild* to the dustbin of history. The emerging 'indifference' of money and the increasing evaluation of the individual make monetary expiation for crimes such as murder morally impossible. Fines are not to be used for crimes that concern the 'innermost and most basic aspects of the person', as recent commentators have also examined at some length.

Thus Young (1989: 64–65), referring to crimes such as rape, argues:

> There exist a small but vitally important number of such crimes in which the use of money is limited. These are normally crimes which are seen to affect cultural aspects of our notion of 'personhood'; there are some things which are still placed beyond the reach of monetary exchange. Although small in number they have immense symbolic significance as they colour general cultural views of the nature of

punishment and of its legitimacy. In these cases it is the prison that is seen as the proper punishment; penal values shift from a focus on resources to a focus on the immediacy of the body and the person and attack that aspect of it which is most highly valued – its autonomy, its freedom.

In Young's graphic phrase, 'who dares fine the rapist?' (1989: 66). But Simmel also uses this argument in relation to understanding what fines *are* now used for. If money fines cease to be any form of valuation of the person, then the fine must appear as a form 'of inflicting pain upon the culprit'. This leads him, perhaps logically, to a discussion of the advantages of the money form in this respect. Like Beccaria and Bentham before him, Simmel (1990: 364–366) spends some time analysing the characteristics of monetary punishment: its infinite graduation to match the seriousness of offences, its minimization of physical injury or incapacitation of the worker, its encouragement to the worker to make up for loss, and the fact that fines are a harsher punishment on the poor than the rich. We will visit these matters in the following chapters. However, two points that Simmel makes in this respect need a little further attention here.

First, he argues that because money is now set apart from the value of the person, then 'the legal retribution for injustice and injury that one person inflicts upon the other becomes more and more restricted to cases in which the interests of the victim are expressible in money terms' (1990: 367). In other words, he sees fines becoming restricted to matters where economic loss is involved. Given that fines came to be almost the default sanction for common assaults in many jurisdictions during the twentieth century, this seems like an odd claim, even if it is a possible deduction from his analysis of the money form. However, Simmel gives himself a let-out clause in this respect. He suggests that because urban areas are dominated by economic interests, then in these contexts the value of a human being (not just his or her economic interest) is more likely to be measured in money terms. In urban contexts, it appears, the monetization of life overpowers the more liberal ethos of the intrinsic value of the individual. At best, this is not really explained, and seems quite arbitrary. Is rural life not dominated by 'economic' interests also? Is city life less dominated by liberal values than country life? Both are possible empirically, if dubious, but neither is remotely demonstrated. The result is that this seems like a weak post hoc claim that potentially undermines his thesis.

This problem would also seem to weaken his argument concerning the meaningless of money and the inappropriateness of its use as civil compensation for deeply personal matters. As with the fine, he asserts that monetary damages will only apply where harm can be equated with a specific amount of money (1990: 369). In some senses, it needs to be noted, this is an empty tautology, since it implies that wherever money damages are applied, then the court felt that the harm *can* be equated with an amount of money. But Simmel is rather more precise, at least with respect to German civil law.

> I need mention here only some cases pointed out by lawyers themselves: the landlord who does not permit the tenant to use the garden despite his contractual right to do so, the traveller to whom the hotel owner refuses lodging despite written assent ... all these people, although their claim to compensation is as clear as daylight, cannot raise this claim because the damage cannot be equated with a specific amount of money. Who could demonstrate the precise amount of money equivalent of these subjective inconveniences and impairments?
>
> (Simmel 1990: 369)

Of course, in the common law domains of contract and tort law, the answer to this rhetorical question is that judges and juries do this sort of thing all the time. Hence, when Simmel extends his point, he appears to come into conflict with contemporary practices in striking ways. Thus he suggests that as money has become so central to contemporary life, then values that cannot be expressed in monetary terms become subject to a 'peculiar practical indifference' of the law 'even though they are theoretically recognized to be of the highest value' (Simmel 1990: 369). Yet this would appear to confront much of the law of defamation, where reputation has been valued in money terms – and frequently very large amounts of money – even where no direct economic loss can be demonstrated. Indeed, under the common law of defamation at the time Simmel was writing, the demonstration of economic loss was not necessary to the success of an action for libel. In such areas of law, the 'highest' human values are frequently, almost routinely, rendered into monetary amounts, even if, like McGregor, this is done slightly apologetically as the 'best' that the court can do. The emergence of categories of 'punitive' and 'aggravated' damages, as well as 'derisory damages', further suggest that money can be used meaningfully in modern law in ways that Simmel can't explain, whatever the overall value of his central insights. Evidently, we need to attend to Simmel's argument about the developing intrinsic meaninglessness of money.

Perhaps we should ignore his point about the city being a specific domain in which economic interest comes to the fore. We could say simply that as more and more of life is monetized, then more and more of life – rather than less and less of it – becomes calculable in money terms. This is the familiar claim, of course, that life itself is being commodified. Simmel invokes the nature of the city and economic interest to explain how such commodification trumps the increasing (liberal) value of individual life. However, there are at least two other possibilities.

The first is that money does not lose its meaning in such contexts. If we think of the jury that imposes damages for harm to reputation, does money – at least under some circumstances – mean something other than the mere trading equation of incommensurables with each other? Does money have its own meaning in such examples? Recalling Simmel's own important point that the meaning of money is not given and ahistorical, could it be that there is not just the exhaustion of meaning from money, but rather changing meanings of money under changing social conditions? Perhaps money always has meaning, ironically even when – for instance as the medium for purchasing commodities – apparently it does not. Indeed, perhaps Simmel's problem in these respects is that with respect to diverse sanctioning issues or settings, money takes on divergent meanings rather than money having one (meaningless) meaning that then ascribes to it a limited range of sanctioning functions.

The second possibility is that that there is no necessary antipathy between the monetization and commodification of societies versus the valuation of the unique individual life. For example, various recent social theorists (Campbell 1987) have associated the rise of an ethic of consumption with the Romantic promotion of the self. The consumption of commodities in this imagery is not necessarily alienating and may be fulfilling. Production may be the domain of self-denial, of thrift, diligence and frugality, of investment and deferred gratification. However, consumption emerged as the alternative domain for expressing and developing the inner self. In Campbell's argument consumption, albeit perversely, came to be the domain of feelings and fulfilment that *confronts* mundane utilitarianism and the Protestant Ethic, and even regards them as the negation of human value. In a related way, others also have identified consumption as a field of resistance (de Certeau 1984). If we live our lives through commodities then these commodities become a vehicle for expression of resistance. Popular music, films, clothing, jewellery and even cars can become commodified ways in which refusal to conform is expressed. Still other theorists pay attention to commodity purchases as the way in which individuality or selfhood is assembled together and elaborated, whether this is an expression of resistance or 'merely' the way a certain subjectivity is formulated through material objects (Rose 1999). Perhaps monetization, the saturation of life by money, is after all not antithetical to the valuation of individual uniqueness and its high estimation. Maybe money is a medium through which new forms of liberalism, new forms of freedom, simultaneously constitute meaning and are constituted by it.

## The governmental meanings of money

As Viviana Zelizer (1994) argued in her foundational work, there are many ways in which money is given value over and above its value as a medium of exchange. As mentioned earlier, 'the rent money', 'winnings', 'housekeeping money', 'ill gotten gains' – in each case money means something specific and is invested with meaningful and emotional content. Furthermore, it can be argued that even apparently abstract money not earmarked in such ways may bear meanings. For instance, financial traders engaged in massive speculative decisions refer to 'ticks' or some other neutral term in order to distance themselves from the idea that they are dealing with vast sums of 'real' money. Despite money appearing at its most abstract in such settings – appearing only as virtual numbers – the traders believe that the very thought of actual money and its implications may affect their judgment and thus needs somehow to be neutralized (Zaloom 2006). For these dealers, money is invested with such powerful meanings, or meanings of power, that it has to be imaginatively erased.

A sociology of money, such as Zelizer carries out, maps the diversity of meanings attached to money deployed in specific ways. A possible reading of her position would be that in the examples to which she refers, it always appears that money has meaning *added* to it. In other words, it is as if money's purchasing power remains abstract and 'meaningless', but specific caches of money are given specific meaning in relation to how they were acquired, the purpose to which they are put and so on. In such an interpretation, there is abstract or untagged money that is not meaningfully allocated and functions in ways that do not impinge on consciousness: ordinary money remains merely the undifferentiated medium of exchange that Simmel attends to. However, Zelizer argues that there is no moment when money means nothing, simply because it only exists in and through social relationships. There can only ever be different meanings of money. Just because some of these meanings may be taken for granted and seemingly invisible in day-to-day life does not mean that they are nonexistent. Quite to the contrary, we could even say that the attribution of intrinsic meaningless to money is itself a meaningful act that gives it various discursive forms of utility and impact. Consider the example already discussed where an objection is made to fining someone for rape or murder because this reduces the victim's life to a mere commodity. Money that buys mere commodities, in such complaints, has very special meanings.

This tension, over money's meaning and/or lack of meaning is not something this book will be attempting to *resolve*. This is an aim in most of the debates surrounding Zelizer's work, in which a central issue is whether there can be a general theory of money or not. For Zelizer (2005) there cannot be such a theory, because money is constituted by diverse social practices, while for others such as Bryan and Rafferty (2007: 150) it is only through the identification of certain abstract universal characteristics of all monies that individual phenomena can be identified as 'money'. My interest is, instead, with certain congeries of meanings, including that of 'meaningless', attributed to money. At this point, we confront a second problem that Zelizer's work raises but skates over. Whose meanings of money are we referring to and how are we to interrogate these? For example, it may well be that the fine levied against the café for having cockroaches on the premises means something quite different to the planner, the inspector, the proprietor, the chef and the customers. Money fines in the eyes of one party may be a strike against the business they love and nurture, for another it is an inadequate punishment for filthiness, for a third it is an unjustified attack on profits, and for yet others it is an exercise in state revenue raising. This cultural question of the popular meanings of money and money sanctions is not a line of investigation I intend to pursue here – although valid in its own right, and even though the issues it raises are hard to avoid. Rather, as far as possible, the focus will be more specifically on governmental meanings. Such meanings exist in the official discourses of those who set out to explain or justify the intended or attributed purpose or effect of the sanction they are creating, proposing or applying. In this way, my focus is empirical, but it is not investigating the distribution of meanings among the population at large, and certainly, not what money 'really' means.

Of course, governmental meanings may vary among themselves as much as do other meanings: law and regulation are often multivocal and contested. Bentham's view that fines are the optimal sanction is not *the* governmental meaning of the fine. However, it is a major and demonstrable thread of governmental reasoning underlying the nature and form of fines in liberal polities. Yet, while for Bentham the fine was a positive and constructive – even optimal – tool of governance, this meaning was not stable or hegemonic. To a generation of jurists a century later the fine represented something rather more negative. For many of these planners the fine expressed in a dismal way the limits of correctional penology. The fine became a sort of residual sanction where nothing better could be imagined. Instead of Bentham's lionization of fines as the ideal sanction of the liberal future, these jurists saw the fine as an index of the limits of the correctional process.

As this example suggests, we may also recognize that fines, like other legal sanctions, are a kind of governmental technology that take their place as components of fairly systematic mentalities or rationalities of governance. Such rationalities imagine problems in a certain way, and develop techniques for solving them in some preferred fashion, to some specific end. They construct subjects who are to be worked upon or with, and create images of subjects that government wishes to create in the name of good government. Thus, nineteenth century tort law made the assumption that legal subjects are (or should be) equipped with 'reasonable foresight', an assumption common to liberalism more generally. Accordingly, the 'just' outcome of a case would be to compensate those harmed through no fault of their own at the cost of those who had harmed them through failing to exercise foresight. In the twentieth century, it began to be assumed that this was both 'inefficient' and 'unjust'. It was inefficient because insurance would be cheaper, and it was unjust because (inter alia) the injured party may be uncompensated being unable to afford the risks of an unpredictable legal process. Accordingly new insurance schemes, such as workers' compensation insurance, were put into place that were less concerned with 'the reasonable man' and more focused on governing distributions of harm.

To borrow Foucault's phrase, all these legal apparatuses, routines, institutions, subjectifications and so on represent not only technologies whereby governments seek to put into effect certain of their plans, but also they operate as '*technologies of freedom*'. That is, fines, damages, insurance and so on, all these monetized forms of legal (and quasi-legal) sanction, work through and upon the freedom of the subjects they are set in place to govern. This may be a strange way of putting things. However, to take just one instance, the development of the categories of 'punitive' or 'exemplary' damages was part of an attempt to make more clear that the prevailing role of damages was to be compensatory – making clear and separate the punitive element that was seen to have existed in earlier rationales for assessing damages. In this way, it was imagined, contract law, tort law and so on appeared to fit better with the domain of the civil society in which a liberal state should interfere coercively as little as possible. Perhaps Durkheim could see this as vindicating his theory of the move from repressive to restitutive sanctions. More simply we could see it as an expression of the prevailing nineteenth century contractual mentality of liberal rule. It expressed a certain vision of what a 'free' society looked like, and of how a 'free' market would operate with the laissez-faire state interfering only to enforce binding voluntary agreements. Such awards of damages also had a didactic and punitive purpose, enforcing the liberal conception of how a legal subject *should* responsibly exercise the 'reasonable foresight'. In such ways, money damages can be regarded as a technology of freedom, of enforcing and reinforcing a particular vision of 'free' subjects.

It is at this point that Simmel's insights into the nexus of monetization and freedom take on another level of importance. Simmel imagines freedom as a given condition – the independence of an individual from the will of others. It has been seen that he regards this vision of freedom as being made possible by monetization. We might see, however, that this was a characteristically nineteenth century vision of freedom rather than the definition of freedom *per se*. It fits with what Isaiah Berlin (1969) termed 'freedom from' as opposed to 'freedom to'. Equally, and importantly, Simmel worked with a single model of freedom, and this fitted with the fact that he saw only a single meaning (or lack of meaning) of money in modernity. However, to take just one instance, money damages in the nineteenth century were a sanction deployed to create or reinforce a certain vision of freedom. Free subjects, in this view, should be responsible and rational calculators who exercise foresight. Those who broke contracts had damages awarded against them in part because they disturbed the conditions that made rational calculation possible. Thus where the breach caused a foreseeable loss, damages would be awarded against the defendant. But where it had an impact that neither party to the contract reasonably could have foreseen, it became unlikely that damages would be awarded in this respect. Likewise, where the victim of an industrial accident could have foreseen it coming and negligently failed to take evasive steps, then she or he could not recover damages. While damages compensated those victims to whom they were awarded, they also acted as a technique for punishing those who failed to exercise reasonable foresight. Thus was a certain kind of freedom to be shaped by law.

To enter the realm of meanings and uses of money in this way, thus does not involve analysis in the mapping of all possible 'social' or 'cultural' understandings of how money works or should work as a legal sanction. As I have stressed, these are matters that Zelizer is especially interested in. However, to follow them all would require a major sociological study of a different kind to that envisaged. This study instead concerns the place that monetary sanctions have as governmental technologies, and the kinds of governmental meanings, rationalities and broader technologies to which they link.[2] The analysis of such governmental mentalities shifts us closer to what Foucault referred to as 'significant statements'. These are the 'meanings' – often given material form in the reasoning of judges, legislators, urban planners and others – that can be identified with enduring and reasonably systematic governmental uses of monetized sanctions. Of course, there is no hard and fast line to be drawn. In particular, it will be clear that to the extent that popular meanings of money in justice collide with those of the law (for example, where fines are regarded as unjustly creating revenue), and they may change government reasoning and practice. And of course much governmental reasoning reflects or comes to shape popular meanings. Such popular meanings, however, become relevant precisely to the extent that they become the objects and issues around which government is formed.

## Monetized 'justice', regulation and control societies

Durkheim deserves enormous credit for raising the question of the interrelationships of legal sanctions across the so-called 'civil-criminal' divide. Criminologists and lawyers alike have tended to emphasize the specificity of the two domains, and certainly criminologists tend to theorize about the nature of criminal justice and penality as though civil law's sanctions do not exist, or are of a totally different nature. However, while this distinction is one that social theory should take into account, at the same time we should regard it as an object of theory rather than a natural kind. It has been indicated already that the separation of civil and criminal law was in part an exercise pursued by liberal legislators, political theorists and jurists keen to distinguish a domain of state coercion from a domain of civil society. Yet this liberal distinction in law has never been a totally successful enterprise. For example, torts are formally defined as 'wrongs' and thus carry with them some unavoidable element of a punitive nature. 'Exemplary' or 'punitive' damages have been developed explicitly as a form of punishment, especially with respect to the corporate sector. In such discourses, monetary damages take on the meaning and function of a fine. Moreover, in the eyes of law and economics advocates (e.g. Becker 1974) fines in criminal justice function both as a punishment and as a form of 'social damages', providing compensation to the state for harm done to the social infrastructure or social order. More recently, many jurisdictions have deliberately blurred the civil and the criminal in such arrangements as the 'civil offence' as a means of more effectively providing punishment and deterrence (Freiberg and O'Malley 1984). Especially with respect to corporations and corrupt organizations, conviction in a criminal court may allow a plaintiff in a civil court to dispense with having to establish the defendant's responsibility for a harmful event, and to seek treble damages.

Money sanctions therefore are an important bridge between these two domains of legal sanctioning. Imprisonment may be exclusively available to criminal law, but money is a sanction shared both by civil and criminal domains. In part, this almost unique characteristic of pecuniary sanctions may be associated with the idea that money does not threaten or take away liberty: it bears the meaning of 'only money', set against 'liberty', for example. Where sanctions take the money form, procedural protections against the state may be relaxed, the criminal-civil divide smoothed over, the distinction between compensation and punishment blurred or these functions conjoined. Through the vehicle of money and its meanings, it may be suggested not simply that there is a blurring of the civil and criminal domains, but that the two become interchangeable in certain key respects, and form a more or less seamless and ubiquitous system of regulation. There are several elements to this idea.

First, Simmel has made the point that money is 'undifferentiated': that, at least in its historical forms to date, it generally is not possible from money itself to determine to whom a parcel of money belongs. Because money is 'undifferentiated', it is very difficult to establish whose money is paying a fine, or paying damages. In consequence, courts do not often concern themselves with who pays a fine, or who pays damages – as long as they are paid. In a rare exception, the English *Road Traffic Law Review Report* (Home Office 1988: 133) considered the question of whether to prohibit payment of fines for traffic infringements by a third party. The report expressed regret at this practice, especially with respect to situations where corporations paid such fines on behalf of their employees. In the view of the Report this relieved the offender from punishment. Thereby it reduced the fine to a mere business expense and reduced its perceived effectiveness. However, it could find no practicable means of enforcing such a rule (see also Bein 1974).

Sometimes, then, money's undifferentiated form is a nuisance to law's intentions. However, I will argue that it is much more the case that this undifferentiated property of money *has come to be relied upon in modern legal sanctioning.* If courts had to establish that it is the guilty or wrongful party who is paying fines then the sanction would not be the ubiquitous tool of criminal justice and bylaw enforcement that it has become. It would be too expensive and time-consuming to administer en masse. It would also involve the state in exercises whereby the finances of virtually all legal subjects would need to become routinely available to forms and degrees of scrutiny that might create considerable political resistance. It is also possible that resistance to much routine regulation, for example with respect to traffic infringements, would have been greater were it not for the case that money can be paid anonymously through mail or electronic transfers of abstract money. With respect to civil law, if courts had to insist that defendants personally pay damages, even were they able to ensure this, then tort law would cease to function in its present form. Insurers pay the vast bulk of damages, and the existence of insurance has been at the root of the expansion of the 'system' of damages. Were this not so, then the law of torts would be capable of remedying only a small proportion of the current range and volume of harms that are its remit. With respect both to fines and damages, we can argue that by short-circuiting the normal requirement that offenders directly suffer the penalty for wrongdoing, the undifferentiated nature of money has contributed greatly to the growth of widespread and pervasive regulation of modern life.

Second, unlike virtually all other sanctions, *money sanctions are always redistributed*: they may be used to fund the regulation system itself or some other activity of government, or they may be used to provide and spread the cost of compensation for the injured. Because money always passes from one owner to another and endures – unlike the 'cancelled' time of a prisoner or probationer – the proceeds of monetized legal sanctions are circulated, linked to other areas of government and to everyday life in a seamless fashion. The flows of undifferentiated money that pass through legal sanctions invariably pass between courts, government offices, police forces, corporate finances, regulatory bodies, insurance schemes, victims and so on. At one level, this is nothing new or particularly interesting: fines have ever produced income to the state, as Bentham noted two hundred years ago. Nevertheless, nowadays the volume of money generated by modern fines has become astronomical, as has the array of statutes, regulations, bylaws and so on for which fines are the sole or principal sanction. Whereas once fines were a cheap sanction, now in some areas – for example traffic regulation – fines are openly admitted to be a significant source of state revenue. They even appear as a line item in state budgets. The value of fines collected may be modulated not simply to reduce speeding, but officially for the reason that they represent a tax on speeders, required to fund safety improvements to the roads. In this way, modern fines can begin to appear as taxes or licenses, or even more accurately as prices. They are costs of living in a certain way in consumer societies. At the same time, through the revenues generated, fines are integrated into circuits of monetized regulation that socialize the costs or harms of the activities of the government. In parallel fashion, money damages are also directly articulated with broader circuits of regulation. We pay for damages each time a commodity is purchased insofar as the price includes the costs of damages or liability insurance. In a significant degree, therefore, modern fines and damages operate as techniques for socializing or spreading the costs of governing risks and harms.

Third, as this implies, *a very large bulk of legal governance or regulation can only exist because money is ubiquitous.* Although the argument can be dangerously oversimplified, the extent of modern legal governance reflects the availability of money in a society that is characterized not simply by the commodification of almost everything, but equally by 'surplus money' – the money to buy non-necessities – the condition of existence of a consumer society. In a consumer society, such surplus money is the vehicle whereby legal regulation becomes immanent, often invisible and ubiquitous in everyday life. Through various of its characteristics, money blurs what is a sanction and what is a price, a tax, a fine, a fee or a licence. Jeremy Bentham (1962) wryly commented that a fine is merely a license paid in arrears. It is a cash payment for an otherwise restricted or prohibited action. This could help explain why if we fail to pay fines we can have our licences to drive, operate machinery or run a business suspended or revoked. If we drive on a tollway we pay a premium for not having an electronic pass that we really should have known was required. Depending on the jurisdiction, this payment is almost interchangeably understood as: a price or premium for the convenience of using the facility without a pass; an administrative fee or levy for the cost of processing the case; or a penalty or fine for carrying out an unauthorized act and disobeying regulations. Many criminal justice jurisdictions in the United States and elsewhere load up fines with a plethora of fees – for funding victim compensation schemes, for funding programmes of government to control 'the problem', even for processing the fine itself.

Money is thus an extraordinarily flexible and adaptable tool of government. It can be a punishment or a compensation, a tool for governing individuals or whole distributions, it can be valorized as a punishment by articulating it with court denunciation, or it can be rendered merely as price or payment and buried in daily life. In this way, money can bear many meanings, often simultaneously. However, in each case, it retains a certain underlying liberal governmental meaning that it is not as significant a penalty as liberty itself. This constant subtext that it is 'only money' is linked to its undifferentiated (but not meaningless) character, to its ubiquity in modern life, and to its use as the principal currency of justice. In certain respects, Simmel had already discerned these features of governing justice through money. However, since his day a series of changes have given this combination of attributes an even greater range of possibilities and domains for extending governance.

One critical development in this respect has been the development of regulatory governance. In Foucault's (1984) sense, 'regulation' is a technology of government that works through distributions rather than through punishment or individual discipline. While examples certainly can be found in the nineteenth century, it is really the rise of social insurances and the large scale development of the insurance industry from the early years of the twentieth century that mark the expansion of this mode of power. As suggested, money damages in tort law were to be imbricated in this development, both facilitating and facilitated by the formation of a nexus between liability insurance and money damages. In turn, this articulation with insurance pushed compensation forward as the principal function of damages while the punitive role – which had been dominant in the nineteenth century – slipped to the margins. In the same process, emphasis on compensation shifted concern away from individual attributes such as negligence and fault as the basis of legal liability. Such punitive or even disciplinary concerns were displaced by distributional categories and techniques – such as 'enterprise liability' – as law's attention to monetary compensation of the injured became paramount. In turn, as the role of insurance in funding damages grew, so the overall liability to pay damages increased proportionately, and the reliance on insurance to pay the damages increased with this. Money accordingly extended its role as the currency of justice through rationalities and techniques focused on distributive justice and risk spreading.

A second and related development concerns the shift toward distributional governance through fines. Like 'penal' damages, the 'penal' fine in criminal justice is punitive and individualized. It is organized around a focus on individual blameworthiness – in this case, guilt and *mens rea* rather than negligence and fault. It 'works' through an ethos of punishing individual wrongdoers through the extraction of money.

However, during the twentieth century, a new form of 'modern' or 'regulatory' fine grew out of and alongside the penal form. Such developments as the growth of motor transportation, and the growth of a consumer society with which this was imbricated, increased requirements for governance to a degree that outstripped any capacity to persist with individualized justice. However, means were at hand to manage the problem. The increasing surplus income that came hand in hand with these changes created a medium through which massive volumes of sanctioning could be effected – for consumers could afford to pay fines. Fines were cheap to administer, provided funds for regulation itself, and their 'only money' form made feasible the erosion of expensive and time-consuming procedures of individual justice. Rapidly growing sectors of justice moved away from discipline and punishment *per se* and became regulatory. The focus on individual denunciation was increasingly displaced by conditions in which the offender – exemplified by the driver committing a minor infringement – remained publicly anonymous and mainly of interest as a fragmented role-bearer. He or she is frequently what Deleuze (1995) has called a 'dividual' rather than an individual. Procedural and related streamlining, necessitated by the volume of regulation, meant that concern with fault was reciprocally displaced with an emphasis on the behaviour itself. This change in its turn lent itself to automation in the registering of offences and the issuing of penalties, thus reducing the costs and increasing the capacity of regulation still further. In the process, each individual offence became less important in itself, and much more important as part of a distribution of behaviours that needed to be shaped. The modern fine, the child also of pressures toward efficiency and universality rather than individuation, had emerged.

Of course, none of this should be read as implying that we have entered into a new epoch of the regulatory society. The money form of the fine and damages linked to the rise of consumer society provided the conditions for massively expanding the capacity of government to govern everyday life. However, the move toward regulation is only one trend, albeit important. This book, therefore, does not announce a new kind of society with a new kind of justice. It emphasizes the extent to which, and the governmental processes through which, money has become the currency of justice. Without downplaying the importance of other shifts, most notably the varying fortunes of correctional justice, it focuses on the enduring and expanding importance of money sanctions. In the modern era, penal fines became and remain probably the dominant sanction in most criminal justice systems; modern regulatory fines are growing at an exponential rate in terms of the scope of regulation and the volumes of money involved; and the articulation of money damages with insurance apparatuses means that money remedies have become a part of a huge fiscal apparatus governing harms. In terms of the volume and the scope of activity governed, and in terms of the proportion of justice they put into effect, other sanctions come a very distant second to money as the currency of justice.

Even so, if any correction were needed against a thesis of the 'triumph of regulation', it is impossible to ignore the fact that the past thirty years has seen a neoliberal counterattack that has revalorized punishment and sought to wind back 'welfare' logics of entitlement to compensation and distributive benefit. One of the tasks of this book will be to register the uneven impact of this sea change in government on money sanctions. Broadly speaking, with respect to damages it has been associated with the reassertion of the nineteenth century approach to damages. Within a reformulated vision of individual responsibility, money has been valorized as a medium through which the negligent are once again to be punished, and harmful actions deterred. Strict liability has retreated in certain respects, and the amounts of money provided in compensation have been subject to ceilings to protect enterprise and especially the private insurance industry. Moves toward displacing tort damages with fully socialized insurance schemes have been thwarted or, where implemented, wound back or modified. With respect to penal fines, the 'punitive turn' has been associated with a relative decline in proportionate use virtually for the first time in more than a century – although without significantly threatening its status as the principal sanction in criminal justice outside the US.

However, there is little or nothing associated with this historic shift in governance that appears to have impacted negatively on the modern regulatory fine. Perhaps this is because of a background value neoliberalism places on 'user pays' and market models, in which modern fines appear as prices, fines and fees. Perhaps it is because modern fines embody a punitive principle. Perhaps it is simply because the revenues have become vital to national and local government. Traces of all such countervailing rationales can be found, but in truth, systematic challenges to the regulatory fine hardly arise.

If, as my analysis will argue, this robustness of money as the currency of justice across the board is inextricably tied to the rise of the consumer society, it may well be that this provides some further food for thought regarding money and the forms of contemporary government. This links to Deleuze's (1995) suggestion that governance is increasingly effected through immanent regulation: regulation that is built into the activities and process of everyday life rather than being exercised in the domains of disciplinary institutions. He points out that our 'swipe-card', credit card or other bar codes and electronic IDs allow or block our entry into various governable spaces. Many of these are sites of consumption: parking zones, hotels, bank accounts, airlines, nightclubs, freeways, commercial websites, etc. We circulate in this securitized system not as disciplinary individuals, but as 'dividuals' – two-dimensional identities stripped of personality (we might say), of motives and intentions. It is an image of governance that evidently aligns well with what I have been outlining here regarding monetized justice, and especially the regulatory fine and compensatory damages.

But Deleuze's image of control societies envisages an arrangement of bans or permits. Certainly, this is an important part of the story. However, as he emphasizes, these circuits of control extensively work through commodified existence. Through the services and commodities we buy, we are linked to a system that works through flows of money. To the extent that they act as prices, money sanctions insert what economists refer to as 'friction' into economic and social transactions. That is, they work through the modulation of resistance. They speed up or slow down flows of action, deter, deflect and facilitate activity as well as simply permit or refuse entry. In Foucault's (2007) imagery, they govern the circulation of things, bodies and actions that we may understand as 'freedom' and 'security'. In this respect, it is important to recognize that money sanctions, and especially the ubiquitous modern regulatory fine – have a certain quality of porosity. Without putting at risk our liberty, we may choose to refuse regulation and simply pay a money price for this privilege or choice. Money sanctions may thus have been constitutive of new ways of being free. Just as they were vital to promoting and enforcing 'the reasonable man', they may now also be vital to the formation of other ways of being free and self-determining.

## Notes

1  It is argued by some that far from being repressive, most traditional societies are more focused on reintegration, and that coercive punishment is a characteristic of modern societies (Lukes and Scull 1983). In general, critics pay almost no attention to Durkheim's argument that the emergence of violent and spectacular punishment in the eighteenth century was associated with the development of absolutist monarchies. These, he suggested, 'distorted' social relations by a political process that artificially re-created the king as the equivalent of the sacred order, and this regenerated repressive sanctions. As well, it is important

to note that his principal point was not so much about the changing nature of criminal justice as about the increasingly extensive and important place occupied by civil law – and especially contractual law and its compensatory sanctions. Both of these points make Durkheim's thesis rather less ridiculous than some of his critics imply, although it still suffers from significant problems, including an adequate analysis of the nature and forms of civil sanctions.

2 It should be stressed here that 'governmental' meanings are not just those deployed by legislators, judges and so on. As well, they include those used by critics and commentators engaged with problems of governance. These latter have to be regarded as 'governmental', both because they are about government, and also because they shape government – whether through resistance or through the fact that they may subsequently become state policy of juridical dicta themselves.

# Chapter 2

# Penal fines

Ever since the publication of *Discipline and Punish* (Foucault 1977), it has been virtually impossible to think about modern punishment without in some way focusing on Bentham's Panopticon. For criminologists, it is fair to say that while Bentham was well enough known already as a founder of classical criminology, until then it had been the rational choice criminal rather than the disciplinary prison that was his trademark. Now the Panopticon appears as the quintessential expression of liberal penology. Working with the lightest possible touch on the body of the offender, it accorded well with liberal rejection of the coercive excess of the Absolutist state. As well, as Foucault argued, it was an institution that made subjects free in the sense that they would conform to the ways of a liberal polity without continued intervention by the state. However, we may well query whether the Panopticon should be considered the liberal penal apparatus par excellence.

While Gertrude Himmelfarb (1968) has pointed out that the poor reception the Panopticon received continued to rankle Bentham into old age, it needs to be recognized that it was the child of his middle years. Between the 1790s and the 1820s Bentham's politics shifted from Tory to Philosophical Radical. He was, to begin with, an advocate of corporal punishment, and his promotion of the Panopticon did not (*pace* Foucault) envisage working simply on the mind or the soul. The 'terror' of imprisonment, with its delivery of 'corporal pain' was one of the key deterrent functions the Panopticon was to perform (Bentham 1962, iv: 122). By the 1820s, however, he had moved far from this position, regarding all punishment as an evil, albeit a necessary one. And it was no longer the Panopticon that was central in his writings. Rather it was those forms of punishment that in his view delivered no physical coercion and that were, in the event of injustice, completely reversible. These were monetary – or as he expressed it 'pecuniary' – sanctions. So much is Bentham associated with the Panopticon, it is hard to credit this fact. Yet it would be quite possible to argue that, rather than the Panopticon, the twinned punishment of the fine and monetary compensation was the ideal liberal criminal justice sanction. After all, it is the child of Bentham's final years, overriding in his estimation the Panopticon. To back up this point, with reference to Bentham in their classic analysis, Rusche and Kircheimer (1939: 206) argued that 'the system of fines (is) the epitome of rationalist capitalist penal law'.

As will become clear I do not wish to make such an argument. Bentham's own shift between two historically specific forms of liberal politics suggest that insofar as liberalism is attached to specific penologies, this nexus will vary with the historically particular forms that liberal governmentality takes. The fine may be associated more with certain forms of liberal political rationalities than other forms. However, the point does serve to underscore the arbitrary way in which the fine has been submerged beneath the prison in criminological theory and research.

## After the Panopticon: Bentham on fines

I have mentioned before that Jeremy Bentham saw a close connection between fines and licences, for, in both is a capacity to purchase an otherwise forbidden deed. Bentham was clearly aware that 'pecuniary forfeiture' linked not only fines to licences, but also linked fines to monetary compensation for harms, to taxation and to insurance. Indeed, through the mechanism of money he envisaged an entire system of security that would be the most perfect imaginable. Two hundred years later, this remains a very contentious topic, the subject of considerable struggle over the meaning of money and its place as a punishment. Contested issues in this respect include whether money can or should be a way of 'buying off' other punishment and moral outrage, and whether money demeans and cheapens human worth when used in this way. Such concerns are salient, perhaps because, as Simmel suggested, money now carries a popular meaning of the commodification of those things most dear to modern human life. By and large, it has to be admitted that Bentham pays such matters little heed. For Bentham, seemingly, money solved almost every problem. But we should pay close attention to his position not simply because he is among the first to make such arguments about fines in an extended fashion, but equally because he linked them directly to the foundations of liberalism on which his work had such a marked influence.

Bentham's terminology at first appears odd or confused, for when he refers to 'pecuniary forfeitures' this covers both fines and compensatory payments – both of which he regards as 'a punishment', in which one party is compelled to pay a sum of money to another (1962, i: 468). He soon distinguishes these into the more familiar forms of fines and damages. With fines, money is simply taken from the offender and put into the general revenue, and with damages money is given to the person harmed. Consequently he refers to the distinction between fines, forfeitures and damages as 'having nothing to do with the nature of the punishment', but rather stemming 'from the accidental circumstances' of the manner in which the money punishment is disposed of: whether respectively to the crown, some other agency, or to the party injured by the offence' (1962, i: 468). Perhaps this is only surprising to a post-nineteenth century reader, for as will be seen in Chapter Four, until the twentieth century civil law damages were primarily regarded as a punishment rather than as compensation. To Bentham and his contemporaries fines and damages appear equally as punishments for they are 'all reducible to the *pain of privation* occasioned by the loss of so much money', while in turn it is 'from his money that a man derives the main part of his pleasures, the only part that lies open to estimation'. (1962, 1: 468, emphasis in original). Indeed, because all sanctions work through pain, and only sometimes through pleasure, elsewhere he assigned punishments and remedies to the sphere of penal law, leaving to civil law the status of 'mere masses of expository matter' (Bentham 1982: 306).

With respect to his use of the term 'estimation' here, Bentham is temporarily glossing over the fraught problem of how to calculate in monetary terms some nonpecuniary harm or pain. By estimation, he is referring first to the idea that money sanctions can be graduated minutely with respect to offences, and second to the idea that money can be made to affect all persons equally. This can be read, especially in a Marxist fashion (e.g. Balbus 1977), as another reflection of the ideological flattening of class by liberalism. One of the enduring, and reasonable critiques of liberalism has, of course, been that in law it regards all subjects as equals, thus effecting massive disadvantage on those without resources. This is vividly illustrated in the law of torts, to be discussed in a later chapter, where it was conveniently imagined in nineteenth-century law that fellow workers could and should be the target for recovery of damages where their negligence caused the accident – even though they could not possibly pay adequate compensation for injury. But Bentham is not attempting such an ideological gloss. Quite to the contrary, he accepts without question that a fixed fine will affect the poor person more drastically than the rich, and argues that the size of a fine should be set by three factors: the gravity of the offence; the value of injury or property involved; and the wealth of the offender. Consequently, with respect to wealth he suggests that the precise 'estimation' of the punitive effect is to be expressed as the ratio of a given amount of money to the offender's total capital. In short, pain will be delivered equally to all by expressing fines as a fraction of their wealth – and in this way he prefigured the 'day fine' still beloved of Scandinavians. For the moment the key point is that he ties the operation of the fine to the felicity calculus of the rational choice actor. For this reason, and because of his belief that this sanction can therefore be delivered with such equality of impact on individuals, the fine already appears as the liberal sanction par excellence. Over and above this, the fine is to be contrasted with imprisonment, because it does not interfere with liberty, while in contrast to corporal punishment, it is not complicated with a degree of 'infamy': the fine does not lay the state's hand upon the offender. For Bentham (1962, i: 579) speaking as a liberal of his times, 'all penal police consists of a choice of evils', and pecuniary sanctions are preferred, because they deliver punishment with 'the greatest economy of force and the most exactitude of suffering'.

Not gainsaying the fine's value as punishment, money's 'peculiar excellence' for Bentham is that it simultaneously adapts itself so precisely 'to the purpose of compensation'. This follows because the felicity calculus was envisaged in such a way that pleasure and pain could be equated: so much anticipated pleasure to be gained illegally would be offset by law's guarantee that pain would follow in proportion. Since the crime would take away pleasure from the victim, then its return in money form would allow the purchase of pleasure to compensate. This is almost exactly the legal rationale behind modern compensatory damages. In the same moment, compensation works as a proportionate punishment to the offender. Moreover, where there was a criminal intention to injure, rather than simply to steal or defraud, Bentham suggests that one would suffer double punishment, for 'in having to pay compensation to one I have harmed, who may be an adversary, I would also suffer humiliation'. (1962, i: 392–394).

Through the money form, therefore, punishment and compensation merge. Hence in the closing passages of his *Principles of Penal Law*, in which he brings together in single point the general result of his lengthy exercise, Bentham argues that 'by good laws almost all crimes may be reduced to acts which may be repaired by a simple pecuniary compensation; and that when this is the case, the evil arising from crimes may be made almost entirely to cease' (1962, 1: 580).

> Everything that can be repaired is nothing. Everything which may be compensated by a pecuniary forfeiture is almost as non-existent as if it had never existed; for if the injured individual always receives an equivalent compensation, the alarm caused by the crime ceases entirely, or is reduced to its lowest term. The desirable object is, that the funds for compensation should be drawn from the mass of delinquents themselves ... If this were the case, security would be the inseparable companion of innocence, and sorrow and anguish would only be the portion of the disturbers of the social order. Such is the point of perfection which should be aimed though there be no hope of attaining it but by degrees.
>
> (1982: 579)

In view of the fact that this was unlikely to be achieved in the foreseeable future, not least because the poverty of most offenders would preclude them making adequate compensation, then Bentham argued that compensation would have to be through insurance. But more properly, this remedy should become a cost on the public treasury, for the state had a responsibility to provide security – to the cost of which the victims had contributed monetarily through taxation – and clearly this protection had proven ineffectual. In this aspect of pecuniary justice there would be the added benefit of a spur on the state to produce a better security of the nation.

In discussing the merits and demerits of the fine, Bentham stresses that one of its prime characteristics is that in the execution of the sanction 'no spectacle is exhibited: the transfer of a sum of money on this account has nothing to distinguish it from the case of an ordinary payment'. Perhaps this is not quite so if we consider the element of denunciation in court associated with pronouncement of the sentence. However, certainly it was to become a primary characteristic of regulatory fines that appear as simple 'prices'. Yet it is not at all clear that he regards this as a matter of concern. Passing quickly over the issue of 'exemplarity' by noting that the fine has 'nothing in particular to boast of' in this respect, he short-circuits possible criticism by immediately linking the idea of exemplarity to the discredited punishments and 'spectacles' of the corporal kind. Thereby the fine is made to appear all the better because of one of its supposed failings. It is as though, for this matured Bentham, the smooth working of a system of pecuniary fines and compensations will better resolve the question of crime than any ceremonial embedded in the 'mere masses of expository matter' that constitute legal procedure.

In many ways, Bentham's rather ruthlessly monetary – yet blithely optimistic – vision provides a framework for thinking about the present. After all he has prefigured something that is central to the thesis of this book concerning the embedding of fines in mundane life as a price of existence. He has made clear the nexus between fines and damages and other monetary sanctions and fiscal impositions. He has established a nexus between the fine and a liberal political rationality and raised the question of the role of insurance with respect to crime compensation – and linked all of these to monetary damages. He joins this assemblage of pecuniary justice together within his own liberal and utilitarian governmental framework. Of such a framework, of course, we could quite readily echo Karl Marx's sneer (1976: 758–759) that 'with the driest naivety he assumes that the modern petty bourgeois, especially the English petty bourgeois, is the normal man', and that therefore Bentham is 'a genius in the way of bourgeois stupidity'. This is a foundation of the Marxist analysis of fine, as will shortly be seen. Alternatively, we could say, first, that it is precisely because Bentham is this kind of genius that he is important for us to attend to: he maps monetary sanctions, and especially the fine, onto a particular rationality of liberal thought. Of course, not all liberal thought takes this shape, and certainly his and Smith's brands of relentless utilitarianism generated considerable opposition. This included opposition from those such as Adam Ferguson (1995) who decried the absence of passion and communal humane values from such a calculating vision. Even so, it is impossible to deny Bentham's currency and influence at the time, and if it ever faded, the work of the law and economics movement over the past thirty years has done much to revive it.

## The mirror of production

The work of the 1930s German scholars Rusche and Kirchheimer has become almost synonymous with a kind of narrowly economistic Marxist penology, in which the system of punishment appears as no more than a reflex of the needs and effects of the mode and relations of production (Garland 1991). While there is more than a degree of truth in this characterization, a just measure both of their achievement and their limits should take into account that they did recognize the theoretical importance of the fine and were the first modern criminologists to do so. Moreover, they did not simply deduce the status of the fine from rigid axioms about bourgeois economy and society, but attempted to historicize its conditions of its development as a principal sanction in modern criminal justice. In order to appreciate this, it is worth setting analysis of their work against the apparently more sophisticated backdrop of Evgeny Pashukanis' Marxist theorization of bourgeois law – written in the previous decade, but seemingly unknown to them.

Because of its identification with the 'commodity form of law', the form of law appropriate to a system of generalized commodity production, it may be imagined that Pashukanis' (1978) treatise *Law and Marxism* virtually throws itself at the question of how to theorize fines. In practice, however, Pashukanis barely mentions the topic. The one passage where this does get raised is only an aside, but nevertheless is instructive. Pashukanis (1978: 181) outlines a general thesis that criminal law 'is a variation of that basic form to which modern society is subject – precisely the form of equivalent exchange, with all its consequences'. Central to an understanding of law, he argues, is a recognition of the isomorphism between on the one hand the abstraction of commodity relations, in which all things are reduced to a universal common denominator, and on the other hand the form of law in which subjects likewise confront each other as abstract, equal and voluntary individuals. In this contractual vision of the commodity form of law, criminal sanctions appear in a particular light: the state is represented as a party seeking damages from one who has wronged it. Thus, 'punishment functions as a settlement of accounts' (1978: 181). In the imagery of commodified relations, this settlement is effected though an abstract medium of exchange: especially time and money. Thus, bourgeois punishment's most characteristic feature is the arithmetical expression of the severity of the sentence:

> so and so many days, weeks and so forth, deprivation of freedom, so and so high a fine, loss of these or those rights. Deprivation of freedom, for a period stipulated in the court sentence, is the specific form in which modern, that is to say bourgeois-capitalist, criminal law embodies the principle of equivalent recompense. This form is unconsciously yet deeply linked with the conception of man in the abstract, and abstract human labour measurable in time.
>
> (Pashukanis 1978: 180–181)

Pashukanis' focus on the labour theory of value projects his analysis to the question of labour time. As the underlying relation shaping law, the commodification of labour swings around the exploitation of the working class through the appropriation surplus value. In other words, the amount of value returned to labour in the wage form is less than the value that labour produces in the time for which wage payment is made. Capital accumulation occurs through the creaming off of the uncompensated or 'surplus' value.

That Pashukanis focuses on labour time reflects two things. First, the tenets of the labour theory of value that for Pashukanis centred labour time (later interpretations focused on labour power). Second, a taken-for-granted focus on imprisonment, and on imprisonment as simply an amount of time incarcerated. While time therefore emerges as central in this understanding of the commodification of criminal justice, this is not the only possible reading of the labour theory of value. The wage form is critical to the labour theory of value, because the money form masks the extraction of value: the wage ideologically appears merely as an exchange of time and money agreed on by contractual equals. In turn the wage form reproduces the dependence of labour on capital because labour can only buy the commodified means of survival, not the means of production. The money form of the wage is, therefore, one mechanism ensuring that labour remains separated from the means of production. Pashukanis, therefore, could have had an easy time incorporating the fine into arguments about the commodity form of law; but it is the prison and the deprivation of liberty for a fixed amount of time that occupies virtually all of his attention. At best, the implication is that money is merely the abstract medium of exchange, and so the fine is intrinsically uninteresting, because money translates to a certain amount of labour time, and thus to a certain amount of time in prison. In this reading, the prison is regarded as the principal or symptomatic sanction, the fine only an adjunct – a view that (although coming from a different political direction) replicates the assumption made by western criminologists.

Writing in the 1920s, Pashukanis' focus on production perhaps reflects the conditions of the poor in his era – although the fashionable excesses of the Weimar Republic and the 'flapper' culture of the 1920s might have alerted him to the wider significance of commodification that was beginning to emerge. For a widening array of ordinary people, and certainly for the capitalist economy, money and what it could buy was perhaps beginning to lose its intrinsic embeddedness in the world of production. Consumption was stirring, but the Marxist entrapment in the domain of production restricted Pashukanis' analysis. The theoretical and political necessity of focusing on the extraction of surplus value meant that to emphasize the domain of consumption as shaping forms of punishment was tantamount to revisionism (as it was, Stalin executed Pashukanis for his deviations). For several generations to come, the domain of consumption was to remain an epiphenomenon for Marxists, an ideological chimera. But in any case, looking beyond production relations simply did not occur to Pashukanis – or to his contemporaries – because the prison dominated criminological consciousness then, as now. There is no obvious nexus between imprisonment and consumption.

All of this was reflected in much communist law, where the fine was normally consigned to a minor role until quite recently. Grebing (1982: 15) points out that in the post-revolutionary years, the fine was held in considerably bad odour in the Soviet Union and was completely omitted from the Leading principles of Criminal legislation of 1919. It crept back only for a few minor offences through the 1920s, usually where financial gain was associated with the offence. The fine was regarded as inferior to reformative sanctions, and was displaced by short periods of 'correctional labour'. This remained true through to the 1980s where fines were seen as inconsistent with the ethos that 'Soviet citizens possess private property as a reward for their personal participation in the process of social production'. It was held that in the Soviet Union the fine ought to be a penalty of insignificant application only, and consequently is to be used only for trivial offences (Grebing 1982: 15) Like the theorists who shaped its doctrines, the Soviet state's focus was unremittingly productivist.

Frankowski and Zelinska (1983: 39) indicate that by the 1980s fines still made up only about three to four per cent of sanctions in the USSR, about five per cent in Czechoslovakia, about ten per cent in Bulgaria although climbing to about 18 per cent in Poland. In their summation they suggest that

> The relatively rare use of the fine in these countries may be explained by the fact that for many years the fine was viewed with a great amount of suspicion. It was suggested by some scholars that this penalty was incompatible with some of the basic ideological premises of socialism. It was maintained that the fine was a criminal measure typical of the capitalist system in which everything, even the criminal justice system, was profit oriented.
>
> Frankowski and Zelinska (1983: 39)

Ironically, despite the focus on production, it could be argued that these state socialist examples illustrate the relevance of governing mentalities on the place of sanctions. The fine's place was driven by the governmental vision of what it was to govern 'well' rather than by the needs of the productive system. The importance of official thinking about the nature of fines is something we will again see when we consider the case of the United States. Despite the Marxist views on the obvious nexus between capitalist production and fines, the most capitalist of all nations exhibits a similar aversion to fines – on the similar grounds that the fine has little or no reformative value.

Rusche and Kirchheimer continued the legacy of Marxist theory, producing what Baudrillard (1984) refers to as 'the mirror of production', the unintentional reproduction in form and focus of the nineteenth century bourgeois obsession with production. Yet they achieved two notable advances over the kind of commodification of law analysis represented by Pashukanis and which was reproduced half a century later by Balbus (1977). The first, as mentioned, is that they actually write at length about the fine, although again managed to do so entirely within a framework of production. The second is that in theory, if not in practice, they allow much more room for the relative autonomy of law. In their classic statement Rusche and Kirchheimer (1939: 6) stress that

> ... punishment is neither a simple consequence of crime nor the reverse side of crime, nor a mere means which is determined by the end to be achieved. Punishment must be understood as a social phenomenon freed from both its juristic concept and its social ends. We do not deny that punishment has specific ends, but we do deny that it can be understood from its ends alone.

Instead, they argue that punishment reflects the 'basic social relations' in a society. Primarily, this does mean that the prevailing system of punishment is to be understood in terms of relations of production. But while they could fairly be described as narrowly economistic this does not correspond to a strict economic determinism. They stressed simultaneously that there can be no general theory of punishment because 'punishment as such does not exist, only concrete systems of punishment' exist, and that 'every specific development of the productive forces permits the introduction or rejection of corresponding penalties' (1939: 3–6). This use of the term 'permits' says no more than that penalties have certain material conditions of existence; it does not go so far as to argue that the nature of punishment is simply an effect of the mode or relations of production. With respect to the fine this is consistent with their ultimate conclusion that 'the application of fines has its natural limits in the material conditions of the lower strata of the population' (Rusche and Kirchheimer 1939: 176). As such, they assume both that all fines are directed primarily at the poor and that under conditions of generalized poverty the fine would not be a viable sanction, because too few could pay it. Both assumptions are questionable, probably wrong.

Rusche and Kirchheimer's analysis of money sanctions begins with the observation that while the fine was well understood in principle by classical criminologists such as Bentham and Beccaria, fines could not be deployed to any degree before the end of the nineteenth century because of the extent of unemployment and poverty. The increase in employment and real living standards into the twentieth century provided the conditions under which the fine becomes a more generally applied sanction. Their evidence focuses on the dramatic shift in proportions of offenders imprisoned and fined in Germany between 1882 and 1932, where the percentage fined increased steadily from 11 per cent to 47.5 per cent, having peaked at 50.5 per cent in 1930 (Rusche and Kirchheimer 1939: 167). Over the same period, the proportions sentenced to terms of over three months imprisonment remained stable, indicating that short periods of imprisonment were being substituted by fines. On the basis of rather thin evidence – none of which for example even indicated changing real income levels and unemployment rates, or relative rates of imprisonment and fines before 1882 – Rusche and Kirchheimer conclude that:

> In general therefore the application of fines in the first half of the nineteenth century was infrequent because the necessity of commuting the punishment into imprisonment would have unduly complicated criminal procedure ... The decline in unemployment and the rising living standard in the second half of the century, however, introduced a fundamental change. Many of the difficulties lying in the way of a fine system lost their force.
>
> (1939: 168)

This rather narrow point is extended by an argument that, as a corollary, during periods of depression the fine becomes less feasible, and consequently short terms of imprisonment become more prevalent. The extent to which the fine can be developed is thus 'decisively influenced by the whole social situation and by the conditions of the various strata', and it is concluded that 'the poorer the population of the country, the less frequent is the use of fines for offences characteristic of the great mass of the people' (Rusche and Kirchheimer 1939: 171–173).

As it stands, this argument rests very largely on three claims. First, an implied statistical correlation although one side of the equation is merely asserted. While I don't want to challenge the correlation's general direction – because unless poor people can usually pay fines the sanction would not be widely used – there are some problems that make this specific interpretation bothersome. In particular, given their own assertion that economic depressions have an adverse effect on the propensity to fine, it seems strange that the severe depression of the 1890s does not appear to have registered more than the slightest hiccup: basically the rise in the use of fines appears unchecked. As well, their own data on fines during the Great Depression of 1929–1933 are problematic. Rusche and Kirchheimer (1939: 169–172) put stress on the proportions of fines that are not paid in full and that therefore result in imprisonment in default. This produced the predicted increase in imprisonment. But the proportion of *sentences* that are fines does not decline as it should, given the severity of the depression. They dip by only three per cent throughout the period. In short, people may be unable to pay, but the courts are only marginally changing their sentencing behaviour. Their own data suggest the possibility that courts do not sentence as a reflex of the state of the economy, but are influenced far more by other considerations. In turn, while there is no reason to doubt that rising real incomes are indeed relevant in certain ways, this casts some doubt even on the argument that the basic shift from the late nineteenth century can be attributed simply to economic conditions of existence.

This doubt is intensified by other arguments they mobilize in support of their claim. To begin with, they spend some time outlining the essentially bourgeois philosophy underlying the fine by identifying various late nineteenth century views that justify the fine. These are Benthamite in form, beginning with official quotes to the effect that as 'money had become the measure of all things' then the fine was an appropriate punishment in a society of commodities, and that 'since virtue is rewarded by wealth, vice should entail impoverishment' (quoted in Rusche and Kirchheimer 1939: 168). Presumably this is meant to show that the ideological conditions to support extension of fines were present, which they may be. But as these are no different to Bentham's arguments and, as Rusche and Kirchheimer have already pointed out that such views had no impact on the viability of the fine in Bentham's time, the best we can say is that things hadn't changed in that 'ideological' respect, not that new juridical reasoning had emerged.

Much the same goes for a second bank of supporting arguments. Pointing again to contemporary legal arguments, they demonstrate the existence of official recognition that imprisonment is expensive to operate, removes the labour power of the offender from the economy, and creates a further cost to society through the need to support the offender's family. While Rusche and Kirchheimer put a Marxist cast on these and related arguments, again they are points raised by Bentham in the 1820s. Since they had been present and prominent throughout the nineteenth century, again the best we can say is that there was likely a receptive environment for expanding the use of fines – but not necessarily a changed environment in this respect. So, everything seems to swing on an undemonstrated and historically questionable correlation between real incomes and the rates of fining.

Consequently, it is Rusche and Kirchheimer's further claims about fines and the poor that are pivotal. They point out, quite rightly, that the problem of inability to pay that dogs the fine system is the source of endless official experimentation to make fines payable, right through from the late nineteenth century to the period in which they were writing. This problem, and the experiments to resolve it, continue to the present day. In particular, they include the rise of the arrangement whereby fines could be paid by instalments – a development implemented across Europe from the 1920s. Rusche and Kirchheimer argue that this innovation served the function of reducing the high proportion of prisoners who were incarcerated because of inability to pay fines – which in England had reached a high point of nearly half of all male prisoners and more than two-thirds of all women prisoners. Rusche and Kirchheimer conclude that scheme would 'empty the prisons and reduce the costs and work of administration'. Certainly, as their data showed, the rates of prisoners who were fine defaulters was lowered, even if the rates of imprisonment were not. Nevertheless, in all of this claim their reasoning is quite wrong in some places and misleading in others.

## The mirror broken

To begin with, it is not tenable to argue that under conditions of poverty the fine cannot operate as a mass sanction. As Sharpe (1990: 20–25) and Briggs *et al.* (1996) have shown, fines were an important sanction as late as the mid-eighteenth century in a social order that cannot be assumed to be materially better off than that of fifty years later. King's (1996) detailed analysis of assault dispositions shows that in the eighteenth century close to 80 per cent of convictions resulted in the imposition of a fine, most frequently of only small amounts of up to a shilling. Sharpe's analysis of the seventeenth century likewise shows that fines were frequent and usually light, usually only from a few pence to a few shillings. As Briggs and his colleagues (1996) argue, the reason why fines were so small 'was that they were imposed on ordinary working people, people whose incomes and resources were minimal'. In short, over a very long period prior to the nineteenth century, fines were a default sanction for minor offences. We should remember the import of Bentham's basic observation that the fine is infinitely gradable, and recognize that this means it can be applied in measure according to the economic circumstances of the time as well as according to the means of specific offenders and the gravity of the offence.

One reason for the widespread usage of the fine in earlier periods is that prior to the nineteenth century, prisons were not generalized institutions for punishment. In one of a very few close studies of such sanctioning, King (1996) found that the end of the eighteenth century and the beginning of the nineteenth century was a period in which a major transformation in penology occurred. Following a pattern matched by that with respect to petty property crimes a few years earlier, the period from about 1760 through 1820 saw the proportion of offenders fined for assault drop from nearly 80 per cent to only 26 per cent. Corresponding with this, the proportion imprisoned rose from less than four per cent to over 50 per cent. (King 1996: 48–50). Nor was this move confined to Britain. As Seagle (1948) has argued with respect to Europe more generally at this time, it was 'the acceptance of the penalty of imprisonment (that) first relegated the fine to a comparatively minor role as a punishment for slight misdemeanours and police offences'. This dramatic shift, King (1996: 64) suggests, is best accounted for in terms of both an increasing punitiveness and changing beliefs in the role of imprisonment as a correctional institution:

> The writings of Howard, Hanway and others, which claimed that hygienic, highly regulated prison regimes – including regular religious instruction, strict work schedules, and an element of solitary confinement – offered a way of reforming offenders, were gaining influence. By the early 1780s, the new climate of reform … was affecting not only decisions about prison construction and prison systems, but also more general attitudes toward offenders. Magistrates and county benches were considering the possibility that minor offenders could be reformed by stricter imprisonment policies.

Already this points to the distinct possibility that the increase in fining that Rusche and Kirchheimer attribute to the material conditions of the poor, is unlikely to be related to the conditions they focus upon – even as a condition of existence rather than a cause. They suggest that the late nineteenth and early twentieth century innovations aimed at making fines more easily paid was a key factor increasing the rate of fining. True, but perhaps this reflects a question they never seriously asked. Why did fines so suddenly appear more attractive than imprisonment if people still had trouble paying them? The question is all the more pointed since we have now seen that the fine had been much more in favour only a century before.

Rather than the fine coming into existence as a generalized sanction only at the end of the 1800s, it would appear that this was the resumption of a status quo ante. Short terms of imprisonment during the nineteenth century *temporarily* displaced the fine from its historically dominant perch. In order to figure out why this occurred, we need to attend to what governing discourses of penality were saying at the time. Again, writing with respect to Europe, Seagle (1948: 250–52) points out that it was not simply states responding to the improving material conditions of their populations that brought fines back into prominence. Rather, the leading criminologists of the time – including Garofalo, Rosenfeld, Wahlberg and Liszt – argued strongly for the fine's restoration. In many respects, this movement merely repeated arguments that Bentham and Beccaria had mobilized, citing the stigmatizing effect of imprisonment, its cost to the family, its administrative burden and so on. But these arguments took on increasing importance as they were proposed by criminologists at a time when 'penal modernism' – the scientific-correctionalist movement – was coming to the fore. Even more significant, these familiar claims were joined by another argument of greater novelty and impact. It was now claimed that short terms of imprisonment were counterproductive: short term imprisonment was seen to be 'converting casual offenders into confirmed criminals' and to have no reformative effect. This argument took two forms. On the one side, there were those such as Garofalo (1885 [1968]: 226) arguing that imprisonment for first and minor offenders was pointless, because 'if the occasion has been an exceptional one, if there is little likelihood of its future occurrence, there is no need of employing any means of elimination'. On the other side was an argument that was to gather strength throughout the last part of the nineteenth and repeatedly throughout the twentieth centuries: that the reformative effect of imprisonment took time, and could not be delivered in periods of only a few weeks or even a few months. Thus Grebing (1982: 8–9) notes that across Europe and Scandinavia

> The common basis here, resulting from the intense national and inter-national discussion that took place towards the end of the nineteenth century, was the widespread recognition of the harmfulness and

futility of the almost universal practice of imposing short sentences of imprisonment. The short prison term was seen to have neither reformative nor deterrent effects; indeed it was criticized for having criminogenic effects, especially on first and occasional offenders. The abolition or, at the very least, the general restriction of short imprisonment was demanded. It was to be replaced by other types of sanction and, above all, by the fine and the conditional sentence. For this purpose the fine would have to undergo a thorough improvement.

Perhaps now we have an answer to another troubling aspect of Rusche and Kirchheimer's argument. If, in fact, the fine's use expands rapidly because of the increasing real income of the population, then why does its increased usage appear to be so closely related to the beginning of a long period of innovation and experimentation that was based exactly on the opposite premise – that people could *not* pay fines unless major 'improvement' was made? As far as we can tell, in the eighteenth century, fines were levied without there being any such devices, the problem of ability to pay being dealt with by imposing fines of small amounts. Why was it at the beginning of the twentieth century that things did not simply revert to this state of affairs?

At least on the face of things, it would appear to be because the intention was to keep people out of prison if possible. But if this aim were paramount, why were fines not reduced to relatively affordable levels as had been the case in previous centuries? More puzzling still, why was it that, as Grebing's research also shows, this was a period in which fines were increased? None of this makes sense if, as Rusche and Kirchheimer argue, a key aim was to reduce costs to the state by keeping people out of prison. In any case, the cost of prisons had been on the agenda since the time of Bentham – the period in which imprisonment had grown to be the default sanction and fines had been displaced. Rather, as the official discourse of the time suggests, the innovations aimed at making fines payable were given priority, because faith in short terms of imprisonment had been transformed. However, fines could not be reduced to trifling levels – unlike in the eighteenth century – because these fines were to appear as a plausible alternative to a significant deprivation of liberty. Basement-priced fines could only be legitimated where prison was not an alternative. Thus, the English Departmental Committee, set up in 1934 to investigate the question of imprisonment in default of payment of fines, commented that one way of reducing the problem would be for the court to 'mark its sense of the character of the case by inflicting a fine of five shillings or less. In that event committal to prison should be an impossibility' (Departmental Committee 1934: 24). But that did not happen.

As Garland (1991: 109) has argued, a general weakness in Rusche and Kircheimer's account is that the analysis simply maps out historical correlations between penal policies and practices and imputed economic interests, assuming that all intervening processes – such as prevailing political conditions and prevailing governmental meanings of penality and its purposes – are ultimately irrelevant. However, to make a plausible case, Garland points out that it would be necessary for them to show how the policymakers recognized the needs of the production system. When we do attend to official and expert discourses that are repeated across many jurisdictions, they do not mention production. Rather, the re-emergence of the fine as a generalized sanction during and after the late 1800s was linked to a belief in the limits of penal correctionalism.

This is not to say that in such cases the fine had a role only as a residual category, for it was still regarded as a punishment in its own right and, in this respect, little or nothing may appear to have changed since the seventeenth and eighteenth centuries. While the rejection of short terms of imprisonment on correctional grounds does appear to have been the critical factor in the rise of the fine in the early twentieth century, this was not the only discourse that was relevant. As Garland (1985) has shown, the 'triumph' of correctionalism at the end of the nineteenth century was never complete. Punitive discourses remained prominent in penal politics, both opposing therapeutic reform in the name of punishment and responsibility, and braiding punishment and correction together in the compromise that Garland referred to as the 'welfare sanction'. Thus, while the re-emergence of the fine was based on the failure of corrections, punitive rationalities were readily available as the stand-in solution. By the 1930s, for example, we find official discourse in Britain regarding the relationship between fines and imprisonment – including the problem of default – in terms that frame the fine more in terms of a punitive scale:

> In the majority of cases where fines are imposed the nature of the offence and the character of the offender are such that a sentence of imprisonment is inappropriate, because it is too severe and liable to have too damaging an effect on the career of the offender. The Court expects that the fine will be paid and that there will be no question of imprisonment. If imprisonment follows because of the failure to pay the fine, the intention of the Court is frustrated ... (because) his

offence is one which the Court does not hold to deserve so heavy a punishment, and it is certain that were it not for his pecuniary default he would not actually go to prison.

(Departmental Committee 1934: 10)

Both correctional and punitive rationalities thus regarded imprisonment for default to be a problem, and – as in the case of the government body just quoted – strongly supported innovations to deal with the 'problem' of default.

However, it may be a mistake to think that the fine appears now exactly as it had appeared in the eighteenth century before the rise of the correctional prison The twentieth century penal environment in which the fine took its place had shifted ground with the rise of the prison and the correctional movement. It might be said that once correctionalism had been invented, the governmental meaning of the fine drifted from being simply one punishment among many, to being one of the few punishments that has no reformative value. This negative meaning, I want to suggest, is highly significant precisely because it helped to open out a distinction that could not have existed in criminal justice prior to the late eighteenth century and which was to develop unevenly through the 1800s. It is a distinction to which Rusche and Kirchheimer (1939: 173) themselves allude, between a domain of penality, which is individualized, correctional and disciplinary, and a domain of *regulation*, which exists in large measure outside of the concern with individual normalization. Fines contrasted with the rest of the penal environment in that, while available as deterrents, they could be separated from individualization – the basis of the drift from penal fines to modern regulatory fines. But before we can move onto this, we must deal with an apparent, and highly significant, exception to much that has been argued to this point: the United States.

## The curious case of America

While in Europe the fine became a sign of the limits to correctionalism, we need to be clear that not every jurisdiction drew these limits in the same way. It could reasonably be expected that the United States, that most prosperous and capitalist of nations, would be wedded to imposing fines for criminal offences. In many ways, a society and economy that emphasizes financial incentives so strongly, and lionizes market processes, is the 'logical' place for this commodified sanction to thrive. In practice, almost nothing could be further from the truth. Certainly, fines have long been the default sanction against corporations in America, but the same is not true for punishments levied against individual offenders, and things have been this way for quite some time. In the 1950s, for example, The University of Pennsylvania Law Review (1953) reported that over 90 per cent of antitrust violations and offences against labour standards legislation, and almost the same proportion of offences against food and drug legislation, were sanctioned by fines at the federal level. When the focus shifted to assault, however, the proportion sanctioned by fines dropped dramatically to ten per cent, in the case of theft dropped to only four per cent, and with 'juvenile delinquency' dropped to less than a third of one per cent. At the state level, the fine has hardly been used as the sole sentence in relation to felonies, but was deployed as an additional penalty in about a quarter of all cases – most frequently as an add-on to a sentence of imprisonment (Bureau of Justice Statistics 2004b).

In the 1980s, a wide array of offences attracting fines more than three quarters of the time in Germany, and more than half the time in Britain, in the United States attracted sentences of fines in only five per cent of cases at the federal level (Gillespie 1981). As well, in such cases, Morris and Tonry (1990: 116–117) have noted that with the exception of fines against corporations, fines in America 'have traditionally been limited to amounts so low that they cannot seriously be viewed as even roughly equivalent to a term of imprisonment ... Under federal law before 1984, the maximum authorized fines were at such low levels that it was hard to argue that a fine could have much impact, actual or potential, on many offenders.' Morris and Tonry (1990: 116–117) also point out that no sentencing guidelines system in the country 'contains a provision for the use of fines in place of incarceration, (while) several jurisdictions including Pennsylvania and Federal guidelines expressly limit the fine to a supplemental role, something to be imposed in addition to the *real* sentence' (emphasis added).

Even by 2004, at the federal US level only four per cent of offenders were ordered to pay a fine (only 3.5 per cent received a fine only), and this was true for only one per cent of those convicted of felonies. This latter figure is all the more striking when we consider that this includes those individuals convicted of antitrust violations, 18 per cent of whom (down from 26 per cent in 2000) were fined. This compares, for example, to the fact that fines were the sentences given for nearly a quarter of all indictable offences in England and Wales (Home Office 2002). Even for the minor offence category of misdemeanours, where the equivalent proportion in England and Wales was nearly 70 per cent, the proportion fined in the US federal courts was only 29 per cent. In practice, the fine has been losing ground over the past decade, no doubt a reflection of the punitive swing in the United States, where something over three quarters of all offenders at the federal level were sentenced to imprisonment (Bureau of Justice Statistics 2004a). At a superficial level, it could almost be said that America seems to have a love affair with the prison, and this has insulated it against the use of fines in 'traditional' criminal justice contexts.

Perhaps this is a clue to the peculiarity of the American case. As noted above, in Europe fines increased in proportion and increased in money value precisely at the time they came to be regarded as a replacement for short periods of imprisonment. Short periods of imprisonment did not decline in the United States in the same way. Fines were *not* seen as comparable to short periods of imprisonment. Consequently, they did not attract significant penalties in dollar value. But why was this the prevailing pattern? One obvious hypothesis would be that the United States has a low commitment to reform and a high commitment to punishment, so nothing appeared wrong with short periods of imprisonment. Reading backwards from the present, punitive era, this might appear plausible. But again is an argument sustainable only if we ignore the official discourses. In fact, the American Bar Association (1971: 126) argued that 'because of its doubts as to the correctional value of the fine, the Committee would express a presumption against its imposition in the absence of a clear affirmative reason'. Such 'affirmative reason' was held to exist where the commission of an offence had resulted in direct financial enrichment of the offender. Likewise, the National Commission on Reform of Federal Criminal Laws (1971: 296) argued against the use of fines 'because fines do not have an affirmative rehabilitative value'. Putting these claims together, Gillespie has concluded (1981: 201) that the explanation to which he

> ... would give the most support, is based on the observation that the central objective of U.S. correctional policy for several decades has been to effect a rehabilitation of offenders. While the achievability of this goal is now seriously questioned, it remains the foundation upon which most existing practices and institutions have been erected. Within such an institutional structure, there is little room for monetary penalties. Fines have the potential to punish, and possibly to deter, but not to rehabilitate. Thus, the dominance of a rehabilitative approach to corrections has precluded a serious consideration of the use of fines.

To this, Gillespie adds the interesting observation that because of the fine's marginality, it is usually overlooked when legislative updates occur. Consequently, the statutory minimum amounts set for fines are overtaken by inflation, thereby accounting for their frequently piddling magnitude. This is graphically illustrated by the fact that into the second half of the twentieth century, fines for some offences in Pennsylvania were still expressed in English pounds (University of Pennsylvania Law Review 1953: 1017).

Of course, one obvious response would be to ask why US policymakers and judges had paid no attention to European developments, which centred correctionalism and had argued against short terms of imprisonment for many years. Although it may appear simplistic, one of the surprising reasons is likely to be American insularism. As late as 1990, Sally Hillsman, a leading commentator on this problem, was able to make the stunning assertion that 'the use of the fine in Western Europe as the dominant criminal penalty springs from these criminal justice systems' straightforward commitment to punishing and deterring the offender', and furthermore that 'the treatment/rehabilitation model of imprisonment never won the following that it enjoyed for a time in the United States' (Hillsman 1990: 52–53). It is amazing that the kinds of reformative argument against short terms of imprisonment commonplace for the previous century in Europe had not penetrated such research-influenced organizations as the American Bar Foundation, nor Hillsman's own institution at John Jay College, even by the late twentieth century. Such seeming insularity may help explain why the American journal *Judicature* could ask the slightly breathless question 'The use of fines in England: could it work here?' (Carter and Cole 1979); and how it could be that as late as the 1980s and 1990s, authors such as Hillsman, Tonry and Morris are raising the pros and cons of techniques for avoiding imprisonment by default with an air that suggests their intended audience would be strangers to basic questions that had been commonplace elsewhere for more than half a century.

Yet insularism was by no means the only reason. It probably interacted with other matters that appear influential, although their impact too is perhaps just as surprising when contrasted with Europe and the rest of the Anglophone world. When Carter and Cole (1979) interviewed judges concerning their views on criminal justice fines, their generalized distaste for the sanction was based on such well-rehearsed nineteenth century chestnuts as the fact that it would have little impact on the affluent and a harsh impact on the poor. Hillsman and her colleagues (1984: 179) likewise found that in their interviews with judges and court officials, the resistance to fines was most commonly based on the imposition of fines on poor defendants who do not have the means to pay; for whom a realistic fine would not produce an amount of punishment appropriate to the seriousness of the offence; and in too many cases would result in imprisonment for default. Such reluctance to fine may reflect a variation on the theme of democratic justice. This would be consistent, perhaps, with the fact that imprisonment for nonpayment of fines was in 1971 deemed by the US Supreme Court to be in violation of the Fourteenth Amendment rights to equal treatment (*Tate v. Short* 401 U.S. 400). This view was supported in the 1983 case of *Beardon v. Georgia* (461 *US* 672) in which it was argued that 'the State cannot justify incarcerating a probationer who has demonstrated sufficient bona fide efforts to repay his debt to society, solely by lumping him together with other poor persons and thereby classifying him as dangerous. This would be little more than punishing a person for his poverty'.

However, while there is no point denying that many American judges do feel this way about the fine, or that this helps explain the fines' comparative under-use, such economically democratic views seem hard to square with the fact that day fines in the United States have been very little tried compared to elsewhere.[1] If the principal objection was inequity on the basis of wealth, then Swedish experience with day fines – which of course was Bentham's own preference – would have provided a well-known and readily accessible solution to the problem. In that long-established model, the day fine is estimated in units of one thousandth of the offender's gross income, with reductions allowed for dependants. However, the day fine appears to have made its appearance in the US only recently and then experimentally in a few states (McDonald and Moody 1992).[2] While it may reasonably be argued that many jurisdictions have considered and turned down the day-fine scheme as a viable alternative, none of these confronted the American resistance to fining *per se*, and arguably had no strong incentive to take up a system that has its problems. In the US, there would seem to have been every incentive from an early date at least to consider an available technique that would have reduced the load on the prison system and reduced concerns about inequity.

Perhaps the bottom line lies at the level of governmental meanings. It is simply that for whatever reason the United States developed a rationality of criminal justice in which imprisonment was far more central than the fine, and fines were made to appear unjust or nonprogressive.[3] In turn, this meant little attention was paid to developments with the fine in Britain and Europe. As the arrangement persisted through time, so it became more difficult to change. Thus, the aforesaid studies show that fine collection mechanisms in the United States were very poorly developed compared to Europe and elsewhere, with the result that overcoming such a problem could appear as a further hurdle to expanding the use of fines. The rationality of the fine in the United States, like most rationalities, created its own conditions of reproduction, by elaborating intellectual defences against possible lines of change, and by not developing or adopting available technologies that would have rendered these changes feasible.

In this sense, it should be stressed, the fine in criminal justice comes to mean something rather different in the United States as opposed to Europe. In Europe and the common law countries other than the US, the fine had emerged as that sanction, which is deployed where correctionalism failed to operate effectively, but that was valued for its punitive effect. In the United States, the fine became that sanction that operated outside of correctionalism, but was devalued for its punitive effect. We are looking at two sides of the same coin. In Europe, because the short term of imprisonment was regarded as invalid, it became essential to make the fine (and such techniques as probation) 'work'. The fine had to be made affordable and practicable. In the United States, it did not, because the short term of imprisonment was not as discredited. This allowed an array of arguments to develop in the US to the point where they became obstacles to change, rather than (as elsewhere) as problems to be resolved. For rank and file offenders, prison rather than the fine remained the governmentally preferred option.

However, there is a mystery here that can only be foreshadowed and will be dealt with in a few pages. Despite what has been said thus far, the fine has *not* been a stranger to criminal justice in America where corporations specifically are concerned. It is the United States federal jurisdictions that pioneered the modern use of swingeing criminal fines in relation to the corporate sector, notably through the Sherman Act and related developments from the end of the nineteenth century. And it is this same jurisdiction that has subsequently innovated a wide array of techniques of monetized justice, including fines, confiscation of assets, equity fines, treble damages and reparations to be deployed against corrupt organizations, the corporate sector and even wealthy individuals. In contrast to the fine levied against rank and file individual criminals, with corporations and executives the fine *was* put to work. Unlike the poor, such targets of the fine would have no problems paying fines, and thus no problems with defaulting.

## Making fines affordable

Much of Rusche and Kirchheimer's analysis of the fine focuses on its use in relation to what they term 'offences characteristic of the great mass of the people', a list of offences that includes various categories of assault, arson, fraud, theft, resisting arrest and so on. Broadly speaking, these are still offences for which the fine is the most frequent sanction in most jurisdictions outside the USA and for which imprisonment remains an alternative to the fine. Insofar as it is still largely the poor who commit such offences, the problem of imprisonment in default of payment, and experimentation with ways to manage this problem, remain central foci in criminal justice. Such issues include: the numbers of people in prison for nonpayment of fines; the critical and the official discourses regretting this state of affairs; the government efforts to find solutions to the problem; the research and the law reform discourses on techniques giving 'time to pay' or of taking the means of the offender into account, or of allowing payment by instalments and so on. I do not want to enter these technical and normative discussions on their own grounds.[4] Rather, I want to investigate more closely the reasons why this became such a focal issue for criminal justice.

It has been seen that the emergence of this problem appears just at that moment when short periods of imprisonment were being rejected as counterproductive. As a result, in many jurisdictions in the late nineteenth century the use of short term sentences of imprisonment declined relative to numbers sentenced to a fine, the launching point of Rusche and Kirchheimer's thesis. Surprisingly, however, numbers of prisoners serving short terms of imprisonment often increased. As Stephen Garton (1982: 97–105) has mapped it in detail for Australia this was the effect of a large increase in the number of offenders being imprisoned for nonpayment of fines. Such offenders made up 75 per cent of all admissions to prisons in New South Wales in the 1890s. What had begun with the fine as a solution to a problem at the limits of correctionalism, and as an innovation intended to reduce numbers of prisoners dramatically, had been transformed into a problem of overcrowding in prisons, coupled with a high profile politics over the injustice of imprisoning poor people simply because they could not pay their fines. The new problem was resolved by the *Justices Fines Act NSW* of 1899. This allowed the poor to pay their fines by instalments and allowed those imprisoned for fine default to pay off some of their fine (and thus their period of incarceration) by work in prison. Over the following 20 years, the latter measure alone resulted in about a quarter of those imprisoned for default gaining remission.

But why did the number of fine defaulters create a new problem of overcrowding if most of them were simply diverted from prison in the first place? At worst, it would be expected that the number of prisoners would decline less dramatically than anticipated. The answer appears to be that, as fines justified the introduction of speedier summary procedures, so it became an attractive proposition to transfer more existing offences to this summary justice circuit. In the Australian case, this transfer involved most forms of assault, most petty property offences and an array of 'moral' offences such as prostitution and brothel keeping. In addition, this apparently resource-efficient assemblage attracted a whole array of newly emerging offences related to liquor, gambling, family maintenance and so on (Garton 1982:102). We see emerging a procedure that renders it possible to expand enormously the volume of court-based governance, and to allow police to process more offenders by reducing the drag on resources created by needing officers in court for long periods.

Money and one of its most prevalent meanings was having an effect. As the fine does not affect liberty, and thereby appears in the form of 'only money', so it became feasible to reduce protections to the defendant and streamline justice. In turn, this made it possible to govern more subjects through the criminal justice system. Looked at in this way, the fine and its correlative summary forms of justice were creating a condition of existence of a regulatory state – the availability of a cheap, noncorporal and rapidly administered form of deterrence capable of being delivered en masse. Of course, some other technology could have been developed to this end. Later innovations, such as the suspended sentence and variations on the theme of the fine, such as 'expiation payments', would perform this function. However, it was the nexus between summary justice and the fine that here began to create a regulatory form of justice for the masses. Then, as now, there is an element of condemnation remaining, but in the streamlining of the procedure, and in the monetization of the sanction, the ritual ceremonial of denunciation in many cases became etiolated. While we must wait a few years for the development of 'on the spot fines' a fault line was appearing that would make such innovations more thinkable and feasible.

As well, it is easy to take for granted the idea of payment of fines by instalments, but this was an entirely new concept. If the fine tradition-ally had been a punishment then it should hurt, and those who did not pay should suffer some other punishment in lieu. Where did the idea of payment by instalments come from? It is difficult not to recognize that, at this time, the first stirrings of a mass consumer culture were beginning. In the insurance world, the invention of industrial life assur-ance had brought commercial insurance to the poor through a collection system (O'Malley 2004). Commercial insurers recognized that the poor had little surplus income and many short-term pressures on what income they did have. Insistence on using the established techniques deployed with middle class customers – involving substantial annual premium payments – therefore would not have created a market for this commodity. Companies such as the Prudential invented a system in which insurers visited the homes of the poor, preferably on payday, and collected small weekly or biweekly contributions. The experiment was hugely successful, and by the end of the century few working class homes were not insured through this technique. The model was quickly applied elsewhere. The invention of techniques of buying through instalments, such as 'hire purchase', in the closing years of the nineteenth century was used to create a market where otherwise none could have existed. It was a high-profile commercial innovation that criminal justice would borrow and adapt – a manoeuvre that unintentionally brought paying a fine and purchasing a commodity one step closer to each other. The whole point of instalments and 'time to pay' provisions did not simply emerge out of traditional penal consciousness. Rather it was the commercial vision of expanding a market by making the fine '*affordable*' (Departmental Committee 1934: 13–21). To the extent that we can accept Simmel's observation that as money became more commonplace so it became less visible and was invested with meanings associated with everyday purchase of non-necessities, so by the same token the assemblage of sanctions associated with streamlined summary justice – the fine and the instalment system – rendered this sanction increasingly distinct. Fines remained a significant burden for many, but they had now lurched in the direction of being just another financial cost to existence for ordinary people.

At the same time, other innovations were being entertained. Many jurisdictions introduced sentencing provisions that allowed, or in some cases required, the sentencing official to take account of the means of the offender.[5] While explicitly geared to reducing the problem of imprisonment by default, this was at the same time a move in the direction prefigured in Bentham's concerns with the equalization of impact. In most instances, this is a relatively easy calculus to perform, usually involving no more than a probation officer's or social worker's report and thus not significantly slowing the administrative pace of the summary justice machine. Perhaps this rather casual approach in most common-law countries reflects the fact that the principal concern is with facilitating the machinery of justice and reducing the risk of imprisonment by default. However, elsewhere the question of equality of impact has been primary and other innovations have emerged. With the day fine, the specific focus is on equalization of impact rather than speed of processing. In Sweden, for example, the size of the fine is assessed in terms of the seriousness of the offence and the offender's wealth, usually expressed in terms of days of income. Court time is largely unaffected by the innovation, as the calculation and verification of what constitutes a day's income becomes an issue for police upstream or justice administrators downstream from the court. However, this ease of procedure is based on the fact that in Sweden, unlike most other jurisdictions, tax records are a matter of public record.

The day fine was first introduced the by Portuguese in 1852 although its origins can be traced back to the French Revolution The Brazilians attempted something like Bentham's model that incorporated a measure of property as well as income as early as the 1830s, so we could say that there is little new about these innovations. Yet regimes have never tired of resurrecting them for consideration, rejection, modification, abandonment or reconsideration. Austria and then West Germany adopted the daily income scheme only in the 1970s, at a time when the English, Dutch and French had been considering but not enacting it for some years. About the same time the Italians rejected it and the Danes – who had operated a day-fine scheme since before World War II and arguably established it in its modern form – abolished it (Grebing 1982: 2–5, 75–77). Australians have been considering and reconsidering the idea of day fines for the past thirty years or more (Australian Law Reform Commission 2005: 120). The Swedes and Finns have long continued with the system, since the 1920s and 1930s respectively, and it was patchily talked about and experimented with more recently even in various US jurisdictions (Morris and Tonry 1990, McDonald and Moody 1992). Its attractions are made obvious in Bentham's discussions, but its difficulties are equally clear. It can be resource consuming. It raises questions of the admissibility of income estimates and perpetual doubts as to whether people can effectively hide their financial status and thus dupe justice. The same offences can be met by fines that in dollar terms can be relatively huge for the wealthy yet tiny for the poor, offending principles of proportionality of offence and sanction. The question of how to translate day fines into prison terms in default creates more differences between diverse income groups; and to add the brew there are objections to state intrusion into offenders' financial affairs. While reformers have pressed for a day fine system in many countries the protection of tax information under privacy provisions represents a considerable obstacle. This has been relevant to decisions not to proceed with the system despite in principle support – as in Australia. (Australian Law Reform Commission 2005: 120).

All these problems, and more, are endlessly set against the deterrent and democratic arguments for equalizing fines' impact. Naturally, the conclusions reached vary from time to time and jurisdiction to jurisdiction. Yet, the very fact that there has been such a persistent grappling with day fines, with the need to take the offenders' means into account in setting the fine, and so on – over almost the entire history of modern penality – indicates that with specific respect to punishing traditional criminal offences, there is a strong sense of money's bearing on individual justice. Whether this sense focuses on making sure deterrence is delivered across social class, or focuses on a sense of fairness to the poor, it is in marked contrast to the category of 'modern' or 'regulatory' fines, to be considered in the next chapter, where most fines – which tend to be both strict liability and strongly tariff based – take no account of such questions. While the point may seem obvious, this brings us back to consider the United States, where the aversion to the penal fine is not at all matched with respect to regulatory fines levied against motorists and retailers, for example. Put another way, while there is a marked aversion to fining in the US, some of which is attributable to concern about poor offenders' ability to pay, this is of virtually no concern with respect to traffic fines and the broader category of regulatory fines they epitomize even where (unusually) imprisonment remains as a sanction of last resort. In this way, it is possible that money is related in different ways to these two forms of justice: the disciplinary and the regulatory; the individualising and the distributive. It is also possible, of course, that penal fines are imagined, with good reason, as levied against the poor whereas regulatory fines are imagined as levied against consumers. This fits too with America's positive eagerness to fine corporations.

## Bentham reborn?

> Lest the reader be repelled by the apparent novelty of an 'economic' framework for illegal behaviour, let him recall that two important contributors to criminology during the eighteenth and nineteenth centuries, Beccaria and Bentham, explicitly applied an economic calculus. Unfortunately, such an approach has lost favour during the last hundred years, and my efforts can be viewed as a resurrection, modernization, and thereby I hope improvement, of these much earlier pioneering studies.
>
> (Becker 1974: 45)

While fines are comparatively little used in the United States in relation to 'traditional' criminal justice matters, the peculiarity is doubly interesting because penal fines have been vigorously championed by the influential law and economics movement – centred on the Universities of Chicago,

Yale and Harvard. To those outside the US, the influence of academic movements on law and policy may be surprising, but in the United States such interconnections can be tracked back all the way to the nineteenth century (White 2003).[6] Some key figures in law and economics scholarship, such as Richard A. Posner – a Reagan appointee to the United States Court of Appeals – have been prominent in the senior ranks of the profession. As well, perhaps the prominence of law and economics analysis over the past quarter century reflects the broader governmental current of the times. That is, as neoliberal rationalities of government have become predominant, then a focus on money as a means of rendering the problems of law intelligible in monetized ways is only to be expected. We might immediately be led to anticipate that in such a politico-economic environment, a Benthamite vision of the fine would be in ascendancy, and the penal fine move to a position of even greater prominence. Obviously, this has not happened. As a consequence, it is well worth taking a slight detour through these writings, both to understand how Bentham has been revitalized, and how this legal discourse relates to changes in legal and political policy relating to fines.

For the law and economics movement generally, the fine appears as the most efficient sanction for criminal justice, and money damages is regarded as the appropriate mechanism for dealing with compensation in tort law (Becker 1974; Posner 1979). Of course, this appears to be a restatement of Bentham's final view on justice, and certainly Becker's classic statement of the law and economics case clearly reflects the nineteenth century utilitarian ideal. To begin with, Becker rehearses most of Bentham's arguments in favour of the fine, and in particular stresses the point that fines are to be preferred because they can fully compensate victims – including the state – 'so that they are no worse off than if offences were not committed' (Becker 1974: 29).[7] To this Benthamite discourse, Becker adds that another advantage is that fines do not inflict the costs of punishment on society, costs including the discounted sum of the prisoners' earnings foregone and the (monetary) value placed on loss of liberty (Becker 1974: 13). Posner goes further and includes in the savings the cost of building and administering prisons and of supporting the offenders' dependents (Posner 1986: 208).

Becker, especially, is so immersed in this image of money compensation that, like Bentham, the question of different meanings of money – and especially the idea that it cannot compensate for certain criminal harms – do not enter the calculations.[8] In this model of homo economicus money is unproblematically equated with emotions and vice versa. He can thus argue in an entertaining, if not convincing, fashion that it is the failure to financially 'pay' for crime fully, including for the costs of imprisonment, that results in the anger and fear directed at ex-convicts. He suggests that punishment in the form of imprisonment is never enough for the public, because even though time in prison has been served the offender has not thereby 'paid his debt to society' but indeed has only added to it! Becker strikingly argues that *as a result* ex-prisoners are subjected to postrelease stigma and punishment, for example, with respect to their postrelease social acceptance or work opportunities. By contrast, because fines compensate and have no significant net administrative cost, in this economic imaginary 'anger and fear of appropriately fined persons do not easily develop' (1974: 29). Of course, it may simply be that the fine is a lot less visible in its delivery, related to less serious offences, and leaves fewer social traces than imprisonment, and so attracts lesser stigma, but these are sociological rather than economic concerns.

Whether or not this economist's vision (or any of the other of the counterintuitive claims) is empirically true is not established by Becker. By ignoring the possibility that other things may be at work in forming attitudes to offenders, Becker can conclude that the meaning of money in this framework of the penal fine is that of a price. As Ulen puts it with disarming ease,

> Economics has provided a scientific theory to predict the effects of legal sanctions upon behaviour. To economists, legal sanctions look like prices, and presumably, people respond to these sanctions much as they respond to prices. Thus heavier sanctions are like higher prices, and because people respond to higher prices by consuming less of the more expensive good, they argue that people respond to heavier legal sanction by doing less of the sanctioned activity.
>
> (Ulen 1997: 122)

This focus on the fine does not mean that Becker ignores imprisonment, because it is not a monetary sanction. Rather, he converges with Pashukanis's vision of capitalist punishment, for he argues that not just fines but *all* punishments act like prices. Thus, if the price of stealing a car is so many months in prison, then compared to a fine 'the only difference is in the units of measurement: fines are prices measured in monetary units, imprisonments are prices measured in time unit'. (1974: 29). Time and money can be collapsed into each other. Becker's economic rationality – and Pashukanis' promotion of this kind of reasoning as *the* capitalist rationality of punishment – does not allow for the play of other rationalities that would prefer not to equate time in prison with an amount of money, but would regard loss of liberty as a far more morally significant sanction. Yet, there are already some clear indications that this is not so. Even discounting developments in Europe, where a great deal of thought and action has gone into keeping people out of prison on grounds other than cost alone, the American example alone should have alerted Becker that his theoretical account has empirical problems: after all fines have not developed there in large measure precisely because judges and legislators do *not* think that money and imprisonment are equivalent.

This is not the only 'modernization' of Bentham effected in the law and economics literature. As noted, Bentham argued that the difference between criminal law and tort law, between fines and damages, was a matter of procedure only, for both acted as a form of pecuniary penalty. Becker continues this line of reasoning but inverts and extends it. He argues that because law should be about compensation for harm, then criminal law becomes a branch of the law of torts, or as he prefers 'social torts'(1974: 33). The public, represented by the state, would collectively sue for harm to the public good. In effect this is a utilitarian philosophy of law, and one that closely approximates the spirit if not the letter of Bentham's own focus on monetary compensation as the zenith of criminal law's evolution.[9] In this process the utilitarian morality is to the forefront, and thus the meaning of money in fines is heavily inflected by utilitarian principles. As Levitt (1997: 188) stresses, the whole point of rendering punishment optimally efficient through use of fines is to increase social welfare, although of course this does mean socialized welfare but a process of individual responsibilisation, whereby the externalities created by wrongdoers are returned to them in the form of a fine that is equivalent to a tax on privilege.

Yet it would be misleading to cast the law and economics movement as unified on this matter. Posner has argued that welfare maximization of this utilitarian variety is morally flawed. He claims that Utilitarianism is problematic because of its focus on the greatest happiness for the greatest number. This has a great potential for 'moral monstrousness' (Posner 1979: 117). In the extreme example, the extermination of the Jews could be justified by a claim that they were 'so miserable and so hated that their extermination would increase the total happiness of the society'. To avoid such problems, Posner argues that the morality shaping law and economics has moved on to 'wealth maximisation' – which certainly seems to resonate with the new 'post-social' environment, for as he avers it is 'quite opposed to redistributive and paternalistic theories' (1979: 136). In this moral framework,

> ... wealth is the value in dollar or dollar equivalents ... of everything in society. It is measured by what people are willing to pay for something or, if they already own it, what they demand in money to give it up. The only kind of preference that counts in a system of wealth maximisation is thus one that is backed up by money – in other words that is registered in the market'.
>
> (Posner 1979: 119)

The greatest good has disappeared, to be replaced by individual choice and individual wealth maximization. Money sanctions – the fine or tort law damages according to the target population – remain optimal as a sanction, because they are no longer muddied by 'paternalistic' concerns of the sort Bentham enunciated. Indeed, according to Posner in this strikingly neoliberal revision of the fines is even more strongly tied to such wealth maximizing elements as the 'traditional virtues ("Calvinist" or "Protestant") and capacities associated with economic progress'. Utilitarians, on the other hand, 'would have to give capacity for enjoyment, self indulgence, and other hedonistic and epicurean values at least equal emphasis with diligence, honesty, etc.' (Posner 1979: 124). In key respects, Posner appears to have updated Bentham to provide a foundation for the fine that translates it out of nineteenth century classical liberalism into late twentieth century neoliberal orthodoxy. Surely, if anyone in neoliberal government were listening, and assuming that neoliberalism is the dominant ethos in penality, the penal fine was poised to be catapulted into a new phase of growth.

Toward the end of his substantive argument, Becker (1974: 33) briefly notes that 'actual criminal proceedings in the United States appear to seek a mixture of deterrence, compensation and vengeance'. But, apart from noting that these cannot all be achieved at once, the observation simply leads him to state that 'therefore ... if fines became the norm, the traditional approach to criminal law would have to be significantly modified'. Again, had he bothered to lift his sights beyond the borders of the USA – even only as far as Canada – he might have concluded otherwise! In practice, however, despite the already small base from which growth could begin, since the law and economics movement began its promotion of the fine more than thirty years ago the penal fine has failed to expand its domain in the United States.

The reason for this is not hard to find, especially if we attend to developments outside the United States. While modern regulatory fines have grown unabated, as will be seen in the next chapter, penal fines have retreated significantly. In England and Wales, the key period appears to have been between 1990 and 2000. With respect to indictable offences, for sexual offences the use of the fine dropped from 29 per cent to only three per cent; for burglary it declined from 14 per cent to three per cent; for theft and handling stolen goods from 41 per cent to 23 per cent and for drug offences from 62 per cent to 46 per cent. (Home Office 2001: 98–99). As the Home Office (2001: 85) summarized things, over this period there has been 'a decline in the discharge and fine, with a compensating increase in the use of community sentences and custody (that) continued in 2000 reflecting a general shift upwards in sentencing tariffs'. So Garland's 'culture of control' enters the genealogy of the penal fine.

We may have anticipated that neoliberal government with its bias toward economic rationality and market models would have ushered in a heyday for the law and economics movement and thus for the growth of the penal fine. This expectation would be especially marked in the US, where, as White (2003) has argued at length, tort law has undergone changes that are clearly influenced by such pressures. But the reverse has been true for the penal fine. While for offences overall it may still be the case that the fine is the predominant sanction outside of the US, in relation to all the more serious offences in the 'indictable' and 'felony' categories use of the fine has been effectively pushed back by sanctions that operate to capture and constrain the bodies of the convicted. While the fine certainly punishes, the shift in the last two or three decades has demanded more coercive forms of punitive intervention than is available to almost any of the meanings of money that have surfaced thus far in discussion (Garland 2001; Pratt 2007; Simon 2007). In an era of increased punitivism, despite the apparent tailoring of arguments for the fine to fit with a neoliberal rationality, punishment is to a greater extent than before expected to be more than a price, more than 'just money'. Specifically, this means loss of liberty. Foreshadowing analysis in the next chapter, this may help explain differences in the current trajectories of penal fines and the modern regulatory fines associated with regulatory offences. Regulatory fines are still punitive, and perhaps that is one reason why they continue to expand their reach in the current era.

The fate of the penal fine in recent years makes some sense in light of arguments that the punitive turn in penology reflects the impact of neoconservatism rather than neoliberalism (O'Malley 1999). It is often difficult to untangle these twinned rationalities, which have been hybridizing in many regimes since the New Right era of Reagan and Thatcher brought them to an ascendancy. Both strongly favour individualism and a 'small state' (but not a weak state), and they are usually aligned together in lauding market competition, deregulation, privatization, devolution and so on. Both are unremittingly hostile to 'welfare' and the allegedly 'dependent' populations that this generated. But neoconservatives are generally more wedded to forms of social authoritarianism and consequently rather less enamoured of market solutions in all realms of life than is true for neoliberals. A somewhat extreme example would be the contrast between conservative supporters of the War on Drugs, and those neoliberals such as Milton Freedman who deploy economic theory to argue that market forces would govern the drug problem better if only the state stopped distorting things with its prohibition policies. The relative strength of conservatism in the United States, therefore, also may go some way toward explaining this reticence to use the fine, despite its apparent attractions to neoliberal and economic rationalist thinking. If attention is paid to those discourses that argue that mere payment of money does *not* express the moral meaning that should be associated with criminal conviction, then it is not difficult to see a plausible nexus between political conservatism and rejection of fining in favour of imprisonment.

Of course, this can be read as providing a contradictory argument to points raised earlier concerning the equity objections to fining the poor, and claims that resistance to the fine is based on a reformist ethos in American penality. However, this is not necessarily the case. Such arguments were regarded as plausible objections to the fine up to the 1980s, when reformist ideals were still relatively intact. Insofar as these did establish the historically low rate of fining in the US, they could still be operative – although it is likely that both would have been eroded in strength by the culture of control. However, even assuming that both rationales may be at work – a democratic correctionalism versus a conservative punitive penality – rejection of the fine is common to both. Indeed, there is no particular need to see this convergence as new – merely one in which the relative contribution of one rationality over the other has shifted with the rise of the punitive turn.

## Fines, fees, victims and restitution

As one of the pressures that influenced the formation of the punitive turn, the victim movement has made considerable inroads into the discourses and practices of justice internationally (Kirchengast, 2006). The rise of victim impact statements, victim-offender reconciliation programs, restorative justice and the discipline of 'victimology' all register this refocusing of justice onto the 'needs' of the victim rather than on those of the offender. At the same time, the development of victim-centered crime prevention has both reflected and buttressed this reconfiguration of justice, not least through such techniques of community notification associated with Megan's Laws in the United States, and Sarah's Laws in the United Kingdom (Levi 2000). The genealogy of this victim-centered justice and crime control bears traces of a wide spectrum of political influences, including feminist demands for recognition and protection of women crime victims, reactionary politics of vengeance directed at the 'monstrous', and neoliberal visions of victims as the customers of justice (Kirchengast 2006). In this way, victim-focused monetary restitution to victims in criminal justice may represent a site in which neoconservative and neoliberal penal politics could merge in a way that appears not to be the case with respect to the fine.

This configuration of victim justice has particular relevance to the status of the penal fine, because during the last 20 years fines were set increasingly alongside or against restitution and restoration orders, compensation orders and 'restoration fines'. In principle, the restoration order or fine reflects Bentham's original proposal that fines be paid to victims. The concept itself is, therefore, not new; in New South Wales, for example, the Crimes Act of 1900 allowed for recovery of compensation from the offender. More recently, the (Australian) Law Reform Commission (1980: 237) began pressing for restitution to take precedence over the fine where a victim was clearly identifiable. But in Australia, it was not until the 1990s that it was seriously translated into practice. The NSW Victims Compensation Act 1996, the Victims Support and Rehabilitation Act 1996 and the Victims Rights Act 1996 set up a series of victim support agencies and tribunals, and a state funded compensation scheme (which Bentham had also envisaged) for the victims of violent offences. While payment was not made directly by the offender to the victim, the offender could be made to pay back to the fund all or a part of the money granted under the victim compensation scheme. Courts also may order any fine to be paid to the victim rather than the state, with all the usual apparatus of time to pay and taking account the offender's ability to pay (Powers of Criminal Court Sentencing Act NSW 2000). In Tasmania, under similar laws, offenders may be required to pay both a fine and restitution or compensation – but where they do not have the means to pay both then the restitution or compensation has priority (Sentencing Act Tasmania 1997 s43).

In the US, the reticence with respect to fines is not duplicated with respect to restitution orders. Federal Sentencing Guidelines specify that where there is an identifiable victim, the court 'shall enter a restitution order against the offender for the full amount of the victim's loss' (s5E1.1). Furthermore, where it is determined that the offender does not have the means to pay in the foreseeable future the court may order periodic repayments. In California, where a crimes compensation fund is set up, and into which such periodic payments are to be made, the offender has to pay a surcharge of ten per cent to cover the costs of administering the scheme. As well, under the Californian Penal Code (s120.2.4), the court is required to order full restitution unless it finds 'compelling reasons' for not doing so – and the defendant's inability to pay is *not* to be considered a compelling reason. In addition, the burden of proof falls on the offender with respect to any challenge to the amount of restitution claimed. While it is the case that restitution is provided far less frequently than would be imagined from the formal directives, nevertheless large amounts of money accumulate.[10] 'Special assessments' levied against offenders help to fund the Federal Crime Victims Fund, which by 2002 had accumulated over $5 billion in fines, forfeitures, special assessments, mandated contributions from prisoners' incomes and the like (Dubber and Kelman 2005: 40).

After viewing the American resistance to fining at least in part on the basis of concerns about inability to pay, this seemingly represents something of a turnaround: it is as though the victim card trumps other concerns about money penalties for crime. At the same time, however, by a surprising discursive manoeuvre one of the other objections to the fine – its nonreformative character – is neutralized by claiming that the aim of such orders is 'fostering rehabilitation and protecting public safety' (Penal Code 1203.1.j). Just how this fosters public safety is not made clear, but here the meaning of money has been transformed from something officially scorned in the fine, because it is not rehabilitative, to something officially approved in the restitutional fine because it *is* regarded as rehabilitative. The 'responsibilisation' of offenders, by now a familiar process in contemporary criminal policy and practice (O'Malley and Palmer 1996; Garland 2001), revises the meaning of money to represent a form of training in citizenship that would appeal to both conservatives and neoliberals. In this brave new world of victim-centred justice, therefore, redirecting the payment of money from a state recipient to a citizen recipient has a transformative effect on the pecuniary sanction. From being merely punishment, money becomes one of the few 'correctional' sanctions valorized in the new culture of control.

In the United States, especially, this chameleon-like character of money sanctions also comes to the fore when the subject of intervention changes from the individual to the corporation. From the more or less despised residual sanction on the margins of penality, the fine moves to centre stage.

## Fining corporations

It has been a theme in this book that fines are largely ignored by criminologists. However, certain characteristics of corporations have almost guaranteed that they represent a significant exception: with respect to these 'legal individuals' the fine has long been both a central sanction and topic of criminological research and debate. From the governmental point of view, the centring of the fine is not difficult to explain. Corporations are usually assumed to exist primarily to make money, and thus money appears prima facie to be the logical sanction of choice. Likewise, as economic beasts, corporations appear to be the rational choice actors par excellence, and thus eminently suited to monetary forms of punishment and deterrence. As organizations they are not subject to corporal punishment or incarceration, leaving money as one of the few plausible options outside of such politically traumatic sanctions as forcing the closure of a business: the corporate equivalent of capital punishment. Furthermore, because of the scale of their operations, their capacity to do harm is generally much greater than that of individuals, ensuring that the means of their regulation takes on a politically high profile. With respect to the governance of the corporate sector, therefore, fines become very large and very prominent indeed. One effect, not surprisingly, is that criminology here sits up and takes notice of the fine. It is a field not only of considerable research, but also of considerable policy debate and critique. The transformation in attention given to money sanctions is so striking that perhaps it leaves even the casual observer wondering why such criminological interest did not spill over into a focus on the fine more generally. Be that as it may, it is still true that by and large theoretical questions concerning money sanctions have not been centred in this highly active field. Nor, by way of contrast with what literature there is on fines, has there been any of the hallmark critical criminological concern with the burden of punishment carried by the offender. Rather, the key issues for debate with respect to corporations have been how to make fines bigger and more effective; whether the fine can be delivered in ways that have more lasting impacts; how far fines have insufficient moral impact and so on. In short, whereas much criminology has been set against the traditional questions of law and order politics – how best to punish and deter – the change of subject to the corporation turns everything on its head. Here it is the turn of the critical criminologists to play the law and order punitive card.

While the nineteenth century was a period in which fines almost disappeared in 'normal' criminal justice across Europe and America, they were coming to the fore with respect to business regulation through criminal law. We may imagine that this followed simply because, in the words of Baron Thurlow (endlessly repeated in the corporate punishment literature), the business enterprise 'has no soul to be damned, no body to be kicked'. By default, it appears almost obvious that the fine – or analogues such as punitive damages – is the principal weapon of the law against businesses. However, this old saw hardly make sense of the regulatory politics of the 1800s. As Ingeborg Paulus (1974) maps out, even though recent commentators have argued that the fine has little moral bite, in the nineteenth century conviction and fining was widely regarded as a moral affront to justice because of the stigmatizing effect on business owners. Of course companies were smaller then, and owners more directly in control. But if in this way business enterprises of the time turned out to have a body, why wasn't it kicked, or at least imprisoned? Why was money merely taken from its wallet?

Again, one of the critical issues in this early politics was that the company *was* imagined as a 'normal' subject. In Britain, the thirty year struggle to outlaw food adulteration had swung around the question of whether adulteration existed and was harmful. After the poisoning of two hundred people in Bradford, the struggle appeared to end with the passage of the Food Act of 1860. In the new legislation, the fine was the primary sanction. If people were being put at risk of life and health, why was imprisonment not envisaged for such an offence? After all, imprisonment was the normal sanction of the time and given the relatively direct nexus between owners and the operations of their companies, there were bodies to kick. One answer was that the Act was something of a compromise pressed upon an ambivalent government and in the face of opposition from powerful and respected business associations (Paulus 1974: 28). How could respected members of the middle classes be prosecuted as common criminals when, as entrepreneurs, they were performing a highly valued service to the nation? For all that, in the middle of the century fines had almost disappeared from elsewhere in criminal law in favour of correctional prisons; they appeared here and now because imprisonment would have been too much of a leap. Indeed, no one seriously even entertained the sanction.

The fine, in other words, with the implication of its reduced stigma, and the fact that it did not lay hands on the bodies of the middle classes, made this regulation politically palatable. Yet, even when enacted with the fine as its sanction, the law proved difficult to enforce, because the legislation had taken the form of criminal law and required *mens rea*. Criminalizing entrepreneurs in a society that lionized them demanded at least that intent be proven. It soon proved that this rendered the Act unenforceable, largely because it was difficult to establish where in the production chain adulteration had occurred, and thus where responsibility lay.[11] Even though this was partly remedied in strict liability legislation of 1872 and 1875, magistrates clearly regarded it as unjust stigmatization to convict businessmen of criminal offences where no *means rea* applied. This was registered in a refusal to fine, or at worst in the application of such minimal fines as would indicate the court's disapproval of the law it had to enforce (Paulus 1974: 38–43). The monetary value of fines thus emerged – as it was to do again and again with respect to corporations – as a highly moralized issue. The amount of money that offenders were fined was charged with meaning and was certainly not regarded as merely a price or cost of business. It unambiguously and publicly indicated the moral judgment by judges and magistrates – a kind of contemptuous damages in reverse – in which the courts expressed their disapproval of the legislation rather than of the offender. In this light, convictions would have been almost impossible to obtain in the even more unlikely event that imprisonment were made the sanction. The fine emerged not as the only possible sanction to use against businesses, but rather as the only *feasible* sanction in a charged political environment.

Something similar could be seen with respect to the subsequent politics of corporate crime. Legislators and courts have generally remained reluctant to imprison offenders except in high profile and egregious cases. Critics have constantly attacked this state of affairs. Consequently, the questions of the monetary quantum of fines, and the moral and political appropriateness of fines, as opposed to other sanctions, have remained an issue of considerable political struggle ever since. In over a century of corporate regulation, official and academic critics of antitrust legislation have rarely paused in pressing the point that the criminal law provides what are regarded as painfully inadequate fines, incapable either of deterring corporations or of morally denouncing their criminal actions. The point has been endlessly argued that where substantial fines have been legislated, courts are rarely willing to apply the upper end of the range. The almost derisory maximum of $5,000 legislated under the original Sherman antitrust legislation of 1890 resulted in average fines of less than half of even of that amount over the next 20 years (Elzinger and Breit 1976: 55). Another major complaint continues to be that even apparently large fines shrink into insignificance when set against corporate revenues or wealth. Jefferson (2001: 242), for example, notes that when BP was fined £750,000 by a Scottish court for a significant offence, this was only 0.05 per cent of after-tax profits, or the equivalent of a fine of £7.50 for someone earning £15,000 per annum Even some courts have railed against the state of affairs: Judge Robert Jackson complaining in 1944 that 'the antitrust law sanctions are little better than absurd when applied to huge corporations engaged in great enterprise' (*U.S. v. South-Eastern Underwriters' Association* 322 *US* 591 (1944). A decade later Justice Rifkin noted that 'violation of the antitrust laws which persisted from sometime in the early 1920s to the 1940s with respect to which the criminal liability is discharged by the payment of $5,000 hardly seems ... a penalty which is likely to discourage violations of the antitrust laws' (*U.S. vs. National Lead* 114–115 S.D.N.Y., quoted in Elzinger and Breit 1976: 55). Academic critics likewise regard fines as something that 'corporations tend to regard as an insignificant cost of doing business' (Fisse 1990: 215).

One frequent response to this state of things, predictably, has been to raise maximum fines. In the United States the Justice Department recently fined British Airways and Korean Airways $300 million each for price fixing between 2000 and 2006, and prior to that had imposed a fine of $500 million on Hoffman La Roche in 1999. Nor is this limited to American jurisdictions. In 2007, the European Union Competition Commission fined Microsoft $613 million for making it difficult for other companies to make software compatible with Windows, and had previously fined the pharmaceutical corporation Roche more than $650 million for its role in vitamin cartels. Even so, there are still claims that such fines are 'an affordable irritation' (*Times Online*, 27 December 2005). The stakes are raised still further. More recently, Microsoft was fined $1.35 billion for failure to comply with the previous decisions of the European Commission – bringing the total fine against Microsoft for this matter to $2.52 billion (*Ottawa Citizen*, 28 February 2008: D2). This is reminiscent of the fashion in which law and order campaigns raise terms of imprisonment, even though it has not been convincingly established that such fines will have a deterrent effect. While law and economics advocates argue here, as elsewhere, that the fine is the optimally 'efficient sanction', they provide no evidence that fines do deter corporate offending.[12] But perhaps 'efficiency' is not the point.[13]

As Garland (1991) has argued, in courts and politics such reactions and struggles over sanctions more generally do not necessarily reflect a calculation of deterrence but a statement of moral outrage, or at least the political correlates of this. It is, after all, formally recognized that the prescribed maximum fine available does 'indicate Parliament's view (and through Parliament the community's view) of the objective seriousness of the crime in question' (Law Reform Commission 2003: 6.5). Were it the case that the money quantum of a fine did not bear this meaning, then of course much of the political and academic struggle advocating raising fines would be emptied of the moral outrage that so clearly invests it.

Needless to say I am not suggesting that 'irrational' (or rather other than economically rational) responses are the only ones at work. Even the law and economics model was briefly influential in this corporate domain despite its evident ineffectuality with respect to fines more broadly. But even where economic models are constructed with punitive intent, they are often critiqued as insufficiently moral discourses. In the 1990s, the United States Sentencing Commission promoted the 'optimum penalties model'. It required that fines should be equivalent to the money value of all harms multiplied by the chances of escaping conviction. Arguably huge fines could result. But the Australian Law Reform Commission (2003, 6:7) argued against such a scheme because

> At most, the optimum penalties model provides an arguably theoretically coherent basis for penalty-setting in a civil or administrative regulatory context. ... (However) its emphasis on the harm caused by the offence and on "social compensation" means that it fails to mirror the objectives of criminal punishment, especially retribution, deterrence and denunciation.

Likewise, it was also argued that as the probability of capture increases with repeat offending, fines would tend to drop, which 'ignores the social meaning of repeat offending'. In short, the money quantum of fines is bearing a moral load that escapes the view of those who regard money merely as a morally empty medium of exchange.

Fines against corporations therefore are intended to be loaded with social meaning in political and governmental discourses, and I would argue that this too is clear in the discourses of legal and social science academics. Representative papers mentioned thus far (for example, Coffee 1981; Fisse 1990) show a thinly veiled hostility to corporations and to the legal system that seems to let them – and their managers – off so lightly. While I have no difficulties sympathizing with their general position, it is remarkable that such critiques are made without demonstrating the effectiveness of more stringent monetary sanctions. Again, this suggests a mirror image of the conservative law and order politics that routinely calls for more draconian punishments against 'criminals' of the sort who can be imprisoned. Criminologists have few problems identifying the 'politics of vengeance' that drives the punitive turn and 'actuarial justice' (e.g. Simon 1998; Garland 2001). Yet such analyses rarely, if ever, turn their gaze away from the common or garden offenders who overfill prisons, to consider how far the same politics may be driving legal reactions against the corporate sector. Perhaps this is another criminological blind spot associated with the fine to which attention needs briefly to be turned.

The calculation of fines in relation to corporations, like the calculation of civil damages, traditionally takes place within a legislated range (usually specifying only the maximum permitted fine) that leaves plenty of room for the idiosyncrasies of particular courts or judges. As noted, academic critics and even judges question the appropriateness of such discretionary decisions, with the implication that corporations are let off lightly. Such concerns have dovetailed with persistent concerns that in such an sentencing environment, as Brent Fisse (1981: 220) has argued 'fines do not emphatically convey the message that serious corporate offences are socially intolerable. Rather, in this view, they create the impression that corporate crime is permissible provided the offender merely pays the going price'. In short, Bentham's 'license in arrears' argument resurfaces, and persists into the present, as for example, with the Law Reform Commission of NSW's (2003) argument that fines 'may be licence fees for illegitimate corporate business operations'.

In response to such perceptions, and in line with an increasing punitive governmental trend, several more coercive developments have occurred in the US. To begin with, the US Department of Justice Antitrust Division has begun a policy of enforcement through increasing the use of lengthy prison sentences for executives. In 2002, a total of nearly 30 years in prison sentences was handed down with an average sentence of 18 months, and more individuals were sentenced to periods of one year's imprisonment between 1998 and 2002 than in the previous decade (Sideman and Bancroft (2004). More relevant to present concerns, in 1991, the US Sentencing Commission set out guidelines that took the social meanings of fines to heart. The result was a formula for fines that was intended to scotch the fines-as-licensing argument and produce a sort of truth-in-sentencing for corporations. Taking the pecuniary gain reaped by the corporation (unless this was lower than a baseline set in the Guidelines), and adding to this the monetary cost of the social harm created where this resulted from deliberate or reckless intent, it then multiplied the result by a 'culpability score'. The culpability score was based on such mandatory multiplier factors as prior criminal history and any violation of a court order, and such mitigating factors as cooperation and acceptance of responsibility. The resulting overall score (financial gain plus harm in dollars, multiplied by culpability score) provided the judge with the appropriate fine. If the end result was a fine that exceeded the maximum fine authorized by statute, then this statutory limitation should be overridden.[14]

This was a manoeuvre remarkably similar to the Actuarial Justice that Feeley and Simon (1992, 1994) were mapping out at this time with respect to a 'new penology'. While statistical risk modelling was not a key issue in the case of corporate offenders, nevertheless the Guidelines responded to the stimuli of alleged inconsistency and leniency in sentencing by displacing judicial autonomy with an arithmetical tariff that was oriented toward a more punitive turn – what the Sentencing Commission itself referred to as 'just punishment' (United States Sentencing Commission 2007: 8C2.5b, Nagel and Swenson 1993).[15] The punitive turn, in short, is not simply directed at the underclass. While this may be its principal target, as Feeley and Simon argue, the existence of a 'culture' of control, is likely to ramify in directions other than downward.

## Conclusions: the fine as a technology of freedom

In the twentieth century, the rise of the fine to the status of the principal sanction of criminal justice outside America was in no small measure linked to the belief that short terms of imprisonment were not corrective, while at the same time were expensive for the state and disruptive or even criminogenic in the lives of most minor offenders. Discrediting the correctional rationale of short-term incarceration left it as no more than a punishment, and opened up an equation between prison time and the fine. In this respect, therefore, it could be argued that the Marxists and law and economics scholars were right to equate prison time and penal money. However, these economistic accounts cannot be sustained, at least not in any straightforward sense. Only where prison was evacuated of correctional content, only where penal modernism reached its limit, could such an equation be made between penal time and money penalties. Under penal modernism there were two domains of prison time. With longer sentences (usually over six months) the needs of correction were the principal determinant of time – the time required to effect reform of the offender. Sentencing may well be indeterminate where the therapeutic rationality is completely ascendant, or at the very least the period of the sentence will be shaped by the therapeutic diagnoses of the probation officer and social worker reports. In this domain of the welfare sanction there is, at least in theory, no possibility of equating time and money, no translation of the correctional treatment into a cash payment. While one may doubt that the American criminal justice system was so saturated by this correctional mentality that it could not admit the fine at all, as claimed by some commentators, their arguments serve to underline the theme of the limits to money. From within the correctional mentality money provides pleasure, its deprivation inflicts pain, but otherwise it does nothing. The penal fine is a tainted sanction.

In the twilight zone of short-term imprisonment, however, punishment became the medium through which prison time could be translated into money fines: both inflicted pain and little else beside. It was this emergent time/money equation, created by the fine's historically novel role as substitution for imprisonment, that resulted in the need to increase the quantum of fines. Where the equation was not made – as in the USA – noncorporate fines usually remained small. In turn, this novel equation of penal time and money created the need for a set of innovations aimed at making fines affordable and at keeping offenders out of prison. However, the endless and constantly revisited official and criminological discourses surrounding the problem of default, register the fact that the meaning of the fine is *not* discursively equated with loss of liberty – even where the latter was reduced only to punishment. Liberty and money may *have* to be equated, and the prisons may *in fact* be filled with fine defaulters (at least outside the US), but penal discourses lie unhappily with 'regrettable' necessity. Pretty much the same situation exists with respect to the field of money damages in tort law where, despite the fact that damages are the default remedy for all manner of human hurts – pain, injury, anguish, trauma, shame – the courts and liberal jurisprudence endlessly apologize for the 'inadequacy' of this situation.

Perhaps Simmel's argument that modern money cannot be equated with post-Enlightenment humanity and the 'unique personality' now bears fruit. It is not, as he suggests, that the equation cannot be performed. It is performed all the time. However, whenever it is performed it creates ambivalence, a tension with the sacred quality of the individual – of personality, self, emotions, reputation, the body, and most of all liberty. Loss of liberty is thus the bearer of qualitatively different moral meanings compared with loss of money even where both are understood to be capable of equation through the metric of pain.

The assault on the project of penal modernism over the past 30 years could be expected to change the fortunes of the fine as a sanction for traditional forms of offending, To the extent that the correctional project of penal modernism has been eroded, and a rationality of punishment and deterrence has displaced correctionalism, then at least in principle fines now become equatable with all prison terms, not just short terms. But if anything, penal fines have retreated in the last decade or so. Even though a dominant sanction outside the USA, they appear as if punitively marginal, not to be taken seriously as punishment. Likewise, to the extent that the ideology of corrections was at the root of the fine's poor development in the United States, then the door is opened to mass expansion of the fine. In principle, penal fines could have expanded considerably in the past quarter century. This would have been facilitated by influential law and economics jurisprudence that seeks to render the fine the optimal punishment for a society in which liberal, market and entrepreneurial ideals are so salient. As has been seen, this shift in the fortunes of the penal fine failed to materialize. In US criminal justice, if for rather different reasons, the fine also appears as if punitively marginal, not 'real' punishment.

In part, I want to suggest that the penal fine occupies a marginal space in justice, because since the nineteenth century, the centre stage has been occupied by the prison and its associated ideologies. This is registered in the deafening silence about the fine whenever penality is discussed contrasted with the correlatively deafening debate over the prison. The prison dominates modern penological consciousness – the other sanctions are the residuum. This is true, even though by Rusche and Kirchheimer's time imprisonment had long ceased to be the most frequently used sanction in most places. Accordingly, why didn't the fine become the heartland and core of punishment, and the prison the exceptional outlier? Given that the fine is the principal sanction for corporations why shouldn't the fine be central? Why is 'when to imprison' the question on every criminologist and jurist's lips, and not 'when to fine'? True, America dominates criminology and the fine is marginal there. But British and European criminologies are vigorous in their own right and have been highly influential in setting theoretical agendas for the discipline. The same is true with respect to criminal justice and penal administration.

I suggest that the constant in all this is the phenomenal importance of liberty and its deprivation. Because the fine is 'only money', whatever other denunciatory meanings are loaded upon it, and no matter how important and variable these may be in justice, money's underlying and critical meaning is that it delivers pain, promises or denies pleasure, without interfering with liberty. This does not, of course, mean that money sanctions do not interfere with 'freedom' – or rather, with other freedoms. In particular the fine delivers its sanction in terms of the 'freedom of the market'. It functions in this way as the corporate sanction, impacting upon profits, and it functions on the individual offender by impacting on consumption. The fine thus delivers pain while impacting minimally on the freedoms of movement, speech and political participation that we call 'liberty'. In important respects, this also provides a rationale underlying the fact that the principal civil sanction of the liberal state is also money. In such ways, the money sanction is a technology of liberal freedom. But the pivot remains liberty. The way imprisonment appears in prevailing rationalities of government has defined the nature and extent of the domain in which the money sanction's play prevails.

At least, this remains the case for the *penal* fine. Embedded in the moral regimen of criminal justice the penal fine remains articulated to imprisonment through the mechanism of imprisonment by default. All the governmental efforts to make the fine affordable, and by other means to govern the nexus with imprisonment, now take on added significance. If money sanctions are in important ways bounded and given their range and scale by the system of liberty, then disarticulation of fines from the criminal justice system and the possibility of imprisonment may be expected to have significant implications. This disarticulation is precisely the most vital characteristic of what Rusche and Kirchheimer refer to as 'administrative' fines and what Bottoms refers to as 'modern fines' – the regulatory fines that relate to offences said to be 'technical' in nature. Modern regulatory fines are set free from subordination to the system of liberty and tutelage to the prison. For this reason, I will suggest, they have been little affected by the punitive turn: they exist in a different discursive domain. Indeed, more than this, they govern different subjects.

Rusche and Kirchheimer's focus on production relations led them to focus on 'the poor' as the target of the penal fine. To a large extent they continued this focus when they turned to 'administrative' fines. It led them, for example, to typify modern regulatory fines in terms of labour laws and to focus on the burden of such fines on the poor. However, the concern to anchor such 'offences' in the system of production may have been overtaken by events. Of course, fines are issued with respect to labour laws and the poor are still burdened by regulatory fines. But the poor are not necessarily the principal class on whom such regulatory fines bear any more, and at whom – with respect to this class of 'administrative offences' – the regulatory fine system is aimed. If we take the largest single class of such 'technical' offenders, they are neither corporations nor the kinds of worker that Rusche and Kirchheimer had in mind. They are automobile drivers, the great bulk of the adult population in Europe, North America, Australasia and increasingly elsewhere. These are the new and ever-growing 'masses' of the late twentieth century and beyond. Drivers are attached to a new economic category – surplus income – that did not figure strongly in Rusche and Kirchheimer's vision of the world, but that was certainly coming to the fore as they wrote. The subjects of this consumer market economy, we will see, are governed extensively by fines unleashed from the chains of liberty.

## Notes

1   Some commentators in the law and economics literature have suggested still another ingenious explanation for the continued preference for imprisonment over the fine. Levitt (1997) undertakes to resolve a mystery that plagues economic rationalists. If the fine is so much more efficient than imprisonment, why do we still have prisons? The answer, relevant to the day fines, even more than ordinary fines, is seen to stem from 'private information' – the fact that outsiders may not have perfect information about another.

> In standard models of optimal deterrence, which assume perfect information on the part of the social planner, fines dominate jail sentences as an instrument for punishing crime. In the real world, however, punishments using prisons is quite common. ... If criminals either have private information about their own wealth, or have a substantial portion of their wealth in the form of human capital, the social planner cannot simply impose a fine on a criminal who can always claim to have insufficient wealth to pay the fine ... That additional constraint on the social planner dramatically reduces the effectiveness of fines *vis-à-vis* a perfect information world.
>
> (1197: 180)

In practice, the real world manages to impose a very large number of fines without worrying very much about wealth concealment. It seems unlikely that this is more than what Levitt (1997: 191) refers to as a 'theoretical justification for the heavy reliance on jail sentences in the real world'. Again, perhaps Levitt has the USA in mind, which is, as later becomes clear, rather more 'reliant' on jail sentences than any other western nation.

2   Hillsman (1990: 61) has suggested a further thesis that attributes the lack of use of fines to the practice of using 'tariff' systems to set fine amounts. Tariff systems use fixed fine amounts to guide judges in setting the amount of a fine. She suggests that 'because tariff systems tend to equate equity with consistency, they generally result in fine amounts set with an eye to the lowest common economic denominator'. As a result, judges' ability to adjust fines

to an individual offender's financial means is limited, and in turn tends to restrict their use of fines to less serious crimes or to first offenders. Yet this does not explain the very low rate of fining in the US even with respect to minor offences, and most of all appears to suggest that the existence of tariffs is a given that could never be changed. In practice, tariffs are associated with regulatory fines rather than penal fines. The latter nearly always are associated with a monetary range to be adapted by the court to the needs at hand, including the offender's means. Further, as seen already, fines were extensively uprated when they became the alternative to short terms of prison in Britain and Europe. This surely suggests that it is the lack of this ethos in the US that explains why tariffs themselves were not either changed or not dispensed with rather than that the status of fines as tariffs that explains their lack of use.

3 Perhaps the following comment is one that indicates the acceptance of imprisonment. In a statement that to many outside the US would appear quirky, even had it come from a local politician in the 1950s rather than the 1980s, a member of the bench of the United States Supreme Court, J. Blackmun argued as follows:

> MR. JUSTICE BLACKMUN, concurring. The Court's opinion is couched in terms of being constitutionally protective of the indigent defendant. I merely add the observation that the reversal of this Texas judgment *may well encourage state and municipal legislatures to do away with the fine and to have the jail term as the only punishment for a broad range of traffic offences.* Eliminating the fine whenever it is prescribed as alternative punishment avoids the equal protection issue that indigency occasions and leaves only possible Eighth Amendment considerations. If, as a nation, we ever reach that happy point where we are willing to set our personal convenience to one side and we are really serious about resolving the problems of traffic irresponsibility and the frightful carnage it spews upon our highways, a development of that kind may not be at all undesirable
> (1983 Beardon v. Georgia 401 *U.S.* 402, emphasis added)

4 See, for example, the *Criminal Justice Administration Act, 1914*, the report of the Departmental Committee (1934: 19), the Law Reform Commission of Canada (1974) and Young (1989). As both Young and the Canadian report show, the problem of default had not been solved in the long term, for rates of admission to prisons for defaulting were about where they had been at the turn of the twentieth century.

5 For example, the *Criminal Justice Administration Act, 1914* of England and Wales compelled courts of summary jurisdiction to take account of the means of the offender in fixing the amount of the fine, and to allow time to pay unless there were good reasons to the contrary. In detail, the Act could dispense with this requirement if it was satisfied that the offender had the means to pay at once, that the offender had no fixed abode within the court's jurisdiction, or 'any other special reason'. While this resulted in immediate reductions in imprisonment, twenty years later it was already being complained that the courts were not 'taking full advantage' of the arrangement (Departmental Committee 1934: 19).

6  In the mid 1990s, Landes and Posner (1994) made the observation that articles using the economic approach are more frequently cited in major American law journals and cases than any other approach.

7  In this discussion, I will focus on Gary Becker's germinal work. Generally speaking, there are few major differences within the school with respect to fines. However, while there is close overlap between this and the interpretations by others such as Richard Posner (1979, 1986), there are occasional variations on the theme, as well as elaboration, that I will refer to from time to time.

8  A common criticism levied at this point is to ask how a price can be put on such harms. Clearly, other approaches manage this as fines are levied against offences such as assault, and damages are awarded in relation to many nonmaterial losses where they are said to be related *inter alia* to the court's sense of outrage. The economic calculus, however, is rather different. For Becker, the monetary value of the fine would 'equal the marginal harm caused by offences', added to the marginal cost of apprehending them, although Becker admits that 'such knowledge is not easily acquired' (1974: 26–28). Posner operates with a similar calculus that includes as well 'the probability of convicting and apprehending the thief, the costs of the criminal justice system, etc.' (Posner 1979: 121). No 'outrage' factor is built in, because the aim of the fine is not punishment *per se*, but harm minimization. But for this reason, prevention also becomes an issue for this approach. Assuming a rational choice actor, the principal deterrent effect would be achieved by combining these formulae, which would exceed the offenders' net gain from an offence, with an increase in the probability of apprehension. The costs of such improved policing would in their turn be built into the sanction. This does not escape the difficult problem of how to put a money value on harms, such as physical injury, pain and emotional distress. This will be discussed at length in Chapter Four.

9  This is not an uncommon view in official discourse. For instance, the Law Reform Commission of Canada (1974: 29) has argued that with respect to fines imposed for harm to society generally, 'this type of sanction may be looked at as paying back to the whole of the community'.

10 In practice, such restitution appears to be ordered only in about half of all eligible cases. (Beatty *et al.*, 1996: 39) In their 1996 study, this was found to result from a congeries of factors, including the victims' inability to demonstrate loss, the fact that victims did not request restitution, offenders' inability to pay and the court's view that this would be a burdensome penality over and above that already delivered. See also Dubber (2002).

11 The problem had its parallel in civil law, due to the prevailing doctrine of privity of contract. This meant that retailers could always fall back on the defence that adulteration had occurred earlier in the production chain, before it was delivered to them. As no contract existed between the consumer and the manufacturer, as opposed to between the consumer and the retailer, no action lay. In common law, this was overcome in 1932 in the 'snail in the bottle' action of *Donoghue v. Stevenson*, discussed later.

12 Even swingeing increases in fines – and the imposition of treble damages which we will turn to in a later chapter – are regarded as having their effective limits. Most commentators refer to what Coffee (1981) termed

the 'deterrence trap'. That is, as fines increase in value, many smaller corporations – especially those struggling and thus more likely to cut legal corners – become unable to pay the fine. In many respects, this mimics the problem confronting reformers at the turn of the twentieth century and likewise has given rise to innovations to enable fine payment. Best known among these inventions is the 'equity fine' proposed many years ago and advocated by Coffee (1981). Here, the convicted corporation is forced to dilute the value of its stock by issuing shares to a specified value and providing these to the victims or to the state.

13  See, for example, Elzinger and Breitt (1976: 112–137). Usually the impact of fines is taken for granted on the basis of economic theory's assumptions of the rational choice actor – even though such an assumption has been rejected in writings to be reviewed shortly.

14  I am reliant for this summary on the excellent abridgment provided by the Law Reform Commission (2003).

15  Even so, as with actuarial justice, this cannot be understood as a global phenomenon, and indeed in broad terms, like that development, this remains a largely American innovation. In Britain and Australia, for example, there is in existence a considerable body of common law on sentencing deriving from the different tradition in which courts more frequently provide reasons for sentences and are more likely to have their sentences subject to appeal (O'Malley 2004; Law Reform Commission 2003, 6: 10). In Britain, for example, the Court of Appeal has established a series of factors to be taken into account when determining the fine, including the extent and intentionality of the harm; the degree of risk created; the defendant's resources, the impact of the fine on the business, and whether the offence is part of a continuing breach (R. v. F. Howe and Son (Engineers) Ltd. 2 *All ER* 253).

# Chapter 3

# Regulatory fines

From a policy perspective the distinction between "pricing" through civil penalties and "prohibiting" through criminal penalties leads to an obvious question: why should society ever prefer prices over the more effective weapon of sanctions? One reason is obvious. When society wants not to proscribe the activity, but only to reduce its level, it should use prices.

(John Coffee 1992: 1886)

At the end of the previous chapter it was noted that Rusche and Kirchheimer (1939: 173–176) distinguish two classes of fine associated with the modern era. The first and familiar one was the traditional penal fine associated with criminal justice, and this was to be the central focus of their attention. But a second form of fine already had become prominent when they wrote, one they referred to as 'administrative' and that related to more or less mundane breaches of regulations. In their analysis, this in turn fell into two forms: violations of police regulations and violations of labour laws. While there are slight differences between these two forms (primarily related to the class of those being regulated) both were seen to be characterized by the fact that they do 'not penetrate into the offender's life' and apply to 'merely technical offences (that) are not accompanied by any feeling of guilt or wrongdoing'. The concern of such regulation is not with reforming, punishing or incapacitating – 'the state's sole interest in such offences is to compel obedience by levying sufficiently large fines … it levies fines because it dislikes the activity but it is not seriously prepared to put a stop to it' (Rusche and Kirchheimer 1939: 176). The implication is that – apart from the death penalty – only by imprisonment does the state demonstrate serious intent.

In the most significant theoretical treatment of the fine to date, Anthony Bottoms (1983) also focuses on the administrative fine – what he refers to as the 'modern fine' – as a unity incorporating fines for 'motoring offences and the agency prosecutions as opposed to the indictable offences' (1983: 201). Like Rusche and Kirchheimer, he homes in on the issue of the fines' lack of penetration into the life of the offender. The 'modern fine' is distinguished from the penal fine by the fact that 'in an earlier era the fine was often closely connected with imprisonment through the default mechanism: in England and Wales, in 1910 almost 20 per cent of all persons fined were eventually imprisoned for default, but by 1940 this figure had dropped to 1 per cent'. (1983: 201n8). We will need to consider further just why the question of imprisonment is so important to Bottoms, but here it should be stressed that this figure of one per cent is potentially confusing. In practice the rate of imprisonment in default of paying penal fines had reduced little since the early 1900s. As Young (1989: 47) notes, at the time Bottoms was writing in 1983, in the UK, over 45 per cent of annual male prison receptions were for fine defaults. It is a figure that had hardly changed in the 70 years since 1913, when Rusche and Kirchheimer (1939: 169) recorded it at just under 50 per cent. The decline to one per cent default for all fines reflects the phenomenally expanding ratio of modern regulatory fines to penal fines – for by contrast those offenders attracting the 'modern fine' are rarely in danger of imprisonment if they default in payment.

In his exhaustive empirical study of modern regulatory fines in Australia, Fox (1995, 1996) maps out key dimensions of this changing ratio of penal to regulatory fines, especially with respect to the innovation of 'infringement notices' and so-called 'on the spot fines'. In the state of Victoria, these were introduced originally during the 1950s with respect to road traffic offences, especially parking related issues. They encouraged offenders to escape court appearance by paying a fine in short order and without contest. In large measure Fox sees such regulatory fines as a simplified and cheap way of dealing with the exponentially increasing volume of cases that such offences created for the criminal justice system. In turn, their cost effective nature made these fines an attractive technique, which led to their application to more numerous and more serious offences. Fox (1995: 1–6) notes that in 1965 on the spot fines applied to some eleven traffic offences and that penalties were generally for amounts of a few dollars. By 1992, the number of such traffic offences had increased to more than 200, a substantial proportion of the total of 385 traffic offences at the time, while maximum penalties were no longer trifling but ranged up to $900. Over this period too, on the spot fines were adopted as a sanction by a wide range of government and semigovernment departments, and particularly by local governments, as penalties relating to bylaws. In this respect, especially prominent were parking regulations. While stressing that his estimation understated the total number of offences subject to these fines, Fox counted nearly 800 offences dealt with by infringement notices.

By the early 1990s, it had become the case that for every summary charge coming before the magistrates' courts, more than seven criminal matters were dealt with by on the spot fines. While this registers the importance of the regulatory fine in criminal justice, some 123 other agencies outside the criminal justice arena were empowered to levy such fines. In Fox's study (1995: 89–94) police issued only about a third of such notices, with local government issuing about 60 per cent. In a single year, these agencies together issued nearly 2.5 million fines to a total state population of less than 4 million. While traffic offences constituted the vast bulk of matters subject to such regulatory fines (well in excess of 90 per cent), Fox maps out the administrative fine's application to such matters as environment protection, building and housing, food, litter, taxation, public safety, noise and nuisance, customs, mineral resources, shares and securities, gambling, weights and measures, dangerous goods, occupational health and safety, and many others, including labour law (1995: 39–47). In short, it is hard to imagine an area of life that now is not in some way governed through the regulatory fine.

This massive expansion of the regulatory fine relative to the penal fine was not the principal concern of Bottoms – although it will become an important feature of my analysis. I will argue later that the permeation of the regulatory fine into all areas of life, and the sheer volume of such fines in any jurisdiction, renders this type of fine more or less indistinguishable from other monetary forms such as prices, licence fees, taxes and administrative costs. However, Bottoms focuses much more on the observation that imprisonment is rarely the sanction available in default of payment for the regulatory fine. With this more or less accurate observation under his belt, Bottoms then proceeds to use it as a pivot for theorizing the place of fines in contemporary society. Of course, before even moving onto his theorization, an easy criticism of Bottoms would be to point to the large number of exceptions to his claim. In practice, in many jurisdictions regulatory fines associated with 'infringement notices', 'violations' and similar forms of offence may be enforced in default with a term of imprisonment. This is especially so where the offender refuses to pay the penalty rather than simply is unable to pay it. But, in support of Bottoms, it should be noted that as Fox's exhaustive study indicates, far less than one half of one per cent of regulatory fine defaulters is ever imprisoned. For the most part, in marked contrast to penal fines, regulatory fine defaults are dealt with by other means.

In many jurisdictions, regulatory fines, especially those related to parking offences, are dealt with as civil matters from the outset and thus can result in imprisonment only through unusual and circuitous procedures. Even where the matter remains a criminal concern it is possible to point to a considerable variety of responses to the problem of regulatory-fine defaulters. In some cases, courts may issue arrest warrants, or the matter is turned over to the sheriff's office, where this exists, as a form of bylaw enforcement agency. In such cases, fines may be recovered by confiscation of assets as well as by more routine debt collection techniques. In other cases, fine defaults become a matter for private debt collectors. In Scotland, Duff (1993) reports that the fiscal fine was borrowed from Continental practice with the aim of reducing pressure on the courts. Those who accept the offer of a fiscal fine no longer become subject to criminal proceedings, even in the event of nonpayment. Outstanding payments are only enforceable through civil debt procedures and thus cannot lead to imprisonment. In still other jurisdictions, special and relatively bureaucratic courts are established in order to deal with these matters. For example, in the Traffic Courts that exist in many US cities such as Philadelphia, the routine response to default is to charge a further fee for administrative costs and suspend the driver's licence.[1] In other jurisdictions, especially before the mid-1990s, fine defaults simply were not followed up at all, even where imprisonment may technically exist as an available sanction. In the case of the infringement notice system in Victoria, for instance, it was estimated that by 1994 warrants held by police for outstanding court fines amounted to more than $270 million owed by nearly 108,000 individuals and entities (Fox 1995: 123–125). While this appears consistent with Rusche and Kirchheimer's view that the state is not serious about putting a stop to such offending, a key reason for such difficulties was that of tracing offenders and then demonstrating that the specific individual had been the offender – for example, proving that she or he had been the driver on the occasion when a vehicle was recorded speeding. In turn, it was not so much state apathy that explained this 'failure', nor even the fact that offenders routinely ignored notices. Rather it was the unprecedented scale of the problem. Thus, in practice, while sheer numbers of defaults were very large, these represent a small proportion of all infringements – Fox's later work shows in Victoria that over 90 per cent of on the spot fines were paid within the time stipulated (Fox 1999: 4).

As Fox points out (1996: 6), this issue of the sheer volume of cases, and the resulting volume of unenforced notices, was the major determinant in the development of 'simplified' procedures in Australia and the United Kingdom. When these notices were first developed, if payment were not made, the infringement notice had to be withdrawn and the matter proceeded in the conventional mode of a formal charge and summons. 'This brought the matter to court, but the scale of defaulting made this option unmanageable. Sheer numbers created insuperable difficulties' (Fox 1996: 6). The solution was to streamline procedure and increase the throughput of cases by defining nonpayment 'as though it were already an unpaid judicially imposed fine', even though no conviction had been registered. Thus, one of the principal responses to administrative difficulties associated with the increasing volume of regulation has been to overturn traditional principles of justice, and to establish reverse-onus requirements across a broad array of parking and moving violations. Under such innovations, for example, the owner of a vehicle was assumed to be responsible for any violations, even speeding and red light violations, unless she or he could demonstrate otherwise.

I would argue that such responses to fine defaulting are indicative of the 'only money' status of the regulatory fine. The penal fine also may be just money, but it bears with it the probability of imprisonment in default, and is thus linked directly to deprivation of a generalized liberty of movement, employment, association, sometimes enfranchisement and so on. These are liberties common to all adult citizens, indeed in substantial degree definitive of legal subjects in a liberal polity. That such basic and pervasive liberties are at stake for nonpayment is indicative of the implication that the offences – even if initially punished by a fine – are governmentally defined as 'penetrating' to the generalized legal and moral status of the subject. But with regulatory fines, usually what is at stake in default is some other sanction, for example, removal of a specific license – the specially bestowed (and often purchased) right to drive, to sell food, to operate machinery and so on. Rather than threatening liberty at large, it threatens specific and delimited privileges. In line with this, it is difficult to pass by the point that because the regulatory fine short-circuits the likelihood of imprisonment in default, it is liberated from the traditionally onerous procedural rules that are intended to protect the accused in the otherwise uneven contest with the state. I will return to this shortly. But at this point, it is the specificity of the sanction's target that seems vital. The offender normally is not addressed principally as a person, but primarily as a driver or owner of a motor vehicle or in some other specific capacity, such as a proprietor or operator. With parking fines, the subject is erased altogether and replaced by a vehicle registration number. Rusche and Kirchheimer's observation that the regulatory fine does not penetrate the life of the offender is well illustrated here. Liberty is not at issue because the individuality of the offender is not at issue, only a specific role or 'dividual'. In this respect, the fragmentation of the legal subject allows a certain degree of anonymity to be attached to those sanctioned through the regulatory fine. Perhaps too this allows us to add precision to Rusche and Kirchheimer's sense of the 'seriousness' with which the state regards such offences. It may be more precise to say that where the regulatory fine is applied, the generalized moral character and liberty of the offender is not the issue. Rather, it is the continued licence to engage in certain practices.

In this light, the fine becomes akin to a premium, such as may be applied to drivers' insurance policies: an additional cost incurred in order to retain a certain contractual right that has been violated. Consider two examples of sanctions articulated with the regulatory fine. In the first example, the state confronts the fact that drivers opt to park in 'no parking' areas or overstay at a parking meter. They may do so, choosing to pay a premium fee in the form of a 'fine' rather than go to the trouble of moving the car to some other location. In most jurisdictions, as long as the offender pays the fines, this offence may be repeated indefinitely without further consequence. However, this toleration changes where the authority determines that such parking is too problematic to tolerate, for example where the traffic lane becomes subject to 'clearway' provisions at peak hour, or where the area is required for access by emergency vehicles or public transport. Here the frequent response is removal and impounding of the offending vehicle: the 'tolerance' or 'porosity' of the fine reaches its limit, especially where the parking problem affects 'the public interest'. In the second example, drivers may opt to speed or to run red lights, and pay the premium fine should they be detected. Fines are the most frequent response to these offences, but in the name of public safety and the public interest it is comparatively rare for this to be the only available sanction for repeat offending. Beginning in the 1960s, many jurisdictions linked fines to the accumulation of 'demerit points'. For more serious offences the porosity of the fine is reduced. It is still the case that repeat offences may be tolerated – but only to a degree. Once a specified total of demerit points is passed, then the driver's licence is suspended or revoked.[2]

While there is a vital element of deterrence and punishment built into this kind of response, it is also a strategy of risk management. Infractions are tolerated, providing the money is paid that grants this reverse-licence, but where the offence carries a significant burden of risk – as with red light offences or speeding – demerit points work as a risk-indicator. High risk drivers then are subject not simply to another level of punishment, but to a sanction characterized by *specific incapacitation*. If risk-based imprisonment incapacitates the repeat offender in terms of their general liberty and in the name of public safety and risk-reduction, so these sanctions in support of the regulatory fine incapacitate the risky driver, operator of a restaurant or factory, the owner of a risk-prone apartment building, or whatever, only with respect to their risky activity, not their general liberty.

In such examples, regulatory fines appear not so much to be driven by the desire to punish or correct, *per se*, as by pragmatic concerns with rates and distributions of behavioural regulation. Certainly, punishment is often present in rationalities of the regulatory fine (Young 1989; Duff 1993), but rather than being tailored to the needs of a specific individual as in correctional sentencing it is directed at a rational choice actor, in the form of general deterrence. The sanction is delivered 'in situ' rather than in special institutions. While this is true to a point for the penal fines – although that is at least in principle tied to personal court appearances – regulatory fines are delivered anonymously, appended to windscreens, handed out on the spot, or sent through the mail or even email, paid by cheque or electronic transfer. They are embedded in everyday life rather than singled out for special treatment in contexts set about by the trappings of justice.

While this may reflect the triviality of the violations, or more simply the desire to reduce workload pressures on the criminal justice system, there does also seem to be something else at work. Indeed, for most regulatory fines, it is the *characteristics of the situation* that is the primary object of governance: the spaces and speeds, flows and obstructions, the risks of collision, risks to public safety, rather than the specific individual that is the object of governance. The latter, at best, becomes significant only at the risk threshold for demerit points and the like. With such violations as speeding, parking and red-light offences, the focus is on questions related to circulations, flows and volumes – of maximizing the circulation of traffic within boundaries of public safety. Individual deviations become less significant than overall security and efficiency, and in this light the imperative to identify and punish every breach becomes less significant than do the pragmatics of 'efficiency'. On this matter Foucault (2007: 19–20) has something very relevant to offer.

> Discipline works in an empty artificial space that is to be completely constructed. Security will rely on a number of material givens.

It will of course work on site with the flows of water, islands, air, and so forth. Thus it works on a given (that) … will not be constructed to arrive at a point of perfection, as in a disciplinary town. It is simply a matter of maximizing the positive elements, for which one provides the best possible circulation, and minimizing of what is risky and inconvenient, like theft and disease, while knowing that they will never be completely suppressed. One will therefore work not only on natural givens, but also on quantities that can be relatively, but never wholly reduced, and since they can never be nullified, one works on probabilities.

Security in this fashion deals with the future. It is not concerned to correct past problems, to establish rectitude and punish moral wrongs, but to ensure as far as possible that unwanted situations will not occur again – or more precisely, will reoccur only with tolerable infrequency. The result is a government of the imperfectly calculable, distributional future (Foucault 2007: 20). This, he regards as the 'essential mechanism of security'. It is at this point that we must turn to Bottom's landmark analysis.

## From punishment and discipline to punishment and regulation

Following Rusche and Kirchheimer's (1939) comment that such fines do not penetrate into the life of the individual, Bottoms argues that the 'modern' fine is not disciplinary but regulatory. Unlike penal fines, such regulatory fines are not focused on individuals and their motives but on the statistical distributions which individuals compose: regulatory fines are intended to produce aggregate effects on the frequency of behaviours rather than the correction of individuals. In Bottom's view what differentiates the regulatory fine from the penal fine is that the latter is 'dependent still upon the possibility of a disciplinary penalty being applied in appropriate cases' (1983: 197–198) whereas the regulatory fine is not. He times the critical period for the growth of the regulatory fine as during the postwar era between 1945 and 1965, a period which is 'with justification, generally regarded as the time of maximum growth in the influence of the scientific rehabilitation of offenders' (1983: 193). He argues that scientific rehabilitation differentiated the fine and imprisonment in a new way, for as the prison becomes more and more disciplinary and correctional, its distance from the nondisciplinary fine increases. A bifurcation began to open out between more problematic crimes dealt with by correctional sanctions and less problematic offences that are dealt by modern regulatory fines in the community. Penal fines, it would seem (although Bottoms never outlines this explicitly) are a compromise in which those offenders in the no-man's-land between the two are in a sense put on a form of probation. Indeed, probation is one of the other sanctions that Bottoms slots into a 'non-disciplinary' category of sanction on the grounds that for the most part it imposes merely a reporting requirement.

Bottoms' principal concern is with the implications of the modern regulatory fine for the prevailing 'dispersal of discipline' thesis of 1970s and 1980s criminology. This thesis, associated primarily with the work of Stan Cohen (1979), saw the rise of the penal penumbra of 'community sanctions' as part of a process whereby disciplinary control was penetrating civil society. The 'net widening' and 'mesh fining' processes associated with community sanctions were seen to draw more and more people into the orbit of control apparatuses. However, Bottoms argues that some of the most significant sanctioning developments at the time – probation, the fine and suspended sentences especially – were not primarily disciplinary at least in the sense of correctional interventions aimed at normalization (Bottoms 1983: 180). He notes that the English legal system's differentiation between indictable and summary offences corresponds closely to Rusche and Kirchheimers' distinction between 'criminal' and 'administrative' offences, and suggests that while the more serious indictable offences were becoming increasingly subject to scientific correction in prisons, the less serious and rapidly growing array of summary offences were becoming subject to nondisciplinary regulation through fines – so much so that about 97 per cent of summary offences were being disposed of by fines.

In this analysis, Bottoms focused on Foucault's (1984) distinction in *The History of Sexuality Volume 1* between the anatamo-politics of the human body, and the biopolitics of the population. While the former is associated with individuals and discipline, the latter is focused on populations and 'regulatory controls'. Bottoms also highlights Foucault's observation that regulation is becoming increasingly significant, and he draws the conclusion that the rise of the fine is to be theorized in terms of the shift in technologies of government from the disciplinary to the regulatory. Regulatory governance is concerned with behaviours – primarily with obedience rather than with what Foucault referred to as understanding and changing the 'soul' of the unique individual offender. This is highlighted by the fact that many offences associated with the regulatory fine are strict liability offences: conformity is more important than consent; behaviour is more important than intent;

and *mens rea* is largely dispensed with in practice. Thus, Bottoms observes that

> ... the fine as an impersonal and calculable penalty ... fits well into the mind-set produced by this specificity of social control. If the offender has not been, and is not to be investigated as a whole person, it scarcely makes sense to subject him to specific disciplinary and corrective techniques designed to bring the soul in the body into the status of the obedient subject – the focus of Foucault's disciplinary apparatus
>
> (Bottoms 1983: 190)

We can see immediately that this does not apply to the penal fine, which (in intent at least) *is* focused on the individualized offender and a moralized offence that is pursued by police and courts in a fashion identical to many other offences, including those that can result in sentences of imprisonment. By way of contrast, Bottoms (1983: 187) argues that regulatory inspectorates, whose principal sanction is the regulatory fine, are much more concerned with securing conformity than making moral points in courts. Thus, traffic police are 'essentially interested in the safe and efficient flow of traffic, rather than with stamping out morally undesirable behaviour'. Indeed, Bottoms makes the key observation that what had changed with respect to the modern fine and regulation since Rusche and Kirchheimer's time was the rise in volume and use of motor vehicles and the problems of governance this created. Thus, he notes that by the time of his writing, 75 per cent of summary offences were motoring offences and nearly 99 per cent of these were disposed of by fines (Bottoms 1983: 185). He used this observation as the launching point for his principal theoretical contribution.

> In the road-traffic sphere, the primary mode of social control is environmental, through what Karl Llewellyn in his law jobs theory called the 'preventative channelling' of traffic lights, stop signs, parking restrictions, adequate road design and street lighting and so forth. In ... these areas of 'modern crime' therefore we have preventative social control systems backed up by the fine (and other juridical penalties such as disqualification). *Disciplinary punishment is not necessary to achieve control.*
>
> (Bottoms 1983: 187, emphasis in original)

Here Bottoms is mapping out the contours of what a large number of criminologists subsequently were to identify as the rise of risk as a distributional and probabilistic technique for governing problems across a huge swathe of health, financial, transport, environmental, industrial and other domains. Soon after Bottoms published his notes on the fine, other criminologists (Cohen 1985; Reichman 1986; Shearing and Stenning 1985) were registering the increasing marginalization of correctionalism in favour of 'insurance' and 'environmental' techniques that focused less and less on individual offenders and increasingly on actuarial patterns and behavioural regulation. As Cohen (1985: 184) put it, not simply with respect to fines but across the whole correctional field 'no-one is interested in motives anymore, rather it is behaviours'. Within a few years, this shift became associated with Feeley and Simon's (1992, 1994) 'new penology' that centred 'actuarial justice'. This made sentences proportional to risk rather than offence seriousness, and that evacuated corrections from prisons in favour of simple incapacitation and risk reduction. The same shift toward risk was also registered by criminologists with respect to the rise to prominence of crime prevention. This was especially so with situational crime prevention and 'target hardening', techniques that centred crime risk reduction through behavioural channelling (O'Malley 1992; O'Malley and Palmer 1996). In these approaches to the situational governance of crime, insofar as individuals appear at all it is in the form of the abstract-universal rational choice offender. Criminal justice, in short, was seen to be becoming more regulatory. Curiously none of these criminological risk studies mentioned the 'modern fine' that had been the subject of Bottoms' pioneering analysis.

However, this shift is highly significant to understanding the fine, for the rise of actuarial justice and risk-based incarceration in some ways severs the nexus between discipline and imprisonment that Bottoms wishes to centre. If prisons come to be associated merely with risk-reducing incapacitation rather than correction, then not only do they become less disciplinary, but in the same process they also become more regulatory in Bottoms' and Foucault's sense. The concern of risk-based incarceration is not with disciplinary reform but with reducing the risk across the population by removing risky offenders from circulation (Feeley and Simon 1994). This creates a potential problem for Bottoms' analysis, because he suggests that the penal fine is 'dependent still upon the possibility of a disciplinary penalty being applied in appropriate cases' (1983: 197–198). However, to the extent that prisons no longer correct, then the penal fine has no dependent or necessary relationship with discipline *per se*. Rather, its characteristic relationship would appear to be specifically with the prison, and as suggested already, with the sanction of deprivation of liberty. If so, then it is relatively unimportant whether this prison time is filled with correction or is simply the 'empty' time of incapacitation or punishment. What matters is simply the nexus between the penal fine and the threat of imprisonment in default of payment.

In this way, Bottoms' thesis need not centre the disciplinary prison – this is something foist upon him by his decision to link his argument to the critique of the 'dispersal of discipline' thesis. His case could be reformulated to suggest that the move toward regulation has impacted on fines and prison alike. But to pursue this, we need to examine his thesis more closely. For Bottoms, the shift toward regulation was related to three linked features that were associated with the 'change from early industrial capitalism of 1800 to the much more technologically advanced welfare-capitalist society now operative in Britain'. (Bottoms 1983: 187). These were the development of new surveillance technologies, the changing nature of work, and the growth of welfarism.

While Foucault had allowed that factory discipline and the interests of capital were important sites for the promotion and growth of discipline, he did not make this central – a fact that gave rise to both considerable criticism by Marxists at the time, and led to a kind of Marxist rewriting of Foucault's insights (Melossi and Pavarini 1981). In this Marxist view, it was the needs of the production system that gave discipline its prominence in modern life, and it is this theme Bottoms picks up. To Bottoms, if discipline had once been critical to the factory and work relations under capitalism, this was changing with the development of automated production. Worker and machine, he argues, essentially become fused. Discipline is built into the design of the machinery. As the factory takes on the form of technological control that electronically and mechanically sets the pace and quality of production, then discipline of labour ceases to become as necessary. Bottoms, following the leads given by Melossi and Pavarini (1981) and Lea (1979), suggests that the Fordism and Taylorisation of the factory were shifting the focus of control from the factory, where it was no longer essential, to the control of civil society, where legitimation crises were rising. In this he approvingly quotes Melossi (1981: 392):

> The entrustment of discipline to the machine in the Taylorised factory shifts the emphasis of social control to the learning of discipline as a highly automated process, to be carried on for everybody at an early age. For adults, consensus and legitimation are needed.

At the same time social control follows the movement of capital from within the factory to the outside: the city itself, the urban areas must be controlled ... The new epoch of welfare is announced. And with it the era of policing ... Both the welfare system and policing are much older creations but they had their first generalization and massification in the twenties.

Now, Melossi's dating of this double shift to the 1920s is highly significant, as Bottoms chooses to date it at least a quarter century later, seemingly to increase the correlation with his timing of the emergence of the regulatory fine. Against Bottoms, we could argue that in countries such as Britain, Germany and Australia we could quite easily push the date of 'massification' of the welfare systems back to the turn of the twentieth century. As well, automation of the production process in industry was well underway before the 1920s and, as Gartman (1986: 108–109) documents, 'by the early 1930s, automotive manufacturers had wrested from workers nearly every aspect of machine-tool operation loading, clamping, feeding, sizing, reversing, unclamping, unloading. The machines were amazingly automatic, governed no longer by workers but by themselves'. While the post World War II years certainly were a time in which major changes occurred in welfare, and in which Fordist and Taylorist production techniques expanded, nevertheless there is a considerable lag between their first generalization and Bottoms' 'era' of modern regulatory fines in the period after 1945.

This makes Bottoms' timing somewhat problematic, and begins to raise doubts about the close nexus between these factors in production and welfare and the rise of the regulatory fine. Yet Bottoms goes on to make production even more central. In some conformity with the 'dispersal of discipline' thesis that he was critiquing, Bottoms points to a shift away from penal discipline toward 'informal' and dispersed forms of social control in the post-War era, associated with a redefining of the prison as a sanction of last resort. Following the Marxist thesis of Melossi and Pavarini (1981), he saw the prison essentially as a training and holding institution, disciplining the workforce for capitalism. In consequence, Bottoms suggests, prisons become less important to the extent that discipline is displaced from the factory. Rather, the central place is taken by various 'police measures' in civil society associated with use of the new surveillance technologies. Such forms of control focus not so much on individuals but, as he argues, on behavioural order and on 'whole groups and categories'. These new behavioural technologies govern the population not in disciplinary institutions but *in situ* (Bottoms 1983: 191). It is at this point his thesis parts company with the dispersal of discipline thesis: the prison may (or may not) still be disciplinary, but the wider society – including formerly disciplinary sites such as factories – is being regulated rather than disciplined. The regulatory fine is part of this wider social shift from discipline to regulation.

Finally, Bottoms links this set of changes to the development of social welfare, specifically to socialized medicine, social security and public housing. He regards these as essentially regulatory and biopolitical forms of government, for again they are distributive and collective rather than individual and disciplinary. This distributive character, which includes strong elements of redistribution across class, Bottoms sees as resulting from a trade-off by corporatist politics in order to secure worker compliance. Once again therefore, this time via the nexus of social welfare, the rise of the regulatory fine is tied to changes in production. The same process placed great emphasis on the social sciences and their disciplinary expertise. The result was that at the same time the social world was becoming more regulatory, certain state institutions – such as prisons – were becoming more therapeutic and disciplinary. These two worlds, in Bottoms' view, were bridged by various means, but for criminal justice the most vital was the 'social inquiry report'. Basically, this was a formatted analysis of the individual offender's case, used to sort which offenders should be channelled into the welfare-disciplinary prison sanctions, and which could safely be left in the community to be regulated by the assemblage of regulatory apparatuses and sanctions such as the penal and regulatory fines. The prominence of this report indexed the bifurcation in criminal justice and social control: 'summary offences' are dealt with by regulation, more serious 'indictable' offences by the disciplinary prison.[3] (Bottoms 1983: 192–194).

## Rethinking the social context of the regulatory fine

At this point it becomes clear that there are multiple problems with Bottoms' thesis. By the 1980s, when he was writing, the welfare state was being discredited, transformed and downsized, if not dismantled, by successive neoliberal governments. Likewise the welfare-sanction and its correctional prison system was being shaken by the formation of Garland's (2001) 'culture of control'. Furthermore, rather than a corporatist compromise between organized labour and capital becoming increasingly hegemonic, the period was already unfolding as one in which the power of trades unions was being eroded. New forms of discipline were being imposed in the name of creating an 'active' and highly individualized workforce, and many forms of social security were being changed because of their alleged role in creating 'welfare dependency'. Under the proclaimed banner of globalization, automated industries were being exported to the Third World. Mass automated production was being challenged by niche marketing and 'post-Fordism', and worker autonomy was being touted as a key part of 'enterprising the self' associated with a supposed reinvigoration of a competitive economy (Rose 1996; Harvey 1989).

At the very least, all this suggests that Bottoms' analysis of the nexus between changes in the nature of modern capitalism and the development of the regulatory fine is problematic in key respects. The regulatory fine has continued to expand exponentially in volume and application since the 1960s, but in a world seemingly removed from that specific form of production-centred configuration envisaged by Bottoms as its condition of existence. In what follows I want to explore two major themes in this respect, en route to realigning rather than simply demolishing Bottoms' major contribution to the neglected field of the modern regulatory fine. The first is a problem he shared with Rusche and Kirchheimer. His Marxist-influenced focus on production relations led him to overlook the vital importance that consumption was taking on from the turn of the twentieth century – and especially during the postwar years of the 'consumer society' upon which he focuses analysis of the regulatory fine. Perhaps the products and their users were every bit as important as the producers and the process of production. The second is an issue that both he and Rusche and Kirchheimer tend to gloss over: the role of the official visions of the nature of problems, including problems of criminal justice, and most especially the political struggles that defined how these should be represented and dealt with in law. Because of their focus on production, official discourses tended to appear to Marxists as an ideological gloss that did more to conceal than reveal what was going on. However, we have already seen that things were otherwise when understanding the rise of the penal fine, and I suggest the same is true with the regulatory fine. In turn, these two themes, the rise of mass consumption and the importance of governmental rationalities are linked by the problem that Bottoms rightly centred: the proliferation of motor vehicles and traffic regulation.

## Consumption and regulation

Writing so soon after the years of the Great Depression of the 'thirties, we can perhaps understand why poverty remained at the centre of Rusche and Kirchheimer's attention. However, the inter-war years are arguably the period in which the conditions for the emergence of a consumer society begin to appear, especially in the United States. As Gary Cross (1993) has mapped out at considerable length, this is the era in which the existence of surplus income is registered as a governmental category – that is, a category denoting income over and above that required to purchase necessities. It is the period in which economics, especially under Maynard Keynes' influence, began to problematize mass consumption as well as, or even above, mass production. It is worth remembering that the so-called 'Keynesian revolution' centred crises of under-consumption rather than concerns with overproduction, promoting the idea that the key technique for maintaining capitalist growth was to foster mass consumption. This involved not simply the thesis that the state should spend on infrastructure during recessions and thereby kick-start the economy, but equally that the provision of welfare relief would provide demand for consumer goods. It was precisely this assumption, and the observation that the working class was at last generating a surplus as a class – rather than fears of revolution and crisis – that drove Beveridge's (1942) blueprint for the post-War British welfare state (O'Malley 2004).

Thus, I would argue that the post-war years were not simply, as Bottoms notes, the period in which the welfare state grew to its apogee. Equally, as he does not mention at all, it is the period in which the consumer society emerges in a fully fledged fashion. This is important to note for many reasons, but one in particular is that this provides an answer to a difficult question for Bottoms. As noted above, automated mass production was established in the United States by the 1920 and was dominant in key industries by the 1930s. If production relations were as important to the rise of modern regulatory fines as Bottoms suggests, then why was it the period after 1945 that seems to be critical in his interpretation? If, however, we focus more on consumption relations, then Bottoms' timing makes more sense. As Cross (1993) argues, the consumer society – in the sense of mass consumption – did not appear before World War II even though the elite and the middle classes were beginning to form a major market for mass products somewhat earlier. This was not because of limits to prosperity created by the Great Depression and War Austerity. Cross suggests that we should not fall into the trap of assuming that automated production and surplus income simply creates mass consumption that would have appeared but for the depressed 1930s and early 1940s. Instead he argues that there was no necessity that the mass consumer society appear. The inter-war years were a period in which a struggle occurred between the vision of a society in which the surplus income of the masses should be deployed in the unprecedented expansion of *mass consumption*, and a competing but ultimately defeated vision in which this surplus would provide the means whereby *mass leisure* would appear. It is only by the post-war years that this struggle is determined in favour of mass consumption and the consumer society emerges full blown.

In this historical period, it can also be argued (O'Malley 1994) that discipline also undergoes a change. Bottoms' reliance on writers such as Lea and Melossi ties him into a quasi Marxist vision of Taylorism as the model of production for the future. Instead it was a model that was already being displaced by deindustrialization and post-Fordism at the time Bottoms was writing (Harvey 1989). For Harvey, niche marketing, 'just in time' production, and new managerial practices that promoted competition within the factory and the office were the 'postmodern' formation that was heavily conditioning or even displacing the modernist factory. Likewise, in Deleuze's (1995: 180–183) view, it is not so much that the factory is dedisciplined by hypermechanization but rather that 'factories' are being displaced by 'businesses', economic organizations that are 'no longer geared toward production but toward products, that is toward sales and markets'. Thus, 'marketing is now the instrument of social control and produces the arrogant breed who are our masters'.

> Factories framed individuals into a body of men for the joint convenience of a management that could monitor each component of this mass, and trade unions that could mobilize mass resistance; but businesses are constantly introducing an inexorable rivalry presented as healthy competition, a wonderful motivation that sets individuals against one-another and sets itself up in each of them, dividing each within himself.

I don't wish at all to get into the kind of sociology that sees ruptural and total change around every corner. Nevertheless, it is possible to detect a shift in which the discipline of the productivist era, associated with thrift, saving, diligence, and the 'docile body' of the automated factory, is being challenged by a new wealth-accumulating autonomization of many working people. It is a world of 'associates', 'representatives' and 'agents' active on their own behalf in the 'enterprise society'.

The obverse side of all this was the 'deindustrialization' that created the mass unemployability of large sectors of unskilled and heavy industry labour. For this sector of the populace discipline and reform was not so much being transformed into acquisitive risk-taking individualism as becoming irrelevant, because they were regarded as permanently outside the workforce (Feeley and Simon 1994). For this 'underclass' sector of the population, discipline was to be displaced by exclusion and because they became increasingly regarded as risky they were subjected to mass incapacitation. For the other sector of the populace, individualized striving and competition was to be rewarded by a newly licensed hedonism. A new workforce was imagined and encouraged to become enterprising and wealth creating rather than to bend its back in drudgery; to take risks and invest on the stock market rather than diligently save in conservative savings bond; to seek profit and to be rewarded by the capacity to purchase and assemble lifestyles in the marketplace (Rose 1999). To use Mike Featherstone's (1984) memorable phrase, this is not so much an era in which discipline is eroded, but rather one in which discipline became elaborated in new ways: in which 'disciplined hedonism' emerged. Consumption ceased to be something that is problematic and became something to be celebrated. In Margaret Thatcher's (1994) imagery, this was to be the era of the 'active' consumers, whose responsibility was to demand the products they wanted, not the products that were dished up to them. The era of 'one size fits all' may not in practice have disappeared, but in a large measure a new diversity of consumer goods was promoted, catering for new and fragmentary markets. If civil society was changing, it was not so much through the production-focused corporatist compromise that Bottoms envisaged, and that was already in tatters in 1983. It was through a thoroughgoing reformation in which high profile consumption became the legitimate reward for individualized achievement in the workplace.

Of course, the poor have not magically disappeared; quite the reverse. Neoliberalism was strongly linked to the polarization of wealth. Nor has the problem of unpaid penal fines and the imprisonment of many people disappeared, as Young (1989) has shown. Perhaps we see here a rather different understanding of how Bottoms' bifurcation of the 'social control' system was coming about. The expansion of the regulatory fine is relevant to the consumer world of labour with surplus money, of cars and consumables. For the poor another world exists in which penal fines backed up by prison still apply (Baumann 2000).

It is not that the regulatory fine has displaced the penal fine, but rather that the regulatory fine has grown much faster in its scale and application.

So much so that in many ways it may now form a pervasive and embedded part of everyday life in a consumer society – more or less indistinguishable in form, function and effect from taxes, license costs, fees, contractual penalties and so on, with which it is increasingly melded. Such a vision of the regulatory fine can be seen in the fact that traffic and other administrative fines may – like many other demands for payment of everything from water rates to sofa beds – be discounted in the event of early payment or may have administration fees attached to them for late payment (Dubber and Kelman 2005: 74). It may be seen too in the nexus of the regulatory fine with loss or suspension of drivers' licences and even confiscation of vehicles for nonpayment of fines. It is visible in the public outcries that occur that identify traffic 'blitzes' as no more than revenue-raising enterprises, so that fines become a form of taxation. Such political 'outrages' are familiar enough. For example, as this chapter was being written, the *Sydney Daily Telegraph* referred to motorists as 'a persecuted group' because traffic fines had increased threefold in six years ('Taken for a ride', 11 February 2008: 1, 4). Indeed, in jurisdictions such as Virginia, this has become an *explicit* rationale. Identifying speeding as a contributor to traffic accidents, in 2008 the State of Virginia has begun levying extraordinarily high 'fees' attached to fines – up to $3000 – for such offences in order to fund road safety improvements.[4] In Sydney, the *Daily Telegraph* made much of a political struggle between the state government, which justified its actions as both enforcing the law and acting to reduce the road toll, and motorists' organizations that claimed such revenues did not really go into improving roads and that reductions in the road toll were due to better drivers and better vehicles. Fox (1995: 113–116) also indicates that the reverse process also occurs. In 1989, Victoria increased many traffic infringement penalties by between 9 per cent and 175 per cent and dropped the requirement that one-third of such revenues be assigned to road safety programmes Then, he noted, between 1991 and 1992 the state government anticipated increasing fine collections by over 85 per cent and admitted that this was an act of revenue raising – as indeed it would need to be unless it was assumed that it was possible to predict an 85 per cent increase in offending behaviour. Fines in such instance are scarcely different to a consumption tax.

We have, in this light, an array of difficulties that dogs Bottoms' analysis. His focus on production relations appears to ignore the way in which consumption has become more central, and in which regulatory fines are linked to consumption relations and forms. His model of the changes occurring in the production system, upon which his thesis is based, was overturned by neoliberal and globalizing politics.

His assumption that discipline is central to the prison apparatus was badly shaken by the punitive turn and risk-based sentences, and there are clearly problems with the timing of key changes in production and his vision of the postwar years as the era of the regulatory fine. Despite all these historical shifts, inconsistent with his explanation for the growth of the 'modern' or regulatory fine, the regulatory fine has expanded apace.

Broadly speaking, I will suggest that even with respect just to motor traffic regulation there is no single 'cause' of the rise of the regulatory fine, let alone one that renders it merely a reflex of changes in production relations and legitimation crises. Rather, we find a series of rather diverse issues – pre- and post-World War II – that give rise to rather diverse mechanisms and characteristics that are 'typical' of the regulatory fine. Some of these have to do with defining what is and what is not (and who is not) the 'proper' subject of penal discipline. Others have to do with questions of the costs of traffic to the public good, and the politics of taxation and fining as means of funding the costs otherwise externalized by motorists. Yet others are responses to the sheer volume of court business experienced or projected as a result of the growth of traffic violations. None of these seem to have very much connection to the disciplinary prison or the production system as such. Mostly, I would argue, they reflect the ways in which legal and political rationalities made sense of problems thrown up by the rise of a consumer society.

### Genealogies of the regulatory fine

Earlier it was noted that the response to problems confronting enforcement of laws governing pure food and drug provision provided one of the foundations of the regulatory fine. Unable to resolve class, technical and ideological problems associated with prosecuting 'respectable' manufacturers and retailers, a solution was found in creating strict liability offences sanctioned by fines. In this way, 'decent citizens' would avoid stigmatization as the money penalty was given a certain 'acceptable' meaning by linking it to what Rusche and Kirchheimer might regard as a 'technical' question: distanced from bad motives and moral condemnation; distanced from the taint of prison that demolished good character. This was not in any sense because the money sanction applied was meaningless – quite the reverse, it was because it had a certain politically acceptable meaning that it was adopted. The fine, either penal or regulatory, thus does not simply write itself into being through some unavoidable logic, but emerges in a certain form that has its own particular genealogy. In the case of the regulatory fine, such a genealogy is in important ways centred on that set of problems that still dominate its use: traffic regulation. This genealogy begins, not after World War II, but at the beginning of the twentieth century – perhaps significantly at a time when the penal fine was also taking on some of its salient characteristics. In other words, it is not simply that the regulatory fine was invented de nova: its separation from penal fines was to be fraught and imperfect. As with food adulteration, it took a political struggle and changes in official problematics, to allow the courts to imagine most speeding offences as less than criminal, and to draw a wavering and blurry line that distinguished regulatory from penal fines. Here we turn to a preliminary attempt at a genealogy of the regulatory fine.

## A British genealogy of 'speeding'

With respect to moving violations – speeding, dangerous driving and so on – the regulation of traffic speed in Britain during the early twentieth century was a high profile political issue that resonated strongly with a law and order politics. But there was a twist. It was not the riffraff who were the problem; in Britain at this time the automobile was clearly associated with the elite. From the outset, then, the question of inability to pay fines – the bugbear of 'penal' fining at this time and the focus of much contemporary innovation – was never regarded as an issue. As Plowden (1971: 44) puts it 'motorists, however defined, were a minority and a rich minority at that'.[5] Although a speed limit of ten miles per hour existed, in an age before speed could be reliably recorded, it was difficult to prosecute for 'speeding'. Much of the regulation until 1903 relied upon the charge of 'furious driving', for which both a fine and a term of imprisonment were available. Such driving, poorly distinguished from speeding *per se*, was a matter of national political concern. *The Times* (1 August 1903), one of the more moderate critics, complained that the 'road hog' was an upper class deviant who derived

> … from a class which posses money in excess of brains or culture, and which has not had the opportunity of learning insensibly, in the course of generations, the consideration for the rights of others which is part of the natural heritage of gentlefolk. For people of this order the law is an educational influence of the highest value; and when he has once received the ineffaceable stamp of the gaolbird society may be expected, before long, to range itself on the side of the law, and to complete the reformation that it will be the work of the magistracy to begin.[6]

Under the *Motor Car Act 1903*, a speed limit of 20 miles per hour was fixed, with local government bodies empowered to impose a limit of ten miles per hour in designated areas. Police set up speed traps and distance markers and timed speed with a stopwatch. Yet, across the whole of Britain, because of the unreliability of measuring speed, far fewer than a thousand charges of exceeding the speed limit were recorded annually. At the same time there were about 1,500 charges of driving furiously, negligently, recklessly or to the danger of the public.[7] Pressure on the business of the courts was therefore no more an issue than the inability to pay fines. But already new procedures were being put in place with respect to speeding offences. The same Act allowed that the defendant in a speeding charge – but not in the more frequent charge of driving furiously – had the right to opt out of a summary hearing in court, to provide written evidence in defence and have the matter dealt with in chambers. A new procedure was thus invented that took account of this novel class of high-status offenders and allowed for the issue to be contested without this involving court time or ceremonial. Of course, it had always been the case that defendants might opt out of appearing, but then the case would proceed to conviction *in absentia*. Now a procedure was invented that eroded the moral and denunciatory ceremonial of court and introduced a more bureaucratic form of justice.

In large measure this move reflected the fact that the question of speed limits was highly contentious. It was not simply the dubious accuracy of measurement, or even the fact that lack of registration made vehicles difficult to identify, although these made enforcement problematic. Rather the pivotal issue was the view that speeding was a new kind of 'technical' offence. Much political ink was spilled over whether there should be a speed limit at all: a political issue that had close parallels in the United States as well.[8] The 'criminal' offences associated with dangerous and furious driving were felt by many in Britain – and most significantly the motorists' associations – to deal adequately with the problem of speed where it created problems for public safety. Otherwise speed appeared, to a significant sector of the public, including many parliamentarians, to be irrelevant. Such developments in the regulation of speed for its own sake were argued by the influential motoring lobby to restrict engineering and economic progress and give preference to one set of road users (the 'anti-motorists') over another.[9] The fact that the 'offenders' were respectable members of the elite, carrying out an elite pursuit, was never tangential to this innovation. Courts were loath to convict gentry, and magistrates had a marked tendency to believe the word of gentlemen rather than those of working class policemen (Hunt 2006: 174;

Emsley 1993). While the maximal fines for speeding were high for the time, between £20 and £50, actual fines tended to be considerably less, averaging well under £4.

The prominence of the politics that questioned and neutralized the offence of speeding was to be seen in the fact that the Home Office itself had to insist that police enforce the speeding laws properly. Despite hostile claims that fines alone would not deter speeding, and in some cases flogging was called for, the legislation of 1903 created only monetary penalties for speeding. However, the legislation retained the possibility of imprisonment for the other 'dangerous' categories of driving from which mere speeding was distinguished. As with pure food and drug regulation, it was a considerable class and political ambivalence over the question of speeding *per se* that was critical. Many gentry regarded speeding as neither morally problematic nor (absenting furious driving) affecting public safety. In this way, long before the regulatory fine would take on its other characteristics, speeding fines were already being administratively bureaucratized: distanced from denunciation in court and regarded as applicable to offences that were only debatably 'criminal'. It was also the case that no one doubted for a moment – or at least never raised this in the many debates – that such fines need not be set about by the matter of imprisonment for default, simply because default seemed never likely to be an issue given the target population. Before the automobile became a mass commodity, its characteristics as the property of moneyed, *consuming* class had shaped key aspects of what would emerge as the regulatory fine: a fine that is not directed at the traditional categories of offenders at whom the penal fine was and is directed.

Even so, it was clear that there were ambiguities in all this, for the legislation of 1903 did not resolve the 'law and order' politics, which continued in the press of the day. This was not promoted by a concern that the rich motorists could easily afford fines and thus would not be deterred. Rather, after 1903, it was a struggle between motorists and those regarding speeding as nuisance, creating damage to roads and distributing dust across farmers' produce and residents' homes and gardens. The motorists' view was that speeding fines were simply a tax: not a penalty for wrongdoing but a source of revenue to local councils. Speeding, therefore, remained a prominent issue after the Motor Car Act of 1903, but the Act's clear legal separation of speeding from dangerous driving offences created the conditions for a transformation of the class politics. 'Taxation' of speeding motorists, and its nexus with the registration of vehicles became central issues, around which a Royal Commission was set up in 1907. This officially confirmed the view that speeding *per se* was not regarded as a problem of dangerousness. As one contemporary expressed it, this Commission 'showed' that 'the motor-car question is nine-tenths a road question', and the question of the speed limit, now 'finally resolved itself into one of the convenience of the public rather than their safety, as it was pointed out that the dust raised by motorists increased largely with their speed' (quoted by Plowden 1971: 84).

In the wake of the Royal Commission, legislation in 1909 taxed motorists through registration and licensing, and these taxes were to fund a Road Board that would meet the costs of repairing roads damaged by motor vehicles. This had a salutary effect. In Plowden's (1971: 94) words, 'one almost immediate result of the creation of the Road Board was the virtual disappearance of the "motor problem" as it had existed until then … In short tar replaced dust at the expense not of the ratepayers but of the motorists'. A 'law and order' campaign was thus dissipated by what can be regarded as the translation of a fine that operated like a tax into a direct and explicit tax. Speeding had become a question more of an administrative than criminal nature. In this way, issues relating to speeding largely were hived off into problems of taxation, registration and licensing, and such fines as were delivered were regarded as part of this technical assemblage. However, other driving offences were separated into the highly moralized category of 'dangerous', 'furious' and 'negligent' driving – offences that retained their characteristic in law as 'normal' crimes. In contrast to speeding, these offences attracted penal fines – as the legislation also provided for imprisonment both as an alternative sanction and in default of payment.

The ongoing politics of speeding in Britain by no means remained stable. However, through much of the period prior to early 1950s, conflicts largely centred around questions of taxation and traffic infrastructure. With respect to speed, the central question continued to be that of speeding versus reckless driving. In large measure, the courts persisted in dealing with speeding as a 'technicality'. By 1954, there were three million cars on the roads in Britain, yet the speeding fines delivered by the courts averaged roughly the same amounts (per fine) as half a century before, even though the maximum fine allowed had increased considerably (Plowden 1971: 333). Around this time, however, a new problematic was emerging that would begin to change things. Speeding began to change its meaning from being merely technical to being something that was linked with the 'road toll' – which had begun rising during the late 1950s. 'Excessive' but not 'dangerous' speeding no longer appeared merely as a technical offence, because it was now probabilistically linked to a distribution of mortality and injury. It was only now that the question of whether any individual act of speeding was 'safe' ceased to be relevant: speeding was now created *inter alia* as a regulatory offence linked to the problematic of public safety. By the 1960s, the meaning of speed had been transformed. Only now was it enmeshed in the kind of risk-based regulation that Bottoms identified as its key feature. Vehicle characteristics and safety equipment, taxation, road design, licences, driver training and public education about traffic safety had formed a new technological assemblage around what Hunt (2006: 176) refers to as the 'hegemony of safety' in the motoring domain. After this time, more than ever, speeding fines were to take up the character of a regulatory governmental tactic: one technique among many officially aimed at regulating key distributions – the flow of traffic and the 'road toll'. In this sense, Bottoms likely is correct to put emphasis on the post-war years in Britain as the era of the regulatory fine (although in America the timing was quite different, as will be seen). But many of its relevant characteristics had been developed for over half a century, and in relation to issues that had to do with class and consumption, and now national safety, rather than class and production.

Along with this change, and in some senses providing it with its impetus, was the fact that by the early 1960s, car ownership in Britain – which had become became a middle-class phenomenon by the late 1930s – had taken on a mass character. In 1912, *The Times* (20 August) had argued that because automobiles were far cheaper in North America and in countries such as France, the same kinds of class politics that beset English law were largely absent. This situation would improve in Britain 'if motoring became more democratic'. Even in the 1930s – when nearly half of all fines were for traffic offences – a Home Office Departmental Committee (1934: 3), considering the question of imprisonment for defaulting on payment of money sanctions, attributed the remarkable decline in such imprisonment not only to the provisions allowing time to pay, but also 'to the fact that the increase in motoring offences has resulted in the infliction of fines upon a wealthier class of offender'. However, by the 1960s, in Plowden's (1971: 14) terms, Britain had become 'a car-owning democracy'. In this process, car ownership was normalized. It was by now far removed from the luxury pleasure-toy of the rich, and had become a key part of everyday life in a consumer society. This very fact was responsible for the rapidly growing number of speeding offences coming before the court, a phenomenon that, during the 1960s, provided the impetus for the second phase of the genealogy of the regulatory fine, in which its attachment to ceremonial procedures was to be cut asunder even more drastically. But here the analysis is overtaking itself, for there is, of course, another side to traffic regulation critical to the emergence of the regulatory fine: parking offences.

### Fines, fees and the 'parking problem'

The 'undemocratic' nature of car ownership in Britain was largely responsible for the fact that in that country it was not until the mid-1950s that parking emerged as a major issue in traffic regulation. Even in the busy West End of London, kerbside parking was only at 75 per cent capacity by 1953 (Plowden 1971: 328). In the United States, by 1929, 60 per cent of US households owned at least one car (Lebegott 1993: 3–4). Not surprisingly, the parking problem had emerged much earlier than in the UK, and it advanced far more rapidly as a question for government. Already in 1924, over 40 per cent of those going into downtown Los Angeles travelled by car. By 1931 the figure was 60 per cent and in towns such as Chicago, Philadelphia and Boston the figures were becoming comparable. By the early 1920s, traffic congestion attributed to private autos was agreed upon as a major planning problem, but it was also agreed that, by 1925, 'the so-called pleasure car is a business necessity' and automobiles' presence downtown was inescapable (Fogelson 2001: 251–255). Diagnoses of this problem were many and solutions varied, ranging from five-storied streets and freeways to mass transit systems and traffic bans in the central business district. Indisputably, however, by the 1920s parking had become an unavoidable planning and political issue. Retailers, planners and drivers faced a dilemma: too much parking control would affect sales, accessibility and employment; but so too would too little control. The issue was fundamentally a question of the circulation or distribution of life in cities – a question of biopower par excellence (Foucault 2007). Initially, attempts were made to manage the problem by restricting parking in the name of public safety. Loading zones protected the public from accidents. Bans on parking in front of fire hydrants, entrances to hospitals, hotels, emergency service bases and rail stations were all noncontroversial. These were accepted as in the public interest, as were peak hour restrictions on main roads. All these measures were widespread in the United States by the 1920s. More controversial and problematic were parking time limits enforced by fines. These were promoted in terms of speeding up the circulation of customers, but were counted by many planners as having no effect on congestion. Many retailers saw their effect as to deter customers, and many drivers regarded them as a tax or charge for using 'free' public spaces. For reasons of principle and convenience these time limits were widely resisted and officially ignored. As Fogelson (2001: 288) points out, police did not have the manpower required to mark tyres and return to check if cars had overstayed, prosecutors were flooded with charges and shuffled them to the bottom of the heap, while judges were reluctant to convict otherwise law-abiding citizens for unpopular offences. The problem of congestion on the street was thus translated directly into a problem of congestion in the criminal justice system.

One solution to this problem appeared in Oklahoma during 1935 in the form of the parking meter. Two years later there were an estimated 70,000 meters in 160 cities across the US – while they were not introduced into the United Kingdom until the passage of the *Road Traffic Act* 1956. The principal attraction of the meter was that it relieved pressure on law enforcement, both by reducing the number of police required, and providing an unambiguous indicator of parking breach. As was immediately recognized, this invention created a means of taxing motorists, creating revenue for local government at the same time that it reduced the costs of policing and criminal justice more generally. Frequently, the response by local government was to use the revenues to employ more parking police, because this instrument had increased the productivity of each officer – not simply by relieving them of time-consuming labour monitoring parking times, but in the same moment creating a lucrative revenue stream from fines for overstaying (Fogelson 2001: 287–291). Indeed, as parking offences came to be defined increasingly as mere 'violations', many jurisdictions began to employ 'parking wardens', 'city rangers' and other nonsworn and less expensive labour. This removed the offence still further from the domain of criminal justice in all but name. By the end of the 1930s, perhaps the first stage of 'automated justice' had arrived on the scene, and money was the instrument through which this was to be effected. Yet, one of the immediate effects was to *increase* the pressure of business on the courts.

### Bureaucratic justice, traffic offences and the regulatory fine

Beginning in the 1930s, Traffic Violations Bureaus and Parking Violations Bureaus were widely established across the US to relieve this pressure, both in relation to parking and to 'non-hazardous' speeding cases. Parking and 'non-hazardous' speeding and related offences were increasingly dealt with by an opting-in process, in which, unless the charge was contested, the case would be dealt with by clerks in traffic bureaus rather than by courts. In a fashion parallel to motoring law in the UK, a procedural wedge was being driven between 'routine' infringements and 'criminal' offences such a reckless driving and drink driving – offences that were dealt with in courts and attracted penal fines and imprisonment. During the 1960s and 1970s, a new category of 'violations' was invented (Fox 1995: 13).[10] In 1973, the US National Advisory Commission on Justice Standards and Goals recommended that 'all traffic violation cases should be made infractions subject to administrative disposition, except certain serious offences, such as driving while intoxicated, reckless driving, [etc.]' (quoted by Fox 1995: 13). As Fox also points out, various jurisdictions dealt with such routine traffic offences by decriminalizing them. In Michigan, for example, they became 'civil infractions', resulting in 'civil judgments' dealt with generally by fines but also by licence suspension or disqualification, and impounding vehicles. In Britain, likewise, the regulation of these mundane traffic offences punishable by fines was shifting in the direction of an administrative procedure under pressure of the mounting volume of violations. From 1960, parking offences began to attract the 'fixed penalty notices' that have become familiar additions beneath windscreen wipers or attached directly to the windscreen. Under the *Road Traffic and Roads Improvement Act 1960*, such notices advised of a fixed penalty. Issues of mitigation or aggravation were virtually dispensed with. Attendance at court was discouraged further by 'opting in' conditions under which extra fees and risks of extra penalties were associated with disputing the infraction. Individualized justice had been disposed of almost completely under pressure of business. Moreover, 'justice' became a qualified concept because payment of this penalty within three weeks not only expiated the offence, but also, as no judicial proceedings had been initiated, no conviction would be recorded. Offenders could settle out of court. The *Road Traffic Act 1991* took the next step not only of decriminalizing such offences altogether, translating them into matters of civil debt, but of deeming the owner of the vehicle responsible for the infringement. As Fox (1995: 121) shows, the labour required to identify the driver responsible for infringements under the 1960 Act had become insupportable. From now on, not only was such labour externalized to those owners who wished to shift responsibility to another, but also now justice was being delivered to a role, a dividual – an owner or driver rather than an individual.

As Fox (1995: 12–21) documents, this process advanced apace, but carried its genealogy forward with it. The separation of morally reprehensible traffic crimes from those that were deemed not to be dangerous and 'thus' more administrative or technical in nature, had created a qualitative distinction that set the moral conditions under which the bureaucratization of justice could proceed. At one extreme, parking offences appeared as technical, primarily because they were not linked to issues of public safety, and thus would be linked to imprisonment only under rather extraordinary circumstances, if at all. Speeding moved from 'technical' to 'moral' status the greater the risk it presented with respect to public safety. At the point of dangerousness, criminality was invoked in the name of public safety, and the regulatory fine segues into the penal fines and the possibility of imprisonment.

Perhaps this allows some other modifications to Bottoms' observations. First, if the penal fine is backed up by the threat of imprisonment it is because the offence is regarded as one sufficiently *morally* serious to have imprisonment as an alternative sanction, not because of any question of discipline as such. Second, discipline and regulation cease to appear as alternatives. If speeding comes to be defined as problematic because of the road toll, then regardless of the severity of the sanction, the matter is regulatory in Foucault's (and Bottoms') sense. If, say, the risk increases with the excess of the speed over the speed limit, then we shift from 'speeding' to 'dangerous driving' without leaving the domain of risk or regulation, we have moved from low risk to high risk. In line with this, the available sanction changes from a fine to fine/imprisonment. We begin to see that discipline and regulation are not alternatives, as Bottoms' approach sometimes suggests. Rather, as Foucault (1984) made clear, they are frequently articulated together in complex strategies.

Thus, drink drivers may be subjected to regulatory control through risk assessments or random breath tests, and they may be subjected to regulatory interventions such as the regulatory fine or licence suspension if their excess of blood alcohol is marginal. When the blood alcohol content exceeds a certain level, then frequently the driver must undergo a course of disciplinary instruction on the dangers of drink driving, or may be required to attend disciplinary alcohol rehabilitation programmes.[11] Beyond this, many jurisdictions may also provide for imprisonment where severe alcohol impairment, high risk, is judged to constitute dangerous driving. Rather than seeing the 'modern' fine as a regulatory alternative to discipline, it now appears as part of a complex and highly variable assemblage of legal responses to problems of biopower. This complexity reflects both tactical decisions regarding appropriate and effective responses to current offending and at the same time the accumulation and combination of governmental meanings, techniques, apparatuses and so on that have been developed over time to deal with diverse problems. Consequently, with respect to traffic, the large majority of such fines appear as techniques for reducing workloads, for minimizing expenditure, for decreasing risk and reducing political resistance, as well as ways of increasing revenues or effecting behavioural change in individuals and distributions. In this light, tying the expansion of the regulatory fine to direct changes in production relations seems highly implausible, especially when by Bottoms' own analysis they are linked largely to regulation of a phenomenon such as traffic that is in turn linked to many aspects of the life of a modern, consumption-oriented society.

As this implies, it is not argued that the use of the fine can in any way simply be read off from the rise of consumer societies. At best, the emphasis on consumption points to the emergence of certain problems, characterized especially by high volumes of offending that required the invention of new solutions. But the specific nature of these solutions emerged through a web of governmental problematics, definitions, conventions and inventions. Thus, as motorists ceased to be a separable class, and because in a consumer society virtually every driving citizen became almost bound to fall foul of some traffic regulation at some time, then a new problem emerged – the potential criminalization of almost every adult. One response was that to label all such offences criminal began to seem like overkill, but this was never inevitable. The Home Office – which in the early 1900s had to urge police to treat speeding and related offences as real crimes rather than mere technicalities – came to the conclusion in the late 1980s that while 'some offences involving motor vehicles are seen to fall within the category of criminal offences, the majority of road traffic offences cannot readily be characterized in this way'. Its reasoning was that such offences are produced by 'no more than carelessness, misjudgement, a lapse of concentration, a failure to be aware of or understand a relatively technical requirement'. (Home Office 1988: 19) In some official discourses, to continue to treat such actions as criminal devalued the meaning of criminality itself. For the Canadians,

> ... if criminal law's function is to reaffirm fundamental values, then it must concern itself with 'real crimes' only and not with the plethora of 'regulatory offences' found throughout our laws. Our Criminal Code should contain only those acts as are not only punishable, but also *wrong* – acts contravening fundamental values.
>
> (Law Reform Commission of Canada 1976: 19,
> emphasis in original)

Yet, with respect to money damages in the law of torts, it will be seen that 'carelessness' or the 'failure to be aware of or understand a relatively technical requirement' would at various times seem to the courts perfectly adequate grounds for awarding damages as punishments that far exceed any fine. From such a perspective, the governmental definition of the nature of violations is a key factor that separates out the regulatory fine from the penal fine (and I will suggest, compensatory damages from penal damages), precisely because the 'traditional' variants are associated with moral condemnation.

## The meaning of money, freedom of choice and the regulatory fine

If we take such expressions in official discourse literally, then in 'regulatory' contexts, as opposed to criminal contexts, money is to bear no moral meaning; it reflects the 'technical' nature of offences, acts of carelessness, things that are not wrong but merely unwanted, inconvenient, and thus to be deterred. By implication, money takes on a moral meaning when it becomes a measure of moral condemnation in the courtroom. Such fines are linked to imprisonment and deprivation of liberty to the extent that offences are demoralized or appear merely technical, then the mode of their attachment to individuals changes. It becomes possible for the fine to be paid anonymously, instantly, at a discount rate for early payment or a penalty rate for late payment. More often than not the fine is not graduated by the deliberating agency in terms of the case at hand but simply set more or less exactly as a 'fixed penalty': so much for such a speed, so much more for another speed. It is at this point that the 'price' of these breaches takes on not simply a 'meaningless' meaning, but I would argue, a distinctly and purposefully commodified meaning. Here, rather than the moralized and individualized domain of the penal fine, the understanding of the money fine is very close to, or identical with, that of a price. It is not only the absent threat of imprisonment that distinguishes the regulatory from the penal fine; it is also that the absence of this threat is intricately linked with the regulatory fine's character as a routine financial transaction. It is fixed and non-negotiable, it is knowable with exactitude before the offence, there is no necessity for it to be adjudicated unless the payer desires it, it appears simply as another bill to pay, not as an occasion for moralized commentary. And frequently, it is applied to a part-person, a dividual, not the total individual that is the subject of moral condemnation, penal constraint or discipline.

Pashukanis (1978) echoes common parlance in referring to a set period in prison as the 'price' paid for offending, and suggests that this can be simply translated into an amount of money fined. However, I have argued earlier that 'price' with respect to prison takes on a moral meaning rather different to that of a the commodity exchange. Pashukanis and others rather miss the importance of the ideology of liberty and its idea of liberty as priceless. It is this 'priceless' meaning of liberty that explains the retention of imprisonment as a punishment for those morally reprehensible regulatory (especially traffic) offences that endanger or injure others. It provides the premise or rationality behind those arguments – official, popular, academic, radical and conservative – that condemn the use of the fine in relation to crimes of violence and demand long terms of imprisonment (Young 1989). Money that stands for imprisonment, as in the penal fine, does take on some of this meaning. In the penal fine liberty and money may be equated in degree, because the money fine is invested in the court ceremonial, even *in absentia*, with a governmental meaning measuring moral 'wrongfulness' rather than purchasing power alone. The regulatory fine, however, as opposed to the penal fine, emerged as an assemblage of procedures, official discourses and tactics in which monetary penalties are embedded precisely and solely in their sense of divesting the offender of purchasing power and little or nothing else. As Hunt (2006: 180) has argued,

> The consequence of this sort of penalty was that parking tickets and speeding tickets became a familiar experience of law abiding drivers and came to be viewed as part of the cost of motoring in the way that compulsory insurance and vehicle licensing were part of the economics of the motor car.

This too is related to freedom; but to a freedom that differs from liberty: it is the freedom of the market, and freedom of choice.

Freedom of choice emerges as a prominent category in consumer society. As Brett (1995) suggests, freedom of choice is a choice among commodities and most especially the commodities associated with surplus income. The idea of this as a 'freedom' to choose among washing machines, automobiles, brands of toothpaste, could be seen as trivialization of freedom in the sense of valued liberty. But perhaps it reflects a changing centrality of consumption in life. As argued earlier, in a world shaped by consumables, commodities become available as resources for life in new ways, as ways of self-fulfilment, self-identity, politics and self-expression. From this perspective, we live our lives through commodities in ways that have changed since Bentham's time. Colin Campbell (1987) points out that for Bentham, 'pleasure', one half of the felicity calculus, referred to the satisfaction of needs at the level of necessities. Bentham (1962: 578) considered that, as the fine took the bread out of the mouths of offenders' families, it thus worked all the more admirably as an effective deterrent. Nowadays, pleasure refers to a more expansive array of satisfactions to be purchased with surplus income. The 'massification' of the regulatory fine is conditional on its governmentally taken-for-granted meaning as something that can be paid 'on the spot'. Consequently, little innovation has gone into the 'problem' of inability to pay, because the governing assumption is that regulatory fines will not – perhaps even should not – cause serious distress. In this light, we could recast Rusche and Kirchheimers' argument in relation to the surplus income of the masses and growth of the regulatory fine. To put it rather crudely, the fate of the modern regulatory fine is a function of the surplus income of the consuming classes. The sanction has come into being as a means of governing behaviours largely related to consumption, it works through its impact on consumption, and it has expanded in its scope and volume with the emergence of consumer society, especially in the years after the Second World War.

The obverse of this point is no less important, for the regulatory fine and its economic conditions of existence make possible mass regulation as we know it. Without such cost-neutral or even revenue-producing sanctions, made viable by generalized surplus income in a consumer society, the scale of current regulation might not be possible. Without a sanction that can, in a consumer society, curtail pleasure and act as a deterrent without inflicting hardship, it would probably not be possible to create enforceable and politically acceptable regulations in anything like the degree that has occurred.

To repeat, this is not to reduce everything to consumption instead of production, as though we have replaced one determinant of history for another. Consumer society has made the 'modern fine' and its regulatory reach possible, but it has been the governmental and political responses to biopolitical problems that have invented the regulatory or 'modern' fine. This is clear once it is recognized how much has come together – and been put together – in the formation of the regulatory fine: imagining the 'problem' as one of distributions rather than individual morality; developing streamlined administrative procedures such as 'opting in' and 'reverse onus'; developing all manner of specific regulatory technologies from the parking meter and the red-light camera to the on-the-spot fine; reimagining fine defaults as civil debt collection; and so on *ad infinitum*.

All this inventiveness has created the rather diverse regulatory category Bottoms called 'the modern fine'. But of course it did not create it out of nothing. Very largely, I have argued, governmental inventiveness created the regulatory fine as a way (or a number of ways) to resolve problems very largely thrown up by traffic – which accounts for over 90 per cent of regulatory fines – and related threats to circulation and security in modern consumer societies. The inventions occurred in an environment in which relations of consumption increasingly have provided both many of the problems and many of the means through which governments have attempted to resolve them. They have also occurred in an environment in which another key area of law has been developing monetary techniques for governing problems, many of which are also related to traffic and to consumers: the law of accidents – or in the common law world, the law of torts.

## Notes

1 Such courts may issue warrants for the arrest of the defaulter, thereby creating some ambiguities for the question of whether imprisonment is available as a sanction. Again, such blurring at the boundaries is of less importance than the overwhelming difference in rates of imprisonment when considering the general governmental operation of modern fines as opposed to penal fines.

2 In the Australian state of Victoria, drivers with a full driver licence will suffer license suspension for three months if they accumulate twelve or more demerit points in any three year period. Those with a learner permit or probationary driver licence will also suffer suspension if they get five or more demerit points in any twelve month period. In this scale, exceeding the speed limit by 45 kilometers per hour attracts eight points, exceeding the limit by 35–44 km/h attracts six points and so on.

3 Bottoms (1983: 193) complicates his analysis by suggesting that a further bifurcation opens up in the criminal justice system. Promoting the welfare sanction are the senior government officials, prison scientists and probation officers. However, the judges and magistrates are seen to have been left out of this loop, and – to the dismay of the previous group – remain wedded to punitive and regulatory sanctions such as the fine. It is difficult to sort out the priority that Bottoms wishes to attribute to this essentially contingent force promoting fines, versus the more systematic forces that he identifies with the promotion of nondisciplinary regulation and sanctions. In some senses, his emphasis on inconsistencies in 'the state' follows a then fashionable mode of theoretical development in Marxist thinking (itself linked to Poulantzas' (1978) merging of Foucault and structural Marxism). But given that he associated fines with summary justice and trivial offending, it is at first unclear why Bottoms needs to throw in this additional consideration. Some clarification arises when he notes the peculiarity of American distaste for fines and a preference for probation and prison. This he tentatively explains by the fact that because

the welfare system is better developed in Britain than the US, then control by disciplinary institutions such as probation becomes less necessary and fines can be substituted (Bottoms 1983: 194) At a casual glance, this appears to parallel the arguments of Americans such as Hillsman and her colleagues (Hillsman *et al.* 1984), reviewed in the previous chapter. However it will immediately be noted that Hillsman's view is that British and European prisons are less disciplinary than the American equivalents, whereas Bottoms is arguing that in Britain both the prison and the social welfare system are more disciplinary than their American counterparts. In view of other antidisciplinary and 'punitive' changes occurring in both prison systems at the time Hillsman and Bottoms were writing it is probably wise to pass over this speculative and misleading set of propositions.

4  *USA Today* ('Virginia to issue traffic fines as high as $3,000', 15 October 2007, p. 1). In practice, the situation was more complex, for the fine and an extra charge were being merged, to produce a new hybrid. The paper reported that 'In an effort to raise money for road projects, the state will start hitting residents who commit serious traffic offenses with huge civil penalties. The new civil charges will range from $750 to $3,000 and be added to existing fines and court costs. The civil penalty for going 20 mph over the speed limit will be $1,050, plus $61 in court costs and a fine that is typically about $200'.

5  Much of the genealogy associated with Britain and provided here is drawn from Plowden's (1971) fascinating and detailed account. Accordingly, only key points and quotations will be referenced, and I here record my academic indebtedness.

6  Despite important differences associated with the 'democratization' of automobile ownership, a class politics nevertheless emerged in the United States. Simon (1998), for example, reports the following complaint in the *Atlantic Monthly* of 1925:

> … [T]he solid business of professional man is seldom a troublemaker. As his time is valuable, he is likely to drive fast when the way is open; but his sense of responsibility keeps him from knowingly taking chances … The new-rich owner, made arrogant by success, and the spoiled sons and daughters of rich parents, are another matter. They have property without responsibility. Instead of money and a taste for mechanics, the greatest need of the owner today is for the social feeling that accords courtesy and fair play to one's neighbors on the road. It is the lack of this quality, among a newer class of motorists that accounts for most of the avoidable accidents.

7  Plowden (1971: 62) records that at this time there were only about 8,500 motor vehicles in use in the fiscal year 1904/1905, suggesting that although cases were comparatively few, the rate of prosecution was very high indeed, with about a quarter of vehicles attracting fines each year.

8  New York was the first state to introduce a speed law in 1901, although this prohibited speeds greater than were 'reasonable and proper' rather than setting a specified speed limit. The first legislation setting speed limits, a few years later, created considerable opposition among motorists, because they were

seen to ignore the relevance of road conditions, traffic density and so on. Simon (1998: 555) reports that 'by the 1920s a veritable politics of speed laws was in full swing. Pressure from drivers led many states to increase speed limits or to eliminate them altogether in favour of reasonableness standards. To some extent this controversy ... (focused on) the practice of fining violators and the growing apparatus of police organized specifically to apprehend speedsters'.

9 Simon (1998: 555–558) further reports that in the United States various innovations were proposed to match mechanical engineering and regulatory concerns. For example it was proposed that the speed laws be replaced by a regulation that focused on the distance required to bring a vehicle to a stop. This calculus would take into account the tyres, brakes, road conditions, etc. relating to the event. It is likely this would have rendered speed laws unenforceable. However, it is also worth noting that such a complex regulation would have meant that quite an onerous set of demands would have been placed on the police and court systems and would have inhibited the 'streamlining' that was quickly to emerge around absolute speed limits.

10 Much of the following discussion is drawn from Richard Fox's (1995, 1996) invaluable work mapping out this genealogy in the US, Australia and the UK.

11 In the state of Virginia, a Virginia licensed driver under 20 who receives a Virginia speeding ticket will be required to attend an eight hour Virginia Driver Improvement class over and above a fine. In Texas, the 'Texas Drive Safe program' allows for speeding tickets to be dismissed if the driver attends a safe driving course of about six hours. (http://www.texasdrivesafe.com)

# Chapter 4

# Monetary damages

## Introduction

One of Durkheim's most important contributions to the sociology of law was to consider criminal and civil law sanctions together, and within this framework to consider the nexus between restitution as a legal sanction and societies characterized by contractual relations. His observations about the increasing mildness of criminal justice may be challenged in this era of punitiveness. This has been the basis for much 'refutation' of Durkheim's thesis concerning the decrease in retributive sanctions in the modern era. Yet we should also consider that in keeping with his overall proposition, criminal justice has been vastly overshadowed in its reach by civil law, and civil law usually is associated with compensation rather than punishment. In other words, relatively speaking the hypothesis could still be entertained that restitutive sanctions have become dominant in modernity.

It is fair to say that compared to criminal justice, contract law has expanded its reach considerably over the past two centuries. To the extent that societies become fully commodified, contract law is ubiquitous – even if it usually lurks unnoticed in the fine print attached to almost every commercial or employment agreement, and even if most contract and tort law disputes are settled out of court (Macauley 1985; Cane 1993: 5).[1] Embodying many elements shared with contract law, tort law has expanded from a marginal domain in the early 1800s to a central legal field that in important ways governs the array of accidental and unintended harms generated in industrialized and commercial operations (Friedman and Ladinsky 1967). In addition, remedies in contract and tort law have increasingly taken the form of compensation. As will be argued, in contrast to the eighteenth century, the remedies as of right now do not require completion of a contract in breach – which merely ties the parties to their original agreement. Rather it insists that the breach be 'compensated' specifically by the award of an amount of money. Likewise, tort law has become more specifically compensatory and less punitive in the last century, especially through its close connections with the array of social and private insurance apparatuses.

While this reflects the vision of contractual societies supporting restitutive sanctions, nevertheless there is a hidden catch of the greatest significance. Durkheim, like Bentham before him, rather supposed that a modernizing society was one in which contractual individualism would gradually become the telos of social and governmental relations. This was true for the nineteenth century that Bentham foresaw, and upon which Durkheim based his hypothesis. But about the beginning of the twentieth century, the course of liberal governance changed direction in a fashion summed up by Atiyah's (1979) memorable phrase 'the fall of freedom of contract'. The regulatory manoeuvres of the interventionist state, coupled with the growth of trades unions and the emergence of massive corporations and monopoly relations, constricted the play of contract law and thus of contractual damages. In pursuit of 'social' justice, the state imposed legal requirements on contracting parties, for example with respect to consumer protection and industrial safety, that overrode the 'freedom' of contractual relations.

In the same process, the government of many social harms through tort law and tort damages did become more compensatory. However, it did so by moving beyond a narrowly contractual model of law: tort changed in the direction of a focus on socially distributive justice rather than narrowly individualistic compensation. In turn, this shift was imbricated with the expansion of a 'social' approach to governance more generally which invented and then extended the reach of social insurances and other welfare assemblages. Indeed, this process was to threaten the very existence of tort law by displacing it with what were claimed to be more 'just' and more 'efficient' insurance technologies of compensation. Thus, while it could be said that with development of a 'modern' society restitutive sanctions were certainly promoted – as Durkheim foresaw – this was done in many ways *at the expense* of individualistic contractual governance.

Yet, this corrected version is also misleading, for the award of monetary damages in the heyday of the contractual 'era' of the nineteenth century arguably was *not* primarily about compensation. With respect to contract law, it is clear that while compensation did emerge as a governmental model during the 1800s, a primary aim of legal governance was to develop and normalize legal subjects who took responsibility for the foreseeable consequences of their actions. In the nineteenth century, contract law became part of a disciplinary assemblage. While damages were directed at compensation, at the same time they inflicted a punishment intended to reinforce certain techniques of the self in contractual relations. In the case of tort law, which was very closely modelled on contract, much the same was true. Indeed, rather than tort law being associated with increasing compensation, the nineteenth century was associated with a *narrowing* of eligibility for compensation precisely to the extent that the law became characterized by contractual ideologies. In the eighteenth century, responsibility for compensating harms had been associated with a strict liability model. Yet, as will be seen, the growth of such pivotal 'Victorian' liberal doctrines as privity of contract meant that responsibility could be assigned only to a more restricted class of those who visited harm on others. In particular, industrialists and other entrepreneurs would benefit from this restriction on compensation. Workers and the public would suffer. Horwitz (1977) famously, if contentiously, argued that this reflected naked class interests.

However, while legal liability was surely altered in a way that favoured capital, Horwitz mistakenly assumes that the governmental rationale for tort law primarily was compensatory. Rather, it can be argued that the primary purpose of tort law had shifted ground away from compensation with the rise of liberal contractualism. As White (2003: 62) has argued, in the nineteenth century tort actions

> ... had not principally been conceived as devices for compensating injured persons. Compensation had been a consequence of successful tort action, but the primary function of tort liability had been seen as one punishing or deterring blameworthy civil conduct. A conception of tort law as a "compensation system" is a distinctly twentieth century phenomenon brought about by an altered view of the social consequences of injuries.

As with contract law, the main purpose of nineteenth century tort law had been to create and enforce the emergence of a new kind of liberal legal subject: the 'reasonable man' who used foresight and prudence to govern a foreseeable but uncertain future.

Against Durkheim, then, it begins to appear that contractual forms of law are rather ambiguously related to restitution. In the nineteenth century, they are the site of a regime that was at least as much punitive as compensatory. It was only when contractual individualism was reined in by social and distributive forms of justice that restitution emerges as the pivotal rationale of civil law. This suggests once again that instead of 'reading off' legal sanctions as an effect of production relations, in this case the division of labour, we need to look elsewhere. I will argue that it is particularly through consumption relations that these changes are effected. In the twentieth century, protection of the consumer became a major theme in reshaping monetary damages. At the same time, money was to prove the medium through which transformation would be effected. For example, the development of Worker's Compensation in the early years of the twentieth century effectively made liability insurance mandatory for employers. Closely linked with this, in the first third of the twentieth century, a series of developments in Britain and the United States widened the liability of manufacturers for injuries to the consumers of their products. These developments greatly extended the need for public liability insurance. The development of widespread ownership of automobiles extended this further again. Through their shared remedy of money, and its use as the vehicle for redistribution of risk, civil law and insurance began to overlap and integrate. Law's reliance on insurance served to make compensatory sanctioning viable and led to a significant growth in the liability insurance industry. In turn, the operation of this assemblage of tort and insurance meant that a form of private welfare state grew up alongside the state system. As producers and distributors built the costs of liability insurance into the price of products and services, so consumers paid for compensation to those of their number who were in some way harmed by the goods they all purchased. Monetary remedies, prices and insurance form a circuit through which security is provided to the privileged sector that is 'in' the consumer market.

## Money – punishment and discipline

In common law, the idea of specifically compensatory damages is a surprisingly late arrival on the scene. The classic statement in this respect is by Baron Park in *Robinson v. Harman* ([1848], 1 *Ex* 850) to the effect that '(the) rule of the common law is, that where a party sustains a loss by reason of a breach of contract, he is, so far as money can do it, to be placed in the same situation, with respect to damages, as if the contract had been performed'.[2] The choice of words here is very precise, setting up what is essentially a hypothetical 'as if'. In the eighteenth century, the more normal course of the law would have been to require the specific performance of the contract. Of course, this would not be 'compensation' for a broken contract, but simply a requirement that the contract be fulfilled. At that time, some part of the contract must have been performed if it were to be recognized at law. If a load of grain were contracted to be delivered, then the courts would require delivery of the grain or perhaps return of the purchase price. In this arrangement, money damages as compensation need have no part to play. However, during the first half of the nineteenth century several changes were making specific performance problematic.

In the first place, the rise of a volatile and 'free' commodity market created situations in which specific performance of a contract was no longer what the plaintiff sought. For example, a decision to purchase a load of grain may have been based on the purchaser's calculation that the price of grain was about to increase. Suppose the purchase was motivated entirely by an expectation that an opportunity for resale profit would arise. If the contract were breached and the grain not delivered, then by the time the matter came to court, the market conditions may have changed. A remedy of specific performance – to enforce delivery of the grain – may have been worse than useless. The successful plaintiff would be left with a load of grain for which she had no use: the opportunity to profit had been lost, and by now, the market price for grain may even have fallen below the contracted price. In a commodified market, some other remedy than specific performance was needed.

Thus, in the early Australian action of *Kelly v Clarkson* in 1813 (O'Malley 2004), when the court dealt with a case of refusal to accept delivery of wheat at an agreed upon price, it did not enforce delivery but awarded damages of £80 to the wheat seller. Damages were set on the principle that the seller would have to dispose of the wheat on a falling market – and thus suffer an avoidable loss. The quantum of damages was set by the difference between the price agreed in the contract and the price of wheat at time of sale. In this emerging form of remedy, money had ceased to be merely a medium of exchange internal to the contract, but had become abstract capital in volatile 'free market' conditions. What was appearing was a new category in law – an 'expectation interest' – an interest in a calculated future that had been frustrated. Thus it was that in *Robinson v. Harman* the court regarded 'compensation' as being defined in terms of *money*, for making money is now regarded as the point of contractual agreements. More than this, money not only represented specific profits but abstract profit: profit that was never made but that existed only in the rational calculations of the contractors.

The degree to which such monetized abstraction could be extended is well illustrated by the action of *Howard v. Teefy* ([1927] 27 *SR* (N.S.W.) 307), an action over loss of opportunity suffered when a contract to lease a racehorse was breached. The court ruled that the calculation involved was not how much the plaintiff 'would probably have made in the shape of profit out of his use of the horse'. It was reasoned that it was impossible to decipher this. It was dependent on races that were never run, wagers that were never made, and odds that were never set. Instead, the court decided the damages were to be calculated in terms of 'how much his chance of making this profit, by having use of the horse, was worth in money'. Money has now been assigned an abstract meaning but the court gives us no guide as to how it measured this lost opportunity in money terms. In many examples of compensatory damages relating to lost opportunities, it would be possible to calculate the amount of compensation, say, by examining the way prices had fluctuated in the period between the breach of contract and the court hearing, and thus producing a more or less certain estimation of the lost profit. Money replaces money in such cases, even if the money compensation relates to profits never realized. But in examples of lost opportunities of the sort at issue in *Howard v. Teefy* money is being made to 'compensate' for a value that cannot be calculated by any straightforward money-to-money calculus. The court's assessment of what this opportunity is worth presumably was made in terms of an imaginary of the reasonable man, and his valuation of this chance.

As Atiyah (1979: 195) makes clear, such an approach to money and money damages would have been alien to eighteenth century lawyers

> To give the plaintiff what he 'expected' to make on the bargain, without requiring any performance from him, generally seemed, on the contrary, a very strange idea. Indeed it might almost have smacked of usury. Was the plaintiff to get damages for doing nothing? Was he entitled to have his mere expectations protected?

In the eighteenth century, expectation damages would most likely have been refused, and only actual rather than abstract losses compensated (Atiyah 1979: 142–148). However, by the nineteenth century 'compensation' can be read literally as the meaning of money supplied by commodification – in the domain of profit, the domain of production. Money represents capital, and the form of relations in which this is embedded is that which Marx (1976) referred to as 'generalised commodity production'.

In the liberal political vision, this resort to money damages also fitted with, and helped to create, the imagery of the *laissez faire* economy.

The remedy of specific performance had come to be seen as involving the state in an unwanted degree of interference or even coercion. The court would have to stand over the plaintiff in a civil dispute to ensure that he or she behaved in conformity with the contract (Kercher and Noone 1990). A critical feature of the money sanction was its reduction in apparent coercion: as long as no criminal offences were involved, the liberty of the individual to elect not to perform a certain action in the domain of civil society or the economy is preserved. The price of this liberty is the amount the defendant would have to pay in money for any harm to the expectations (or other recognized interests) of contracting parties. In contract law, therefore, the emergence of money damages as compensation brings this area of civil sanctioning into line with what has been said about the fine. In a utilitarian sense, it is the payment of a premium for the right to perform an action that the state disapproves of, but is unwilling to put a stop to by the use of incapacitating sanctions such as imprisonment. Like the regulatory fine, damages in contract law may often result from carelessness rather than a deliberate decision, but in the same fashion, they are a licence 'paid in arrears', or even a 'premium' paid for action beyond the norm. With the emergence of 'expectation damages' of the kind mentioned above, it had now become possible to imagine an 'efficient breach' of contract – where a contract would be broken when the defendant detected an opportunity that would deliver surplus profit over and above the damages that would in consequence arise in a civil action. Even though courts often frown on such calculated breaches, in utilitarian terms these are economically efficient acts in which a net gain is produced. Money damages at law have become a part of the currency of commodified relations.

Of course, as with fines, payment of damages will be enforced coercively if necessary – but normally they are just a morally loaded money transaction. Yet, while there is a relative reduction in coercion when compared to previous sanctions such as specific performance, it is clear that money is also a key punitive device in the service of discipline. Money damages serve to promulgate and enforce emerging norms of contractual relations even while acting to compensate those harmed by breach. This was clear, for example, with the establishment of money compensation for harm to expectation interests: from the time they were invented, any contractual party who failed to make 'reasonable' calculations of how a breach would harm the other party's reasonable expectations would run new risks of having to pay compensation. A liberal vision of the prudent subject exercising calculative foresight was being enforced by money sanctions at those points where failure act to appropriately created harm to others.

Thus, in a line of decisions beginning in 1854, the common law courts began to establish clear guidelines as to what constitutes 'reasonable foreseeability' in contracts. For example,

> Where two parties have made a contract which one of them has broken, the damages which the other party ought to receive in respect of such a breach of contract should be such as may fairly and reasonably be considered as arising naturally, that is, according to the usual course of things, from such breach of contract itself, or such as may reasonably be supposed to have been in the contemplation of both parties at the time they made the contract, as the probable result of the breach of it
>
> (*Hadley v Baxendale* [1854] 156 *ER* 145)

The decision in *Hadley v Baxendale* set in place certain ground rules for reasonable dealings that – through the guarantee of law and its money sanctions – were to provide an enforceable regime for government of business relations. *Inter alia*, the court's ruling meant that in the event one party to the contract stood to gain or lose in some unusual fashion from the contract, unknown to the other, or as the result of some possibility the other party 'reasonably' did not consider as bearing on the contract, then the award of damages would be restricted to what the court decided was reasonably foreseeable. The court reasoned that 'had the special circumstances been known, the parties might have specially provided for the breach of contract by special terms as to the damages in that case' (*Hadley v Baxendale* [1854] 156 *ER* 150). Previously, it was the breach itself, not what had been or should have been foreseen, that was relevant (Barton 1987: 41).

For Patrick Atiyah and others this is regarded as a 'triumph of the entrepreneurial ideal', because 'the idea of responsibility based on the foreseeable consequences of one's action was central to utilitarian philosophy'. This is a fair call, even though in practice it probably owed little to the theorists of liberalism and more generally emerged from the changing practical requirements of entrepreneurs who employed lawyers and thereby generated cases (O'Malley 2004; Wrightman 1996: 7–75). As Barton (1987) expressed it, with respect to damages 'the history of the law of contract, from the early eighteenth century to the twentieth, is the history of the process whereby matters of fact were converted into matters of law'. Compensatory monetary damages were now set in place not simply as a reflection of the commodification or capitalization of economic relations. At the same time they provided a sanction that *enforced* these relations and also produced the liberal 'reasonable' subject – all of this while appearing through the medium of money as not affecting the liberty of law's subjects.

Much the same kind of development was occurring with respect to money damages in tort law, which in the nineteenth century was very closely tied up in the ideology of contract.[3] Whereas in eighteenth century law the emphasis had been more on the harm rather than fault – although falling short of anything like a universal doctrine of strict liability for harm – during the nineteenth century foresight came to be the central issue shaping both liability to pay damages and access to compensation at law (White 2003: 14–15; Gregory 1951).[4] In this way, money damages enforced prudence and foresight primarily through two broad doctrines – privity of contract and negligence – worked out in the nineteenth century.

Privity of contract represented an attempt to come to terms with new situations increasingly coming before the courts in the nineteenth century. The old law had put great stress on a generalized liability for harm to others, because most injuries were likely to occur in relations between people who knew each other, more or less on a day to day basis and so owed each other duty of care as familiar citizens. In particular, this applied to the personal and paternalistic relations existing between 'masters and servants'. However, in an urbanizing and industrializing society, relations between strangers were becoming far more the norm, and relations in businesses and industries becoming far more distant in social, organizational and supervisory respects. As well, individuals were increasingly imagined as autonomous, the free and voluntary subjects released from the paternalism of the old order. Responsibility and paternalism sat in an uneasy relationship in this new order. In such a society perhaps it is not surprising that a 'reasonable' way of governing such contacts between strangers was to apply the norms of contractual relations: responsibility for others was limited to commitments voluntarily undertaken. Relations between strangers had of course existed before – but the new industrial and urban settings not only magnified the scale and frequency of such relations. As well, as Rabin (1981: 945) has argued, they also created new types of risks for strangers not generally confronted by old law.

This was true, for example, with respect to the rapidly growing field of transportation. Thus, in the case of *Winterbottom v. Wright* of 1842, it was ruled that the driver of a coach who had been injured because of equipment failure would have no claim to damages from the coach manufacturer, because no contract existed between them. In the view of Lord Abinger, presiding, 'there is no privity of contract between these parties, and if the plaintiff can sue, every passenger or even any person passing along the road, who was injured by the upsetting of the coach might bring a similar action. Unless we confine the operation of such contracts as this to the parties that enter into them, the most absurd and outrageous consequences to which I see no limit, would ensue' (*Winterbottom v. Wright* [1842] 152 *ER* 402). Of course, this may now appear itself as an outrageous statement. However, we view this from an era in which a much broader sense of social responsibility has become the norm, largely as a result of changes developing in the twentieth century. As many contemporary commentators – from Henry Maine to Emile Durkheim – also believed, in the nineteenth century contract as a form of sociability was displacing ascribed status as the telos for an entire society and appeared to very many as both 'free' and 'just' compared to the authoritarian *ancien regime*. Harm to an unknown driver, capable of looking after his own risks, and not within the sociable circle of contractual relations, appeared both reasonably unforeseeable and outside the realm of daily duty to strangers.

Negligence – in legal terms also an invention of the middle years of the nineteenth century – worked in terms of the same framework of liberal relations. In Baron Alderson's words, negligence is 'the omission to do something that a reasonable man, guided by those considerations which ordinarily regulate the prudent conduct of affairs, would do, or doing something which a prudent and reasonable man would not do' (*Blyth v Birmingham Waterworks* [1856] 11 *Ex* 784). To punish negligence by the award of damages against a defendant in like manner reaffirmed reasonable foresight and prudence. Consider, for example, the so-called 'fellow servant' or 'common employment' rule. In 1837, Lord Abinger in *Priestley v. Fowler* ruled that a worker injured as a result of the negligence of fellow employee should have no right of recovery from the employer. Indeed, in words foreshadowing his ruling in *Winterbottom v. Wright*, he had stated that '(if) the master be liable to his servant in this action, the principle of the liability will be found to carry us to an alarming extent'. By contrast, under the previously dominant principle of *respondeat superior*, it was settled that the master was indeed responsible for the acts of his or her agent – something that 'made sense' in a world where masters and servants were closely connected by all manner of 'paternalist' bonds of social superiority and duty (Friedman and Ladinsky 1967: 52–54). Now, however, in a world of contractual relations between independent and equal strangers, it was reasoned that this was unjust. How could the employer foresee or be held responsible for injuries resulting from the negligence of a worker's fellow employees? As freely acting agents, the employees were expected to be responsible individuals in their own right. As well, being 'on the spot' they were best placed to act preventatively. To relieve these individuals of the duty to apply reasonable foresight and take appropriate precautions would, it appeared to the court, be likely to create more rather than fewer accidents.

Money damages 'worked' punitively in this liberal utilitarian imagery, through the same circuits of governmental reason as the fine. Payment of damages meant the foregoing of pleasures and satisfactions, and thus acted as an encouragement to conformity with the emergent relations and subjectivities of classical liberalism. By extension, similar rules enforced by the denial of money damages were created where a worker was injured as the result of an accident that she or he should have foreseen. This doctrine of 'contributory negligence' – almost absent in law prior to the middle of the nineteenth century – followed the pattern of creating self reliant and independent subjects, whose responsibilities in these respects were a 'natural' corollary of their freedom (Friedman 1973: 410). If the plaintiff could be shown to have contributed in any significant degree to his injury, then an award of damages could be denied altogether.

Finally, the law had much to say about accidents that followed from the nature of the work, such as chemical injury in the tanning industry, or burns in a metal foundry. These harms, it was argued, must have been regarded as more than a remote possibility by the employee at the time of forming the contract of employment. A worker's failure to have considered such an issue demonstrated irresponsibility – a lack of foresight and diligence in his own interests. The worker was thereby assumed to have made a 'voluntary assumption of risk' (*volenti non fit injuria*, or '*volenti*'), and to have offset this by negotiating a higher wage. Having thereby been paid a premium wage for taking a risk – which of course was rarely the case in practice – the employee could have no right to compensation. It was not the law's business to treat adults as though they were incapable of prudent self-government. This line of reasoning is most famously developed in the United States with *Farwell v. Boston and Worcester Railroad Corp.* In Justice Shaw's words, whoever is employed 'for the performance of specified duties and services for compensation, takes upon himself the natural and ordinary risks and perils incident to the performance of such services and in legal presumption, the compensation is adjusted accordingly' (45 *Mass* (1842) 57).

While monetary damages did compensate, and while restriction of access to damages in the nineteenth century did work to the detriment of one class rather than another, more specifically they worked in tort law in a disciplinary fashion on all supposedly equal and autonomous legal subjects. Money damages enforced specific norms of reasonable foresight and care on workers just as in contract law they were doing so primarily among entrepreneurs. Liberalism in the 1800s accepted the Benthamite view that money damages work *simultaneously* to punish and to compensate, and that punishment and deterrence were probably the principal rationales of contract and tort law. While not only money can perform this double function, the money form also has specific properties that facilitate this. It might be said, for example, that to imprison a subject for criminal negligence provides both punishment to the offender and compensation to the victim. However, in such a model the state cannot appear but as an interested party in an act of coercion. Where negligence falls below the threshold of a criminal offence, which is by far the norm, the exercise of state coercion becomes problematic especially in *laissez faire* liberalism.

Because the money form appears as an act of compensation in which the state does no more than arbitrate between private parties, coercion remains at a low threshold – it can be punitive, even explicitly so, but like the fine does not lay hands on the offender. Ironically, because money can be attributed with this Janus-face, the distinction between what is punishment and what is compensation is necessarily problematic. Unlike, say, imprisonment, it is not clear what the purpose of the action is from the form itself. Prison is not just time, but specific kinds of action – while money is undifferentiated. Its meaning (as with the penal fine) has to be announced in some fashion. Consequently, during the later nineteenth century, when the common law began to draw a line between punishment and compensation, discursive problems emerged. In order to create 'pure' compensation, somehow 'punishment' had to be separated out and made different – a distinction of little concern in the previous century or more. Moreover, in the face of money's bland face, ways had to be invented to ensure that damages were being granted in a 'purely' compensatory fashion.

## Distinguishing punishment and compensation

In accord with what has been discussed thus far, Ogus (1973: 5–6) has pointed out that before the late nineteenth century 'compensation in the modern sense' was only one purpose that was intended for an award of damages, and certainly among these punishment of the wrongdoer figured prominently: 'large awards of damages in a civil process were regularly employed to punish or deter wrongful conduct' (1973: 28). In addition, juries, especially, were not to be switched on and off at will in this respect:

> ... the ability to use damages in a civil action as a means of punishing the defendant lingered on. Within the wide ambit of the jury's discretion exercisable when damages were "at large", that is, where an exact pecuniary loss was not claimed, there was ample room for a pecuniary element in the award. Indeed in the eighteenth century, the power of the jury to express its view of the defendant's conduct by awarding large damages was regarded as a constitutional right.
>
> (Ogus 1973: 5)

While Ogus refers here to a lingering 'confusion between compensation and punishment', of course this is a kind of history in reverse – as if these are natural categories that *needed* to be untangled rather than distinctions that had to be *created* as distinguishable rationalities.[5] I am not implying that the idea of compensation as distinct from punishment did not previously exist. Rather, my point is that compensation as a category that *has* to be separated out from punishment was not something that greatly concerned either Bentham, the jurists or juries of his time. Even more to the point, compensation had to be invented in a certain form that was not clearly articulated in common law until the middle years of the nineteenth century. Compensatory damages had become a form of money that did not seek to set up a status quo ante, often this was impossible – as in cases of injury or lost opportunities. Now money was also compensating for a *hypothetical* status quo that would have continued to exist or that would have come to exist but for the wrong. This has been seen to be the case in contract law in *Robinson v. Harman* of 1848, but, likewise in 1880, it was stated that compensation in tort law is 'that sum of money which will put the party who has been injured in the same position as he would have been if he had not sustained the wrong for which he is now getting his compensation or reparation'. (*Livingstone v. Rawyards Coal Co* [1880] 5 *App Cas* 25,39).

Nevertheless, once invented, it takes a particular kind of legal rationality to imagine compensation as if it were distinct from punishment. Take Ogus (1973: 29–30) once more as an illustration. Focusing on the invented distinction between 'exemplary' (or 'punitive') damages[6] and compensation, he suggests that there was

> ... confusion between "exemplary" and "aggravated" damages. For a long time the common law had recognised that actual loss to the plaintiff might be aggravated by the defendant's aggressive or malicious conduct on the ground that it injured the plaintiff's pride or dignity. The law would in short compensate the plaintiff for his justifiable humiliation. To the extent that damages are awarded on this basis they are, of course, compensatory and not punitive. But since both exemplary and aggravated damages are dependent on the defendant's conduct, the line between them is sometimes difficult to draw and a reading of the early cases does not clearly reveal which was the subject of the award

Indeed, the suggestion is made that such distinctions between compensation and punishment only became possible when juries – to which questions of damages were almost entirely left until the early nineteenth century in England and Wales (Atiyah 1979: 425) – were replaced by judges. To put this another way, having invented the distinction, it then required a 'trained' eye to implement it in a standardized or 'just' fashion. In this light, the distinction between punishment and compensation, far from being a natural kind, appears instead as a technical divide capable of satisfactory implementation only by expertise.[7]

As suggested, the divide between punishment and compensation represents a difficult task to the extent that the money form does not make evident where one function begins and the other ends, and in this governmental imagery only the eye of the judicial expert can be relied upon to discern the separation. Even then, the court's difficulties remain palpable. In the leading Australian case, Justice Windeyer later expressed the contrast as follows:

> Aggravated damages are given to compensate the plaintiff when the harm done to him by a wrongful act was aggravated by the manner in which the act was done: exemplary damages on the other hand are intended to punish the defendant, and presumably to serve one or more of the objects of punishment – moral retribution or deterrence.
> (*Uren v. John Fairfax & Sons Pty. Ltd.* [1966] 117 *CLR* 149)

While seeking to make the distinction clear, the court highlights the fact that, in both forms of sanction, the focus is a 'wrongful act', and thus a punitive meaning remains available even in 'aggravated' damages, at least to those courts and juries concerned with moral condemnation.

At the same time, however, the distinction was clearly important within the imagery of the 'non-coercive' domain of civil law. Thus, more than a century after compensation was established as the aim of damages in contract and tort law, the English leading case of *Rookes v. Barnard* ([1964] *AC* 1129 (HL) 1221) was still wrestling with the perceived problem that courts were allowing punitive considerations to influence awards of damages. Lord Devlin argued that exemplary damages 'usurped' a function best left to criminal law. In this decision – which, it should be stressed, has not been strongly embraced in the United States, Canada or Australia – the court ruled that punitive or exemplary damages should only be awarded under restricted circumstances, except where expressly authorized by statute. First, Devline argued that exemplary damages may be awarded where there has been 'oppressive, arbitrary or unconstitutional action by the servants of the government'. Second, they can be awarded where 'the defendant's conduct has been calculated by him to make a profit for himself which may exceed the compensation payable to the plaintiff' (*Rookes v. Barnard* ([1964] *AC* 1129 (HL) 1226)).

However, this attempt at clarification contributed to another point of blurring or convergence. Clearly enough, punitive monetary damages and fines levied against corporations are very little different – except with respect to procedural issues (Mann 1993). This is even more so where conviction in a criminal prosecution under American antitrust laws serves as *prima facie* evidence of responsibility in an ensuing private action, and conditions relating to damages are provided by criminal law. Thus, under the *Clayton Antitrust Act* (1914 section 4), 'any person who shall be injured in his business or property by reason of anything forbidden in the antitrust laws may sue … and shall recover threefold the damages by him sustained, and the cost of suit, including a reasonable attorney's fee'.[9] Here, the punitive nature of the money damages is both explicit and mandatory, and its rationale has been elaborated in the courts as being a deterrence against violations of antitrust laws that might otherwise go undetected or unprosecuted because of the limited resources of the Department of Justice (Schleuter and Redden 1995: 516). Not only are these damages punitive but also their governmental rationale is to promote privately initiated actions as a form of prosecution facilitating the potential award of massive damages (Elzinga and Breit 1976: 66). In addition, reference to the issue of costs makes clear not only a further incentive to bring private action, but also an additional and intentional sanction in itself.[10]

Now, it would be easy to get tangled in a debate as to whether these awards represent significant punishment against rich corporations (Stevens and Payne 2002), or over whether civil awards of this nature carry the same weight as criminal sanctions *per se* and are thus not to be preferred even if the procedure is less taxing on the prosecution (Carson 1974).[11] These political questions are obviously normatively important, but from within the present analysis the issue rather is that money is a sanction with effects relevant at the procedural level. It is precisely because the money form of sanction is regarded as 'less coercive' than sanctions directly affecting liberty (prison, probation, etc.) that this kind of mobilizing of civil law as an adjunct to criminal law is possible. In part, this is simply because, especially with respect to compensatory damages, the punitive element can be valorized (as it was in the nineteenth century) or it can be left to speak *sotto voce* as the latent effect of damages that have compensation as their formal goal. But even with respect to punitive damages, money's meaning as 'less coercive' helps contribute to the differing levels of proof and of limitations on evidence that characterize civil versus criminal law.

## 'A just measure of pain': compensatory damages and nonpecuniary losses

> You must take some sum which you think is reasonable for the defendant to pay and for the plaintiff to receive, and I can help you no further than that.
>
> > (*Scott v. Musial* [1959] 2 Q.B. 432 per Paull, J.)

> No money can compensate for the loss. Yet compensation has to be given in money. The problem is insoluble.
>
> > (*Ward v. James* [1966] 1 Q.B. 296 per Lord Denning)

Where compensation, rather than punishment, is at issue, the amount of damages to be awarded often may be calculated in a relatively straightforward fashion – because what is at stake is money compensation for money lost: the costs of hospital treatment, lost profit, lost income, damage to property and so on. In many respects, this formula applies also in insurance, and it is with respect to such concerns that insurance and tort law overlap so closely in function. However, a division opens up where compensation for nonpecuniary losses is at issue. In most insurance, and especially with respect to such relevant forms as workers' compensation, the award or benefit is directly linked to the calculation of economic losses in past, present and future. Tort law, however, provides additional remedy with respect to such matters as pain and suffering, loss of reputation and a variety of 'emotional' harms (Laster and O'Malley 1996). It has been noted already that with respect to both contract and tort law, it is clearly decided that 'compensation' is to be defined in terms of an amount of money. The problem created here is indicated in an apparently straightforward statement of the nature of damages: 'It is well settled that the governing purpose of damages is to put the party whose rights have been violated in the same position, so far as money can do so, as if his rights had been observed'. (Asquith LJ., *Victoria Laundry (Windsor) Ltd v. Newman Industries Ltd.* [1949] 2 *KB* 539). While obviously consistent with the nineteenth century cases establishing compensation as money, this often-quoted statement makes clear the central dilemma of how to equate money with something that may not appear to have a money equivalent. Not questioned is the fact that money has to be the remedy. At the same time it is made clear that in some important sense money is likely to be regarded as inadequate in this respect.

In the Australian case of *Lee Transport Co Ltd v Watson* ([1940] 64 *CLR* 13–14), Dixon J. remarked that 'it is right to remember that the purpose of damages is not to give perfect compensation in money for physical suffering. Bodily pain and injury are not the subject of commercial dealing and cannot be calculated like some other forms of damage in terms of money'. Put with a slightly different inflection, Luntz states that such harms 'cannot be evaluated according to the rules of the market place; do not represent commodities that can be bought or sold' (Luntz 1990, para 3.1.2). Given such statements, and holding in mind Simmel's (1990) remarks on the *Wergild* and the meaning of money, it would be prudent not to jump to the conclusion that money damages represent a simple commodification of human life. However, the question remains, if that is not the case how did we arrive at a point where such matters were given money value?

In the institution of the *bot*, the Anglo-Saxon precursors to compensation for nonpecuniary loss, a kind of table of maims – strikingly akin to a twenty-first century table discussed later in this section – was established.

> If a thumb be struck off, XX shillings. If a thumb nail be off. Let bot be made with III shillings, If the shooting finger be struck off, let bot be made with VIII shillings. If the middle finger be struck off

let bot be made with IV shillings. If the little finger be struck off, let bot be made with III shillings.

(Quoted by O'Connell and Bailey 1972: 88)

The apparent parallels, however, are a world apart. In the institution of the bot, the distinction between punishment and compensation is unclear, and the meaning of money was not the same as that in a fully commodified economy. It would seem, rather, that the function of the table was more in the order of a fine or punitive damages, registering the existence of a wrong that money marked and measured. Like Wergild, the bot's function was at least in part political pacification. In a weak and fissionable state, the award of bot provided a means of institutionalizing conflicts that otherwise could get out of hand. Much the same appeared in the early law of defamation. In an effort to reduce to the risks of disorder, old statutes of *de scandalum magnatum* – criminally prohibiting the libel of magnates – in the late fifteenth century were adapted into civil law to provide for the award of damages among the nobility as a means of reducing violence and, especially, duelling (O'Malley 1981). Given the significance of honour among this class, it is highly unlikely that payment of damages had any implication along the modern lines of commodifying the harm. Money was rich with other meanings, signifying the wrong to intangible reputation.

By the early twentieth century, however, matters were very different. In line with the commodification view of money damages here, and probably the most frequently asserted view, is well summed up by an Ohio judge in 1919

Award of money damages can in no sense make the plaintiff whole nor undo the suffering which as been undergone. Money can in no sense be considered an equivalent for pain and suffering. The award of money compensation for pain and suffering and physical injury must therefore be founded upon the fact that money judgment operates to afford the plaintiff feelings of satisfaction, pleasure or gratification which in the eyes of the law, will operate to offset the pain which has been undergone. In other words the possession, control, ownership and purchasing power of money is deemed to afford the plaintiff the power of gratifying other desires and of pursuing happiness, and of resulting feelings of content or of an otherwise pleasurable nature'.

(21 *Ohio St LJ 1184* [1960])

Here the vision is that damages provide resources for the purchase of pleasure equivalent to the pain or loss of bodily amenity created by the harm. The point is made even more clearly by Justice Windeyer in *Teubner v. Humble* ([1963] 108 *CLR* 507) who suggests that 'insofar as money can in a particular case give pleasure or provide comfort, money can properly said to compensate for pain and suffering'.[12] Now, this could be read almost as giving the lie to many juridical statements to the effect that the harms being compensated 'do not represent commodities'. If the pain and suffering are not commodities in themselves, they are equated with an amount of money that is envisioned as purchasing pleasurable commodities. It can safely be assumed that Marxists, of the sort represented by Pashukanis (1978) would see the judicial protests as a spurious claim: to equate a harm with an amount of money whose purpose is to buy commodities is to render the harm a commodity; the rest is talk. This was the view, for example, of Abel (1982: 195–196) who objected to the payment of money compensation for workplace injuries, precisely because it commodified the persons and bodies of workers and the emotions and suffering or ordinary people. In his words:

> … damages commodify our unique experience by substituting the universal equivalent – money … If damages for pain and suffering commodify experience the recent expansion of tort remedies for injuries to relationships commodifies love. Damages are now paid for the loss of the society and companionship of a parent in wrongful death actions; for loss of consortium of an injured spouse, lover, parent or child; for witnessing or learning about an injury to a loved one; for mistreatment of the corpse of a loved one, for negligent information about the death of a loved one; even for injury to loved objects. Such compensation affirms several symbolic messages. All relationships have a monetary value and hence can be bought and sold.

However, while it is easy to sympathize with the spirit of Abel's argument, can the insistence of the courts and their interpreters on maintaining the divide between the commodified form of compensation and the 'human' harm be dismissed as a form of false consciousness or duplicity? I doubt this. After all, these official discourses on compensatory damages *explicitly* recognize the dilemma of commodifying human pain and suffering and hence seek always to create a distance between the harm and the remedy. The recurring phrases such as 'the best that the courts can do', 'not perfect compensation', 'so far as money can do so' all register this discursive manoeuvre. The manoeuvre appears necessary precisely because of the meaning given to money by the courts: ironically it is exactly that commodified and rather disdainful meaning Abel and other Marxists would insist on.

Perhaps the problem for the courts is simply that noted already. Money has been specified as the means of compensation, because other means of redress appear too coercive. If the harm has not been deemed criminal, then especially a liberal state has a difficult line to walk. Other forms of intervention, even demanding an apology, let alone inflicting corporal punishment or taking away liberty, require the courts to compel conformity and interfere with the liberty of the subject in a matter that is represented as a private dispute. Money, however – a pacifying device in the bot and wergild – appears noncoercive in such ways. In addition, money's usage in ordinary life – in the world of civil society – as a universal equivalent makes it available as a remedy for an almost infinite array of civil harms. If courts must give remedy for such diverse harms, and somehow appear to be providing an intelligible and consistent scheme of compensation, then money makes itself available as a common currency of justice. In the face of money's functionality in a commodified society, the courts' ambivalent but resigned response becomes intelligible. We have already seen a similar kind of response with the example of the punitive fine.

Here, it might be recognized, we have returned to Bentham's felicity principle and the money calculus that he applied to this in the discussion on fines. In the case of the fine, happiness is measured in money terms and taken away from the offender to a degree slightly in excess of the pleasure afforded by the proceeds or the performance of a crime. With compensatory damages, money for purchasing pleasure is awarded to the 'victim' in proportion to the pain or injury suffered. However, while this suggests the utilitarian basis of contemporary compensatory damages (and given that much of the associated doctrine developed in the nineteenth century this seems a more than plausible nexus), it still leaves unexplained just how human pleasure or happiness is to be measured in money terms. Here, the discomfort of the courts is intensified.

In one of the classic texts on the subject, Ogus (1973: 198) appears to render the question purely subjective:

Damages for pain and suffering can hardly be assessed on any scientific basis. There is no method of objectively assessing pain.

Everything must depend on evidence both of the victim himself and his medical assistants. But how does one translate linguistic concepts like "very severe" or "harrowing" pain into monetary units? How can we relate what medical opinion means by "severe pain" to what the victims, or the man on the Clapham omnibus describe as "severe pain".

Possibly this would be still more problematic where the issue is mental pain and suffering rather than physical. Ogus concludes that 'there are no answers to such awkward questions'. Were this actually the case and there were 'no answers', then the law would be without any means of assessing damages for pain and suffering. In practice, as Ogus himself suggests, the answer in practice lies in a form of common sense, by reference to the man on the Clapham omnibus. As far as case law is concerned Ogus considers that this calculus of equivalence appears as a question of social conventions of the time, to be resolved by application of the 'reasonable man' test. In this imagery, while none of us might be able to explain how to price something like the loss of a child, harm to our reputation or a disfiguring injury, it is legally imagined that the reasonable person can do so if pressed. Thus, Salmon L.J. argues that 'damages must be real and amount to what the ordinary reasonable man would regard as fair and sensible compensation for the injuries suffered' (*Gardner v Dyson* [1967] 1 W.L.R. 1501).

This would be consistent with the traditional technique of the courts to put the matter to a jury: to allow 'ordinary' men and women to make such 'reasonable' judgments of harm and to determine their money equivalent for compensation. In the United States, where this tradition has been more robust than elsewhere, key problems of measurement and meaning have given rise to considerable case law. It is argued that juries give sometimes highly variable, 'capricious' and sometimes surprisingly large awards of damages (Ogus 1973: 198). Of course, it can be argued that as there is no normative basis other than the reasonable person test, then there is no basis to claim that juries give 'outrageous' awards without reference to some other 'reasonable person'. To some degree this other reasonable person is provided by the judiciary in appellate courts. Quite a volume of case law has emerged on how to regulate juries in order to make them 'reasonable'. The principal technique in this respect has been standardization. In the absence of any means of scientifically establishing pain, suffering, humiliation, grief and so on, then objectivity is reached through creating norms by other means. In the words of Lord Diplock, 'justice' is largely to be found in the standardization of amounts of money, yet not in money itself:

> Non-economic loss ... is not susceptible of measurement in money. Any figure at which the assessor of damages arrives cannot be other than artificial and, if the aim is that justice meted out to all litigants should be even-handed instead of depending on the idiosyncrasies of the assessor, whether judge or jury, the figure must be 'basically a conventional figure derived from experience and from awards in comparable cases ....'
>
> (*Wright v. British Railways Board* [1983] 2 *AC* 773)

Such norming is itself facilitated by the establishment of the money form of damages as the remedy as of right – the remedy to be applied universally unless special reasons intervene. Thereby a criterion was unintentionally created in terms of which the 'consistency' or 'calculability' of justice may be measured across the diversity of injuries and harms. Conversely, such apparent comparability creates consistency between cases as a problem requiring a solution. Reflecting this, a good deal of the relevant case law involves the devising and justification of some form of metric or even mathematization of the relationship between nonpecuniary harm money – a modernist way of giving money a standard and *calculable* meaning in terms of the experience of harm.

Reviewing a considerable body of American law, O'Connell and Bailey (1972: 103–110) suggest that the most prominent and contro-versial of these calculative efforts is the attempt to put a monetary value on some specific kind of pain and suffering and then multiply this unit amount by the number of days that have been undergone in this condi-tion. Apart from noting various safeguards that surround such a system of calculability, such as instructions from the judge or the intervention of appellate courts, O'Connell and Bailey (1972: 105) list four principal reasons put forward by courts to support such a schema:

> First, if it is permissible to state the total figure sought for pain and suffering, it is no more speculative to state the per diem figure and the plaintiff should have the right to explain the components of the lump sum. Second, a mathematical formula is just one way to aid a juror in making a reasonable award, and the jury should not have to make a blind guess. Third, since there is no real yardstick to measure pain and suffering, use of a mathematical formula cannot be said to mislead the jury .... Fourth, a mathematical formula is

considered an illustration and not evidence. The defense can either refute the formula altogether or use its own formula to argue for a lower figure.

Perhaps predictably, those courts disputing the use of such an approach have focused on the 'fact' that the foundational unit of calculation – the equation of money with pain and suffering – is not itself founded in science and cannot, therefore, be processed into a precise formula. In *Ahlstrom v. Minneapolis*, it was argued that 'to permit a per diem evaluation of pain, suffering and disability would plunge the already subjective determination into absurdity by demanding accurate mathematical computation of the present worth of an amount reached by guesswork' ([1955] 68 *NW* 891 per Christianson, J.).

Of interest here is not so much whether the attempt to mathematize the monetary meaning of such harms does or does not make sense: clearly to many courts it makes good enough sense. It is rather the struggle itself – the contest over the meaning of monetization of harms that is important. It is a struggle between the effort to render money damages somehow rationally intelligible through a grid of calculation, and the opposing view that the meaning of money damages is situational – a matter of the judgment of the reasonable man faced by a unique situation. This latter is a view frequently met within other common law domains. In Australia, for example, Justice Windeyer of the High Court expressed the opinion that

> Compensable loss depends not only upon the severity of the plaintiff's injury but on the consequences for the individual. No two injuries are really the same and the consequences of apparently similar injuries vary infinitely for different individuals. Thus results given in different cases may be harmonious in principle, although appear disproportionate when the physical injuries alone are regarded.
>
> (*Papanayiotou v. Heath* [1970] *ALR* 110–112)

In this view, highly variable awards of damages cannot be accused of being capricious, because they reflect the nuanced reading of the judge or jury. In either case, however, money makes this question particularly acute, simply because the decisions of the courts are rendered in *exactly* comparable units of monetary measurement. Ironically, while the courts complain about money, it could be said equally that money is not at all the problem *per se* but is the register of the problem – for it 'reveals' disagreements about the nature of the harm suffered by the plaintiff. If the problem is viewed from this angle, then the problem changes. No longer is the question how to standardize the total harm by multiplying a subjectively calculated unit of injury or pain. Now it becomes how to standardize the injury and pain so that they will produce consistent units of measurement!

Partly under pressure from this last form of reasoning, in Britain and many other jurisdictions, the calculation of damages has gradually slipped from the hands of juries to become the decision of judges.[13] Significantly, where this has occurred, tariffs have emerged as a form of standardization. Indeed, this was always likely given that primary reasons given for this shift to judicial awards include the claims that juries are rarely if ever aware of the damages awarded in similar cases, too often allow elements of punitiveness to enter their decisions, and thus produce highly variable awards (Ogus 1973: 198). In such contexts, courts may admit to the fact that the amount of damages is 'reached by guesswork' but at least the guesswork will be standardized and rendered more predictable. In this way, the 'reasonable man' has been translated into a metric that could be expressed as 'the general consensus of opinion of judges trying these cases' (Diplock L.J. *Hennell v. Ranaboldo* [1963] 1 W.L.R. 1393.). Thus, in Britain, the Judicial Studies Board produces regularly updated *Guidelines for the Assessment of General Damages in personal injury cases* (Judicial Studies Board 2002). Here, after the ritual incantation to the effect that 'since no monetary award can compensate in any real sense', and recognizing that 'no two cases are ever precisely the same', the assertion is made that 'justice required that there be consistency between awards' (Lord Donaldson 2002: i).

The resulting table of maims is highly detailed, amounting to several hundred different categories of injury, each of which is defined and linked to a monetary range of damages awarded. For example, foot injuries are differentiated from leg, ankle, Achilles tendon and toe injuries, each of which constitutes its own category of maims. As with each of the other categories, foot injuries are divided into several – in this case eight – subcategories! Thus, amputation of both feet is assessed at between £87,500 and £105,500, amputation of one foot at between £43,250 and £57,500 both being 'treated as similar to below knee amputation because of the loss of a useful ankle joint' (Judicial Studies Board 2002: 51). Seemingly more subjective are the lesser categories – lesser because of the amount of damages awarded – of 'very severe', 'severe', 'serious', 'moderate' and 'modest' foot injuries. For example, the 'serious' category is assigned damages of between £13,000 and £20,000. This is defined as follows:

> Toward the top end of the bracket fall cases such as those of grievous burns to both feet requiring multiple operations and leaving disfiguring scars and persistent irritation. At the lower end of the bracket would be those injuries less severe than in (d) above [i.e. 'severe'] but leading to fusion of foot joints, continuing pain from traumatic arthritis, prolonged treatment and the future risk of osteo-arthritis.'
>
> (Judicial Studies Board 2002: 52)

The point at issue, it needs to be stressed, is not whether this represents reasonable compensation according to any other standard, or even represents a ridiculous exercise according to some imagined other 'rational' calculus. Either judgment would land analysis in a quagmire of its own making to add to that of the law. Rather, attention is directed to the ways in which the body is divided into precise physical components – legs, ankles, toes, Achilles tendons, etc. – for the purposes of analysis. Then, a variety of experiential, abstract, economic, aesthetic and physical elements are combined into a category of injury and pain. 'Future risk', 'continuing pain', 'irritation', 'disfiguring scars', 'grievous' burns and so on, are rendered together to produce a governmental grid through which money is to be given a stable compensatory value.

Into this process of rendering the incalculable calculable are added specific characteristics of the legal subjects. With respect to 'facial injuries', for example, 'in cases where there is a cosmetic element the courts have invariably drawn a distinction between the awards to males and females, the latter attracting the highest awards' (Judicial Studies Board 2002: 55). In more complex fashion, reference is also frequently made to the age and life expectancy of the victim (Judicial Studies Board 2002: 1). Where pain and suffering are at issue, consistent with the happiness principle, courts have taken the view that that the shorter the remaining life span of a plaintiff then the less pain and suffering she or he will have to endure – and thus a lesser amount of damages is required to provide compensation under this head (*Clarke v Kramer* [1986] *WAR* 54). In turn, this calculation is complicated by the observation that knowledge of the curtailment of one's lifespan itself creates pain and suffering and courts recognize that this too needs to be built into the award of damages (Luntz 1990: 3.2.2) Conversely, in *Benham v. Gambling* ([1941] *AC* 157: 201–204) the view was taken that the amount of damages would be proportional to the amount of happiness that has been foregone.

Money damages are thus awarded according to a judicial metric arrived at by a standardized calculation, normatively set by juridical constructions of the reasonable person's estimation, in money terms, of the amount of pleasure required to compensate for harm. Of course, this immediately reveals a second problem that courts bypass where possible. How much money do what sorts of pleasures cost on the open market? Potentially, this could unravel all the carefully constructed metrics reviewed above. Should a plaintiff receive more money if he or she has expensive hobbies compared with another plaintiff who gets their joy from inexpensive rustic pastimes? In part, courts bypass this issue by the practice of not specifying what commodities damages should be spent on. This remains the prerogative of the plaintiff, who is held to be in the best position to determine which pleasures best provide solace. At the same time, however, the emphasis on standardizing the harm side of the equation and allowing damages to be 'read off' from this, masks the variability in the monetary costs of what would generate 'equal' amounts of pleasure across diverse plaintiffs.

At this point, one further 'money effect' appears. Because the form of compensation is money, Abel and others' views to one side, then courts are *not* forced to commodify harm. The amount of money appears 'merely' as a measure of harm and an award of solace. Money is distanced from the act of commodification not only by the jurist's insistence on the invalidity of commodifying harm, but also by the fact that the money is only the means to purchase commodities, it is not the commodities themselves. If this seems a ridiculous matter of hair splitting, consider the alternative rhetorical question raised at the beginning of this book. What if the courts directly awarded commodities – the BMW, the villa in Florida and the diamond necklace? Money in the form of damages may indeed have its purpose in buying pleasures as solace, but by distancing the award of compensation from the commodities it can purchase, it allows the courts leeway to argue against the commodification of harm.

It is worth noting that this same dilemma seems never to be a concern to the insurance industry, where various matters of injury, life, 'priceless' art work and so on are routinely assigned a money value. In part, this is because values are agreed upon contractually: the parties to an insurance contract agree on the value of the risk to be transferred to the insurer, and the premium is set accordingly – frequently calculated on the basis of actuarial data. In this way, the technique for pricing the 'priceless' is the market. For example, in the case of a priceless art work, insurance will be set at a price that the insurer recognizes to be the 'market' rate and

that the policyholder finds acceptable.[14] As with the courts, as Ericson
and Doyle (2004) have shown, judgement of value by insurers may also
be 'subjective', for example where there is no way of assessing the risk
involved. As with the courts, while there is seemingly no way of pricing
the priceless, the institution of insurance demands that it be done. As with
the courts, the valuation process involves comparison of the case in hand
with 'like' cases: the insurer creates a metric for measurement. And as
with the court, the insurer will be aiming for *compensation* – a price to
be paid that is equal to but does not exceed the loss sustained.

In some ways, this last point completes a monetary circle. If the courts
do create a metric in terms of which damages are standardized, then the
courts have mimicked insurance strategies. Pooling together cases from
the past, a grid is established in terms of which damages awarded for
the case at hand – and future cases – can be calculated and predicted.
Judges take on the role of the insurer, applying a grid of compensation calculated more or less actuarially. In this respect, it is not simply
that a *calculable justice* is achieved, something that Max Weber (1954)
might have foreseen, but also that an *insurable justice* is optimized.
To the extent that this does not emerge – as in the United States, where
juries still extensively control the award of damages – one result may be
the creation of insurantial crises such as is argued to have emerged in
the 1980s. We will return to this issue shortly. However, these marked
similarities between insurance and courts bring insurance and the law
of damages not only into interdependence, but also even to mutual
substitutability.

## From punishment to regulation

> The introduction by statute of compulsory liability insurance, first
> for road accidents and later for industrial accidents, has changed
> the whole focus of the law of torts from penalising tortfeasors to
> compensating their victims.
>
> (Cane 1993: 202)

The punitive and disciplinary implications of nineteenth century civil law,
especially in relation to foreseeability and its spin-offs such as negligence,
were almost from the beginning set against alternative imageries that were
focused on the 'injustices' that these concepts and doctrines produced.
Clearly, very many of those injured as workers and consumers were
denied any form of compensation as a result of the contractual imaginary
and the fault-based mentality of the law of torts. Toward the end of the

nineteenth century, especially under the impact of trade union politics, the courts began to voice increasing concerns about the inadequacy of the existing ways of providing tort remedies.

To begin with, judges and legislators began to recognize that tort law was inaccessible to most working people who could not afford the legal costs involved. When coupled with the low degree of predictability with respect to outcomes, this was seen to place a considerable burden of financial risk on the shoulders of people in no position to bear the consequences (Friedman and Ladinsky 1967: 57–64). 'Exceptions' began to be created to rules such as 'volenti' and contributory negligence as courts observed that 'the progress of society' demanded change. Thus, with respect to the fellow servant rule it was noted in 1891 that 'the tendency of the more modern authorities appears to be in the direction of such a modification and limitation of the rule as shall eventually devolve upon the employer ... a due and just share of the responsibility for the lives and limbs of the persons in its employ'. (*Parker v Hannibal & St. J.R.R.* 109 *Missouri* 397). In addition, trade unions and charitable organizations were not only arguing against such 'injustices', but had identified certain industries as having characteristically high and enduring rates of workplace accidents. In this light, questions of individual discipline were perceived merely to determine which specific individuals would be injured, rather than whether a certain rate of injuries would occur (O'Malley 2004). The issue of negligence appeared merely to reduce the burden of costs to industry rather than to govern risks and prevent accidents as previously had been argued. At this point, the appropriate form of governance of accidental harm began to be levered away from the individual, and away from questions of fault and negligence, toward governance *of* distributions *through* distributions.

The earlier development of insurance during the nineteenth century, and especially of social insurances from the 1880s forward, provided a model in terms of which such distributions could be governed directly and, it was believed by many, more 'justly' and 'efficiently'. In its pioneering German form, the cost of a workers' compensation insurance scheme was to be shared by state, employer and employee – as mutual beneficiaries of the productive power of labour – in a contributory social insurance scheme. But in the legislation set up in Britain, the United States and Australia during the ensuing thirty years other diagrams of social insurance were invented. In the United States, for example, a common model was that introduced in Wisconsin in 1911 where participation was 'voluntary'. However, accompanying legislation removed or greatly reduced the effectiveness of many of the protections in tort law available to employers – such as the fellow servant rule, contributory negligence and *volenti*. At the same time, employers were authorized to insure themselves against such liabilities through the private insurance market. Few took the risky route to ignore insurance. Elsewhere, as in Britain, participation in the workers' compensation insurance scheme was compulsory. Whichever model was developed, it resulted in a massive expansion of the liability insurance market (Atiyah 1997). In this moment, as Friedman and Ladinsky (1963: 71) note, the individualized and punitive deployment of money damages was being displaced by a regulatory scheme based on actuarial principles. Injuries were not to be compensated by tort cases, whose outcomes were unpredictable, and whose damages were awarded by juries that were motivated by many considerations. Instead, compensation would be determined by tribunals whose awards were calculated on the basis of schedules largely shaped by the actuarial calculation of economic losses to workers consequent upon their injury. The 'meaning' of money awarded was now stabilized and standardized. In workers' compensation law, calculable and strictly 'compensatory' awards largely displaced 'incalculable' jury-driven damages. In this formula-driven model, compensation provided equivalence – replacement for lost income or expenditures required in the wake of the harm. Unlike tort law, compensation was not to be given for nonpecuniary harms, only for those harms that affected the economic viability of the individual. Money was to replace money foregone rather than the many 'incommensurable' harms that money damages were required to compensate for in tort law.

Predictability and calculability were thus a central issue much earlier than was to be the case in remaining tort law. But there was another process at work in this shift, perhaps more clearly articulated in Australia – for example in the *Workers' Compensation Act (Victoria) 1914*. Here, legislation largely displaced fault-based principles in tort with a scheme legally requiring employers to take out insurance to cover such risks with one of a number of private insurance companies. The implications were immediately clear to commentators at the time:

> ... the object is to make the trade, business or industry in which accidents happen bear the burden of responsibility of providing for those injured or for the dependents of those killed in the course of working operations; [but it is also] that the employer will necessarily add the cost of such compensation or the insurance to provide for it

to the expense of the trade, business or industry and pass it on to his customers and thereby to the community generally.

(Quick 1915: 23)

By transferring the risk of injury to compulsory insurance, and by transferring the cost of this insurance indirectly but wholly onto the end consumer as a component of prices, a form of indirect social insurance was established which subsequently has become widespread (O'Malley 2004).

In this process, money's role dramatically shifted away from a punitive or disciplinary function, especially where no-fault insurance was implemented as in workers' compensation. In many jurisdictions, one of the most significant shifts of this kind related to the development of no-fault and compulsory motor vehicle insurance, especially as attention focused on the systematic and actuarial properties of accident rates (Simon 1998). The development of state governed traffic accident compensation schemes to govern the costs and impacts of physical injuries, the costs of which are frequently built into vehicle licensing and registration fees, further eroded the disciplinary function of money. Risk spreading became more central than risk allocation. While tort law continued to govern material aspects of traffic accidents, such state schemes increasingly marginalized tort law damages – either by removing access to common law, or by greatly limiting the access to damages and the amounts of money recoverable (e.g. Stewart and Stuhmcke 2005: 10–16).

Elsewhere, this 'socializing' model was to be elaborated in some of the foundational developments in the emerging field of 'consumer law'. In the United States case of *MacPherson v Buick Motor Co.* [1916] (*Court of Appeals*, 217 *NY* 382), motor vehicles were defined as part of a class of 'imminently dangerous' products. While this discourse of dangerousness had not yet harnessed a statistical component, it nevertheless implied that manufacturers would need to take their expanded liability into account, with a strong implication that they would have to insure against this. Likewise, in England, Lord Atkin's landmark ruling in *Donoghue v. Stevenson* (1932, *AC* 580) displaced the narrow duty of care imposed on manufacturers by privity of contract (in *Winterbottom v. Wright*). In its place was established a far more expansive duty that seemed to strengthen the requirement for disciplined foresight. This required that subjects

… must take reasonable care to avoid acts or omissions which you can reasonably foresee would be likely to injure your neighbour.

Who then in law is my neighbour? The answer seems to be – persons who are so closely and directly affected by my act that I ought reasonably have them in contemplation as being so affected when I am directing my mind to the acts or omissions that are called into question.

(1932, *AC* 580)

Here, the explicit assumption of the court was that the rise of a consumer society (the case involved contaminated soft drink) was no longer compatible with a narrow contractual form of liability for harm. Thus, through the process of widening the disciplinary duty of care to the level of 'the social' or 'the market', the court effectively strengthened tendencies toward the compensatory and distributive nature of justice. Each consumer insured all other consumers. As White (2003: 148) has remarked, tort actions were no longer imagined as two-party affairs, but rather as 'three party' affairs in which society was the third interested party, based on an emergent assumption that 'society was an interdependent entity in which the misfortunes of one person affected others. That assumption was fundamental to early twentieth century reformist thought'. Manufacturers, among others, could no longer be protected by the chain of narrow contractual relations that effectively separated them from their ultimate consumers.[15]

In 1944, the incipient socialization of tort law that had been implemented in Donoghue v. *Stevenson* in Britain and *McPherson* in the US was pushed one step further when *Escola v Coca Cola Bottling* eroded the negligence requirement and began a move toward strict liability by centring the consumer. It was argued that 'consumers no longer approach products warily but accept them on faith, relying on the reputation of the manufacturer or trade mark ... The manufacturer's obligation to the consumer must keep pace with the changing relationship between them'. (quoted by Simon 1987: 71). In 1963, in *Greenman v. Yuba* (59 Cal. 2d. 900) the court pushed this further still and at the same time accelerated a shift from contract to tort with respect to product defects. The court viewed strict liability as applying to a manufacturer 'when an article he places on the market, knowing that it is to be used without inspection for defect, proves to have a defect that causes injuries to a human being'. And later 'that the aim of this 'is to ensure that the costs of injuries resulting from defective products are born by the manufacturers that put such products on the market rather than by the injured persons who are powerless to protect themselves'.

In short, this changing relationship was a reconfiguration of the imagery of contract, for no longer are the two parties regarded as equals. In the three decades that followed Escola, both statutory regulation and tort law further registered the impact of a view that consumers needed protection (Cane 1993; O'Malley 2004). The concept of 'enterprise liability' with which this was associated in the US assumed that industries were in a much better position to know about the harmful potential of their products than consumers. It no longer mattered whether a product was inherently dangerous (as in *Buick*), nor whether the manufacturer was at fault – the burden of risk was to be shifted categorically.

In Priest's (1985: 461–464) influential view, this shift could not be attributed to social factors, such as the increasing wealth of American society at the time, in part because the period in which most critical developments occurred (the early 1960s) was no more prosperous than other proximate years. Nor could such a focus on prosperity explain why law shifted away from a model of contractual equality. Rather, Priest's broad argument has to do with the intellectual history of American tort law, and especially with the emergence of a 'theory' of enterprise liability. This theory has its foundations in the work of Fleming James, the dominant scholar of the 1940s and 1950s, who promoted the vision of tort law as a system of social insurance. More specifically, James promoted the idea – already commonplace in workers' compensation law – that manufacturers were best placed to bear the burden of risk in relation to accidental harm, because they could pass these onto consumers through price mechanisms. James' vision was continued and developed in the work of Kessler, who centred this 'insurantial' vision of tort law on the figure of a helpless modern consumer. The resulting synthesis of such work, in Priest's eyes, provides the model of enterprise liability.

Now, we have seen already that in the United States legal scholarship plays a much more important role in the development of law than is the case elsewhere, and Priest therefore *prima facie* has good grounds for arguing that the form of enterprise liability reflects intellectual development. It is an invention that did not emerge, at least in the same form, elsewhere in the Anglophone world where prosperity was also marked at this time. But equally there are no grounds for thinking about this development as if it were not firmly grounded in the development of a consumer society. This is not simply to argue that, without the development of consumer society, such an intellectual tradition would have been meaningless. This much is perfectly obvious: the government of a consumer society through consumption is the explicit project of these reforms. But in pressing forward the intellectual argument alone, Priest overstates his case. Priest would have to explain both why the highly influential law and economics movement *failed* to have any impact with respect to the penal fine in America, and why it *was* to have a substantial impact (as seen shortly) on subsequent developments in tort law that was to reverse enterprise liability. Both developments reinstate punishment in terms of economic arguments, yet are markedly different in their influence. This suggests that there is after all a necessity to attend to the broader political and social environment into which such intellectual innovation is inserted.

The 1960s were the high watermark of welfare regulatory state interventionism, coinciding with a period of rapid expansion of the consumer society. Nothing guaranteed that enterprise liability would take off, but the convergence of theory and environment is marked even in Priest's (1985: 519) own terms:

> Enterprise liability ... appointed the judge an agent of the modern state. Negligence and warranty law were by their terms addressed solely to the one specific incident of product use before the court. Enterprise liability theory, in contrast, charged the judge to internalise costs and distribute risks. Enterprise liability theory also allowed judges to join the effort to aid the poor. Indeed the theory conceived of courts as possessing unique powers to achieve these ends to achieve these ends in comparison to alternative branches of government. Massive legislation would be required to aid, in any equivalent way, every poor person in every product purchase.

The arguments of the enterprise liability scholars fell into line with a much broader trend toward welfare and distributive government at the time. While later pressures by the law and economics scholars fell into line with a punitive turn with respect to damages, and were thus translated into policy, their arguments favouring fines did not square with an equally punitive criminal justice environment and were consigned to irrelevance. In short, enterprise liability was a creature of its political and economic times. Yet is it important to recognize that this is not simply a way of governing welfare through private law. By requiring near universal liability insurance for manufacturers and distributors, and by requiring that the premiums be passed on to consumers themselves, such development linked tort damages to prices, to insurance and, even as Priest (1985: 519) also recognizes, to taxes. Money is the means whereby these circuits of security flow together, perform overlapping or parallel functions and become immanent in everyday life.

As an insurantial characterization of tort law came more and more to be taken for granted, and as the dependence of the entire apparatus of damages on a complex array of state and private insurance schemes became established, arguments gathered strength to displace tort law altogether (Stapleton 1995). If, through the commodity market, most accidental harms were being insured and the cost being distributed across the whole society, then in the name of 'efficiency' why not introduce a direct insurance system to displace tort law?

These arguments, increasing in prominence through to the 1970s as they moved from the academic margins to policy-making commissions and inquiries, centred on four main points. First, tort law, considered as a social risk-distributing apparatus, has transaction costs roughly equal to benefits: that is, it absorbs as much money in determining rights to redress as it distributes in compensation. From a 'social compensation' viewpoint, this is costly and inefficient as the costs can be viewed as costs to society 'as a whole'. Insurance schemes have far lower transaction costs with a far simpler and speedier system for provision of compensation through tribunals. Second, because of the procedural complexities of tort law and the uncertainties associated with establishing negligence and duty of care in their various forms, outcomes are always uncertain. In consequence, many injuries remain uncompensated while others are perhaps more lavishly compensated than necessary. Not only did this appear unjust, but in terms of the social distribution of resources it also appeared arbitrary and suboptimal. Third, some critics stressed that the tort law compensation process is slow and compensation is often deferred for many years with harmful consequences. Both problems are argued to create social costs down the line. Medical expenses have to be paid in the interim, substitute sources of income may have to be found, many plaintiffs – and especially the poor – may be forced to settle to their detriment, and so on. Finally, payment in tort law is on a once-and-for-all basis, unlike insurance that provides payments over an extended period as required. The lump-sum payment of damages was held to create 'inefficiencies' and possible uncompensated costs associated with latent injuries that emerge only later. Conversely, because they are calculated on a lifetime basis such awards of damages cannot take account of possible recovery or diminution of incapacitation. Insurance, it was argued, could improve on all these problems. On the basis of this social imagery, most of tort law was displaced by a social insurance scheme in

New Zealand during the early 1970s. The *Accident Compensation Act* (1972) provided compensation for the majority of accidental injuries, including those associated with criminal victimization, as well as accidents in the workplace, domestic and recreational settings. The model proved tremendously influential and gave rise to much talk of 'doing away with tort law' (Sugarman 1985) and the 'death of contract' (e.g. Gilmore 1974).

## From compensation to punishment?

The Australian, Canadian, United States and British governments, among others, set up inquiries to investigate the promise of such a scheme (Keeler, 1994). In Australia, an even more comprehensive national compensation scheme was proposed – following the report of a commission headed by one of the architects of the New Zealand system. However, a change of federal government in 1975 saw a more conservative and neoliberal regime elected and the scheme perished. Much the same fate befell the initiatives that generated the parallel Pearson Commission in Britain a few years later. In a strong sense, the tide that had been running so strongly in the direction of a distributive and insurance model, and against the valorization of individual responsibility through the law of torts, now changed direction rather radically.

Apart from the abandonment of such plans for national insurance schemes – even the New Zealand scheme has been wound back in the ensuing years (Palmer 1994) – tort law itself was being re-engineered under the influence of neoliberal and economic critiques. These were based especially on assertions that: the law of negligence had been wound back too far and protected feckless plaintiffs; that incentives to safety on behalf of manufacturers were reduced sharply because of the widespread imposition of strict liability provisions on businesses; and that many plaintiffs were being awarded far too much by way of damages, creating chaos in the insurance industry and unjust enrichment of the few. In the 1980s, one of the most visible responses was from the insurance industry in the United States, where it was claimed that damages had become so large, long-tailed and unpredictable that the industry was unable to guarantee indemnity. In turn, this meant that insurance was either made unavailable or insurance premiums became prohibitive. In turn, this lead to the high profile suspension of all manner of services and goods that were argued to be in the public interest – ranging from public playgrounds to the development of new drugs. Against this, others argued that this was nothing more than a cynical manoeuvre by the industry to have damages capped and thus to reduce damages liability (Keeler 1994: 351). Whatever the debate, as Priest (1987: 1522–1523) pointed out, what mattered was that the Justice Department attributed the problem to the increase in corporate liability and skyrocketing damages, with the result that tort reform was the solution.

Together these various pressures helped generate a retreat from social and no-fault insurance, moves to reinstate negligence, and statutory caps on damages. The ensuing revisions took different forms in different jurisdictions, but the direction and general shape of change toward individual responsibilization and the increased protection of enterprises is consistent.

In Australia, for example, the theme of personal responsibility with respect to tort law reform was very prominent. The premier of the state of New South Wales complained not only that the law had 'drifted away from the concept of personal responsibility' but also that the law reflected a 'culture of blame', which needed to be confronted. This was also the view expressed by the Australian Government's *Review of the Law of Negligence*, which envisaged a need for measures limiting liability and the quantum of damages arising from personal injury and death. Perhaps most explicitly it was given voice by the Chief Justice of the NSW Supreme Court, who took the view that

> There has been a significant change in expectations within Australian society, as elsewhere, about persons accepting responsibility for their own actions. The idea that any personal failing is not your fault, that everyone can be categorized as a victim, has receded. The task is to restore an appropriate balance between personal responsibility for one's own conduct and expectations of proper compensation and care.
>
> (Quoted in Stewart and Stuhmcke 2005: 19)

Statutory reforms in most Australian states revitalized the defence of contributory negligence, in three states allowing the court not to award damages at all where it felt such negligence by the plaintiff was sufficient. Likewise, voluntary assumption of risk was revived as a complete defence where a 'reasonable person' would have thought the risk obvious – even were it not prominent or conspicuous – or where the risk is regarded as unavoidable and inherent in the nature of the work.[16] More generally, legislation expanded the range of harms held to be 'reasonably foreseeable'. Whereas common law's standard test had been that in order to qualify as reasonably foreseeable, a risk had to be 'not far fetched or fanciful' (*The Wagon Mound* No. 2 [1967] 2 *All ER* 709), the *Civil Liability Act* 2002 in New South Wales imposed a new standard that 'the risk was not insignificant', a phrase 'intended to indicate a risk that is of a higher probability than is indicated by the phrase "not far fetched or fanciful"'.

Such reassertions of individual responsibility and negligence – duplicated in many common law systems – are closely linked to what White (2003) regards as the 'unexpected' persistence or resurgence of negligence over the past quarter century. Compared to what would have been predicted in the 1970s the erosion of 'enterprise liability' by doctrines of negligence has gathered pace. As noted, enterprise liability and similar concepts were characterized by a set of distributive assumptions that not only favoured plaintiffs, but also served to operate as a substitute or subsidiary technology of social insurance (Nolan and Ursin 1999). Indeed, the prevalence of such approaches in the United States has been argued by some (Priest 1985, Atiyah 1997: 11) to make tort law operate more or less explicitly as a welfare system:

> Because the U.S. was much slower to develop an extensive welfare system than England or most European countries, the judges there appear to have regarded it as their function to step into the breach. For some 40 or 50 years some 'liberal' judges in America have taken an extremely pro-plaintiff line in personal injury cases ... (and) have widely used tort law, in conjunction with juries, to plug the gaps in the welfare system and to ensure that accident costs fall on industry

Beginning in the 1970s, advocates from the law and economics tradition began to stress that the savings and efficiencies generated by 'welfare' alternatives to the tort law system were illusory. For example, efficiency calculations that favoured no-fault insurance and strict liability tort law, it was claimed, had failed to take account of the deterrent effects of tort liability. Strict liability and no-fault liability removed incentives to avoid accidents, whether in the workplace, the market or on the roads, and so inflicted a greater human and financial cost on society than any putative savings effected by administrative efficiencies. Richard Posner (1986), for example, is quite happy to accept that the tort system does not operate well as a system of compensation. Compared to insurance, he argues, it is the case that transaction costs are high and that the allocation of compensation is inefficient and insufficiently predictable. In his view, however, tort law's

> ... economic function is not compensation but deterrence of ineffi-
> cient accidents. If the system yields substantial savings in accident
> costs, its heavy administrative costs, which relate primarily to deter-
> mination of liability – the determination whether they accident was
> uneconomical – may be justified.
>
> (Posner 1986: 187)

The law and economics approach was also highly critical of no-fault insurance as the primary means of funding tort law damages in automobile cases. From 'an economic standpoint' no-fault insurance is highly inefficient, because it allows 'even the most dangerous drivers to buy liability insurance at rates only slightly higher than normal' with the effect that such schemes are 'not at all concerned with creating better incentives for accident avoidance' (1986: 187). As this makes clear, 'efficiency' may be a modernist touchstone for good government, but a divide has opened up between the social-liberal vision of efficiency being delivered through a socially distributive, social justice based scheme of no-fault insurance, and a neoliberal and law and economics vision of efficiency being produced through individual responsibilization and the deterrent effect of money damages working on legal subjects through market mechanisms.[17]

At the same time, a line of moral rationality developed that focused on the 'injustices' generated by socialising risks through enterprise liability. Enterprise liability schemes were now argued to have the effect of sheeting the costs of compensating injuries back to persons who had not intentionally or carelessly contributed to injuries – such as consumers of a tort defendant's products, or safe automobile drivers of cars in states with no-fault automobile accident plans (White 2003: 247). A key critic of such 'welfare' trends in tort liability has expressed it thus:

> The current system for tort liability for personal injuries is not a sys-
> tem of personal responsibility ... it is actually a system of insurance
> but a very peculiar kind of insurance system in which those who ben-
> efit do not pay premiums. It thus operates much more like a welfare
> system in which those who are injured seek benefits under insurance
> policies which they have not themselves bought or paid for. To this
> extent I find the consumerist ideology more real than that of personal

responsibility, and to my mind this means that the law of personal injuries cannot be defended by moral arguments about corrective justice. In practice, it just does not operate as a system of corrective justice but of distributive justice ... and from that perspective it is evident that the whole system is grossly unfair.

(Atiyah 1999: 3)[18]

Perhaps Atiyah's vision of the welfare orientation as 'consumerist' is justified, for it was associated with a shift toward consumer protection in contract law in the same era. However, at the same time we need to be more specific. It is not that the new developments were to be anticonsumer. Rather, as White has argued, it was imagined that strict liability worked against creating a *'responsible consumer'*, because it 'might encourage enterprises to build in the projected costs of products liability lawsuits into the market prices of their products, rather than conveying more information to consumers about the product's risk' (White 2003: 280).

Atiyah's assumption of 'fairness', of course represents a rather different vision of justice than that of the social justice rationalities that had informed the growth of enterprise liability and its related developments throughout the twentieth century. Rather than a social vision in which collective responsibility is primary, it is a vision of individual responsibility linked to a free market in insurance. In such an imagery, the dominant assumptions have been that punishment will return through the medium of money penalties that bear more directly on those who create harms to themselves and others. Fault-based third party insurance and, even better, first party insurance, in which individuals insure themselves against risks created by others, would both deliver a disciplinary effect through increases in insurance premiums linked to risky behaviour. As well, instead of having to accept a 'one-size fits all' social insurance scheme, individuals were imagined as purchasing their insurance to suit their personal risk tolerance. At the same time, reliance on this scheme would relieve enterprise from the 'unjust' burden of damages awarded against them even where they had acted with the utmost care. An associated retreat of tort law from strict liability provisions would – through the same monetary mechanisms of premiums and prudence – restore the motivation of producers to minimize negligence and thus reduce risks to others.

While all of these arguments have been challenged and disputed, the heyday of enterprise liability and its parallel models is behind us. Of course, this is in line with the retreat of social and welfare rationalities more generally since the 1970s, and with their partial displacement by market-based and individualistic models. Mobilized by neoliberal governance, this raft of changes has sought to return torts to something more akin to the punitive and contractual framework that characterized nineteenth century law. As if echoing the so-called 'punitive turn' in criminal justice, arguments have surfaced that retribution – in its symbolic role rather than its role as a producer of economic efficiency and risk reduction – should be restored to law. While in the 1960s, as seen, the English courts sought to marginalize any such 'punitive' or 'exemplary' damages under the 'hegemony' of compensation theory, now it is frequently argued that it was a mistake to move away from the idea that civil law should punish.

> Roman law with its penal law of civil wrongs, was branded as in this matter curiously immature. It failed to detach itself from the primitive urge to private vengeance. Declining resources expose this as no more than a choice made at a time of faith in the power, efficiency and benignity of the state … Policy, not logic was at work. And the policy which was chosen has done harm. Rooting out punitive damages can now be seen to deprive society of useful private initiative and to reduce to helpless grumbling against an inefficient bureaucracy individuals who might otherwise have been encouraged to go to court themselves. Alienation of the citizen from the law is only one cost …. It is impossible to avenge contempt unless the court can award the victim a sum which satisfied the need, not to compensate the loss, but to condemn and avenge the outrage.
>
> (Birks 2003: viii)

It may appear unlikely that this dream of vengeful damages will come to pass. But at best this is so only outside the US where it has been seen already that punitive damages and a politics of outrage are certainly available to aggrieved parties confronting convicted corporations.[19] That a new register of the 'punitive turn' extends the scope of this penal culture of control into civil law is no doubt something of importance to note for criminological theory. Money is given renewed capacity to punish and to register denunciation, and in this way money damages now increasingly replicate in civil law the function of penal fines.

## Conclusion

It would have been tempting, especially during the 1960s and 1970s, to read the course of legal compensation as following down the same track that Anthony Bottoms had laid out with respect to fines. It was a course from punishment and discipline to regulation, seemingly generated by changes in the economy. Tort law was being eroded and in some domains and jurisdictions being displaced, by the encroachment of social insurances and related schemes that provided monetary compensation for accidental harm. Even where tort law remained in place, negligence and related punitive and disciplinary logics were being displaced by strict liability, enterprise liability and the like, that shifted attention away from the discipline of individuals and toward the social distribution of harms and their consequences. Moreover, with respect to tort law, especially outside the US, there had been a move toward the standardization and metrication of damages, rendering them more calculable, more like an insurance scheme than a process of individual justice.

In this process, the money form of the sanction played a key role. It was the money form that made possible, and was made possible by, the development of insurance and its articulation with the legal system. Liability insurance grew as the market for its commodity was expanded by changes in tort law. Tort law could not have changed in such ways, increasing manufacturers' and others' liabilities exponentially, had it not been the case that insurance existed as a means of paying for this. Of course, theoretically insurance could have been dispensed with insofar as enterprises can build damages into prices. In practice, this is an option only for governments and very large corporations. Insurance and damages appear to have converged as regulatory technologies that turn harms into money and in the name of 'compensation' redistribute the money across time and social space. The principal mechanism whereby this is affected is the pricing of commodities in a consumer society. The principal process whereby money damages were to effect compensation – other than where they merely replaced other money – was officially understood to be the purchase of pleasure.

At the same time, in other rationalities money damages clearly are governmentally understood to deliver punishment. As economic theorists from Bentham to the Chicago School aver, and was assumed throughout the nineteenth century, money damages are a deterrent, and work 'efficiently' to prevent harms by sheeting home externalities to those who produce them. In key respects, the genealogy of money damages is shaped by a struggle over which approach to damages – compensatory or punitive – shall predominate. But what is constant in this long, slow and ongoing struggle is money. The struggle is over how money is to work and what money is to mean – not whether money should or should not be the remedy. Money is more or less taken for granted. It is for this reason that even those who seek to revitalize tort law as a punitive and preventative apparatus do not seek to dislocate damages from insurance but to change the form of insurance from third party and social insurance to first party and private insurance. Punitive turn or no punitive turn, the regulatory or distributive component of the apparatus of damages is inescapable. In good measure, it is this fact that differentiates the 'penal damages' of the nineteenth century from their twenty-first century echoes. The massive expansion of legal liability has meant that money damages are now locked into complex monetized circuits, mediated by insurance, that permeate all aspects of life in a consumer society.

## Notes

1  For example, Cane (1993: 168) reports that in England fewer than one quarter of personal injury cases ever get to trial.
2  Money damages is a remedy limited to tort law and to breach of contract. This excludes, for example, monetary awards in restitution. Damages generally refers to payment that is compensation for loss, whereas awards in restitution are focused on correcting an unjust enrichment. While there are many arguments pro and con concerning whether money awarded in equity cases should be defined as damages (McGregor 1997: 4–6) the differences are largely procedural, and not a matter that this book is concerned about.
3  For a more detailed discussion of these developments, see O'Malley 2004, Chapters 2 and 4.
4  Horwitz (1977: 98) notes that as late as 1841, it was still possible to find it argued in case law that 'for all civil actions the law doth not so much regard the intent of the actors as the loss and damage of the party suffering ... he that is damaged, ought to be recompensed'.
5  This complexity and plasticity of the attribution of meaning to money is furthered with respect to 'nominal', 'derisory' and 'contemptuous' damages. These serve to mark that a legal right has been infringed but that no significant loss has been established. Usually the award is a very small amount of money and costs are awarded against the plaintiff. The award signifies the court's disapproval or contempt for the plaintiff in bringing the action even though she or he has won the case.
6  The terms 'punitive' and 'exemplary' are interchangeable. In the United States, 'punitive damages' is the term of preference, 'vindictive' and 'retributory' damages are terms also in use (Luntz 1990: 1.7l.1–1.7.5, Morris 1931).
7  It is still frequently argued that the distinction cannot be made with any reliability or even that as aggravated damages are applied where no compensable harm has occurred (for example where the issue involves publishing a photograph of a patient in hospital) then the distinction is invalid (Beever 2003).
8  The Australian High Court has held that exemplary damages can be awarded in many other categories of cases. Likewise in Canada, where they are awardable if the defendant's actions are 'malicious, vicious, brutal, grossly fraudulent, evil, outrageous, callous, disgraceful, willful or wanton'

(Schleuter and Redden 1989: II: 646–647). In the United States, it is frequently the case that punitive damages are awarded where 'there is no effective criminal remedy to complement civil redress' for harms where the conduct involves conduct that is emotionally or physically bruising to the unfortunate victim, but of little consequence to society at large'. (American Bar Association 1995: 669). In the latter case, the difficulty of distinguishing punitive damages from compensatory 'aggravated' damages is evident.

9  While this appears as a relatively new innovation when applied to corporations, Luntz (1990: 1.7.3 note 1) points out that under Edward I, double, triple or even quadruple damages could be awarded as 'penal and exemplary damages'. This was repeated in a statute of 1623 concerning monopolies (Elzinga and Breit 1976: 63).

10  In practice, courts have ruled that as plaintiffs free-ride on the state-funded prosecutions, then some portion of the punitive damage award should be returned to the state, thus blurring the civil-criminal divide still further (White 2002: 594–595).

11  Simpson (2002: 49) argues that, in any case, the equivalent 'crimes' lack moral impact assumed by Carson:

> Many corporate violations are regulatory offenses – crimes that lack the moral offensiveness and blameworthiness associated with Ford's behavior [i.e. the Ford Pinto affair]. Regulatory offenses are not immoral in their known right but rather illegal because they are prohibited by law – that is *mala quia prohibita*; Because there are no moral prohibitions against these acts, successful deterrence is purely a matter of effective legal sanctions.

12  To add to the complexity Posner (1986: 182) suggests that damages are automatically subject to a multiplier over and above that which a 'normal' subject would need by way of compensation. For example, 'since the loss of vision or limbs reduces the amount of pleasure that can be purchased with a dollar, a very large amount of money will frequently be necessary to place the victim in the same position of relative satisfaction that he occupied before the accident'.

13  Ogus (1973: 208) estimates that at the time of his writing far fewer than two per cent of personal injuries cases were assigned to jury trials in England and Wales.

14  Ogus (1973: 198–200). It could be argued by economists, that the reasonable man test is no more than an exercise carried out daily by the market. If the market can give a money value to objects such as paintings and rare animals, then the same technique could be applied to the assessment of damages for nonpecuniary losses. In the one American case where this approach was tried (*Baker v Pennsylvania Co.* 21 *A* 979 [1891], the question was posed as a barter: what sum of money would be required to induce a person to undergo the pain and suffering in question. Ogus (1973: 199) dismisses this out of hand by suggesting that it cannot be assumed that 'market conditions are in any way relevant to the assessment of nonpecuniary losses', and moreover 'the notion that the willingness to submit to pain and suffering has a "market value" is of

course wholly artificial'. Just why this is any more 'artificial' than where assessment is made by a judge or jury is not explained.

15 White (2003: 15–45) makes a strong case to argue that such broadening of the duty of care was linked to the triumph of a scientific ethos in American jurisprudence and the associated preference for universal principles rather than the narrow and particularistic ones that have been inherited from earlier law. While this likely contributed to change, this positive approach to law (and more generally, the impact of scholarly jurisprudence on law) was markedly less influential in Britain and common law countries of the British Commonwealth where such trends were also marked. Perhaps more significantly, the impact of considerations specific to the growth of changes in industrial and consumer relations are given priority in my account, because these were the issues raised in the official discourses concerned.

16 For a detailed discussion of these changes and the related matters discussed in the remainder of this paragraph, see Stewart and Stuhmcke 2005: 187–214.

17 In all of this, of course, there is a morality. Not just the morality of individual responsibility, but a utilitarian vision. At least tailored to Posner's specifications of a negligence-based model, 'the common law may be viewed as an effort to attach costs to the violation of those moral principles that enhance the efficiency of a market economy'. In turn, this moral vision is elaborated to the extent that there is a clear 'economic value of such moral principles as honesty, truthfulness, frugality, trustworthiness, consideration for others ... hard work and avoidance of negligence and coercion ...' (Posner 1986: 195–196).

18 For a greatly expanded account of this imagery, and of Atiyah's preference for a first party insurance scheme to largely replace both tort law and third party insurance, see Atiyah's (1997) *The Damages Lottery*.

19 Again, the exceptionalism of the United States is interesting, for whereas Americans deploy punitive damages with a degree of gusto against corporations, elsewhere this is not necessarily the case. In fact, punitive damages generally are only likely to arise for intentional torts in Australia, because there must be an element of contempt for the victim, while intentional torts are only a very small species of civil actions. Moreover, in Australia relatively small amounts of punitive damages are imposed on corporations (*XL Petroleum (NSW) Pty Ltd v Caltex Oil (Australia) Pty Ltd* [1985] 155 CLR 448).

# Chapter 5

# The currency of justice

Unlike liberty, money can be digitized. For this reason, we may anticipate that while there are limits to how many people may languish in prisons, the domain governed through monetary sanctions – and especially through regulatory fines – is likely to continue to expand almost exponentially. It is not difficult to imagine a world in which each behavioural transgression committed, or each degree of licence taken, is registered electronically and billed to us electronically together with the usual warnings, disclaimers and conditions that accompany most market transactions. Along with our other bills, fees and taxes, these fines will be paid electronically as well. It is a scenario already substantially in place with respect to traffic regulation. While it can be pushed into a paranoid imagery of technocratic despotism, as Deleuze (1995:175) sometimes envisages it – from another viewpoint, it is quite consistent with a vision of freedom associated with consumer societies. Money is sufficiently ubiquitous that these impositions almost may be taken for granted. While a constraint on our power to spend, fines of this sort do little or nothing to constrain or threaten our liberty, nor is it intended that they do so. Such sanctions govern through 'freedom of choice' – indeed we may think of them as a technology of such a freedom. As responsible consumers we pay for our choices and for the routine mistakes and failures of foresight that characterize everyday life. Regulatory fines are thus quite consistent with governing the consumer society that has come into being since the end of the Second World War and has burgeoned in the past 30 or 40 years.

This is all the more the case, because such monetized regulatory governance is consistent with the emergence of risk as a telos of consumer societies. As Jonathan Simon (1987) noted, because it governs through categories and distributions risk can offer a form of moral tolerance that is more relaxed than government through disciplinary techniques, and better fitting for social relations governed increasingly by consumer-led markets. Government through speed humps, seat belts, insurance, CCTV, parking fines, and so on is not so much interested in ensuring the conformity of each individual to a right-thinking norm. It does not touch the 'soul' of the subject. Rather its concern is with the secure distribution of behaviours and things. Individuals are left to 'float' within a monitored space in which deviance is less the problem than riskiness, in which conformity is less to do with moralized norms than with the potential for harm. Here, money is also put to work, as the commodities we buy are already risk-proofed through manufacturing standards, vendor licences, health and safety regulations, customs regulation and so on. Such governance works to constrain and shape behaviour not through visible coercion and intrusive examination, but seemingly through our own consuming desires. As risks increase, fines, prices, fees, premiums all tend to increase. Other, less risky and less expensive choices become more attractive. Money becomes a way in which risks are rendered governable and through which freedom of choice is shaped and expressed. Money sanctions, and especially regulatory fines and compensatory damages, are a part of this complex and almost seamless circuitry through which such governance works.

This diagram maps roughly onto the contours of 'control societies' discussed by Deleuze (1995). In both, government increasingly is immanent within the circuits and flows of freedom of choice. The subjects of government are not so much the unique individuals constituted and governed through still robust disciplinary practices, but instead are fragmented dividuals that are the stuff of databanks, pattern recognition software, markets and a plethora of other distributions. The distributions are primary and the dividuals – consumers, drivers, homeowners, taxpayers – are the component means through which the distributions are governed. As William Walters (2006: 192) has summed it up

> Nothing better captures the ethos of the control society than the password, which can materialize in such forms as the credit card, the passport, the reward card, the identity card and the electronic ankle tag … Control resolves its subject matter into coded flows. If control societies resemble networks of privatized consumption and information, circuits of desire and lifestyle, these are networks whose every node is a potential gate or filter. Linked in a dynamic relationship to the database and the risk profile, the password distributes access and status. It constitutes privileged populations who enjoy the rewards

of credit, mobility and information. But at the same time it filters out a risky, excluded remainder.

But the fact that money can be digitized not only allows it to act as another – often merging – conduit or circuit related to control but also it allows for more than the relatively crude mechanisms of blocking and filtering flows. In the circuits where regulatory fines and penal damages are deployed exclusionary manoeuvres of the sort outlined by Deleuze and Walters are the techniques of last resort, mobilized only when the more porous mechanisms of pricing are not adequate for security. Money in its various regulatory forms allows for more subtle, graduated and variable processes. Like prices, regulatory fines and penal damages have the effect of slowing down and speeding up flows, of shaping the volume of distributions by degrees, and of making actions less or more attractive through price modulation. Such friction or resistance can be increased or decreased in tiny increments if required, creating an admission price or a money penalty fewer and fewer would be prepared to pay until the optimal distribution is achieved.

Only where risk is deemed unacceptable does exclusion cut in. In the case of regulatory fines, this rarely takes the form of general incapacitation or loss of liberty. Such drastic resort as imprisonment is often virtually impossible and always proportionally rare as the back-up to this sanction. Far more frequently, the exclusionary back-up sanctions deny access to a privilege, to some right of access to things and places or to the performance of certain specific (and often purchasable) rights. In Deleuze' examples, this is epitomized by the denial of digitized credit. In the case of regulatory fines, it is more frequently exemplified by other forms of specific incapacitation such as licence endorsement, suspension or cancellation, closure of premises, impounding of cars parked in tow-away zones, and so on. Again, much the same applies with penal damages, for once products become sufficiently risky that they generate more than the occasional tort action, more restrictive regulation is likely to cut in, in the form of prohibitions on manufacture, suspensions of import licences and so on. Such incapacitations and exclusions do not threaten our liberty; they erode particular and 'surplus' freedoms, often in the name of risk reduction. Correspondingly, they do not bear upon us as individuals, as would be the case with loss of liberty or criminal conviction that bear upon the whole legal and social entity. Instead they bear upon that aspect of us that is licenced or privileged – the relevant dividual. The 'dividualisation' of the subjects governed by this sanction and the articulation of this to a dividualisation of sanction (for example, impersonal fines backed by licence cancellation) is one facet of this governmental tactic. The risk-creating dividual is incapacitated, but the individual of which this dividual is merely a facet or fragment, remains at liberty. For the same reasons such regulatory fines can become anonymous – targeted at owners, proprietors, drivers and so on, and accordingly can be monitored, delivered and expiated privately and anonymously.

Bentham's felicity calculus is hard at work in this diagram of governance, not so much by inflicting pain through withdrawing necessities as he envisaged, but by the denial of those pleasures that circulate in the surplus economy of desire. Regulatory fines have been deliberately designed in this fashion, to be paid 'on the spot'. Damages are simply built into prices that we elect to pay. In the case of regulatory fines, to the extent that they appear as 'only money', as touching upon the money that flows almost unnoticed through our hands on a daily basis, they do not necessitate the time and resource-consuming administrative paraphernalia associated with trial and court hearings. By progressively dislocating these penalties from the threat of imprisonment in default of payment, it became possible to streamline their processing. Financial and other incentives are put in place to encourage the maximization of administrative throughput, offering deductions for prompt payment, penalties for late payments, fees for exercising a right to contest the notice, steeper fines if unsuccessful, and so on. The court or tribunal hearing appears as another optional service for which the user pays. Conversely, in this genealogy inability to pay emerged as a much lesser problem than with penal offences and offenders. Some mechanisms were put in place to take account of this, notably time-to-pay, the instalment system of the consumer economy. But this was not the shibboleth that it became in criminal justice, because in planning terms regulatory fines were aimed at consumers, retailers and others imagined as able to pay, rather than at the poor who may well default. Indeed, in many jurisdictions, the difficulties associated with criminalizing are further etiolated as the whole process of regulatory fining is carried out in the private sector – for example, where monitoring traffic offences and infringements (which, remember, make up 90 per cent of regulatory fines) is contracted out to security companies. The revenue generated by such fines, fees and penalties thus may either create a revenue-neutral 'state' regulatory system that is thereby almost infinitely expandable, or a sector of private industry in which opportunities for profit are associated in proportion with the increased policing of security.

If this scenario represents the realization of one of Bentham's dreams – a self-funding system of pecuniary security based on the fine – another aspect of this imaginary of wholly monetized justice was likewise to appear within a century of his death. For Bentham, it will be recalled, the distinction between civil and criminal law was of little importance. Both delivered pain and should be regarded therefore as part of a system of punishment. In large measure, this view was far from being as outlandish as it now appears. In the nineteenth century damages were primarily regarded as punitive. Damages were part of a liberal project to shape and foster the responsible liberal subject. Certainly, they provided compensation, and Bentham among others lauded this state of affairs. But the primacy of punishment was indexed by the fact that the law's focus on establishing negligence and similar faults as the basis for liability to pay and for entitlement to receive damages, meant that compensation became harder to get than had previously been the case. As Bentham recognized, the nineteenth-century law of damages thus had much in common with the penal fine: damages were sheeted home to the individuals responsible for creating harms, and by and large there was little or no insurance available to soften the blow.

Of course, this restricted the 'system' of damages to a very small scale affair. Damages could not be large, few could pay them and thus be worthy of suing, and many of those harmed would not recover compensation unless free of fault themselves and able to demonstrate that they were victims of negligence. Indeed, put together with the fact that penal fines were themselves a very marginal sanction in criminal justice through most of the 1800s, and regulatory fines virtually nonexistent, then it can be seen immediately that until the turn of the twentieth century, money sanctions constituted only a small part of justice. Insofar as money was the currency of justice, it was a very small economy indeed. Between this time and the middle of the twentieth century the situation was to change in almost every conceivable respect.

First, after the 1880s, it is possible to argue that the penal fine was invented as a sanction that marked the limits to correctionalism. During the ensuing half century, penal fines became the dominant sanction in virtually all liberal jurisdictions outside the United States. This was not the resurrection of a largely defunct mode of punishment made possible, because poor people had suddenly become able to pay. It was the creation of a penalty that was articulated in specific ways with the modern prison. Where it was perceived that short terms of imprisonment were counterproductive, fines were introduced as a way of registering the offence and punishing it. The unanticipated impact of this shift was a considerable increase in rates of imprisonment for defaulting on payment of fines (thereby indicating that a new capacity of the poor to pay was not the key issue). Because fines were regarded as a lesser sanction, 'only money' that did not immediately touch upon the liberty of the liberal subject, court protections for the offender had been lowered. 'Summary justice' resulted in an increase in the number of offenders in court, and a corresponding increase in both the proportion and number of offenders sentenced to fines. A second result was even higher rates of imprisonment for default. This was not only because of the increased throughput of offenders, but also because the fine could not be reduced to trivial amounts – it could not be reduced below a threshold that was consistent with the fact that these new penal fines stood in lieu of a period of imprisonment.

The dilemma was partially resolved by adopting market solutions: allowing offenders time to pay, allowing for payment in instalments, tailoring the fine to fit the means of the offender and so on. Fines were to be made 'affordable' by the introduction of novel techniques that allowed relatively large fines to be applied to poor people – a form of hire purchase justice. The combination of the administrative ease of use of the fine, its cheapness as a sanction and its facilitation of streamlined administrative procedures, allowed the penal fine to expand rapidly. Instead of a residual sanction penal fines rapidly became the principal sanction, creating criminal justice (outside the US at least) as a predominantly monetized assemblage. In the twentieth century, the currency of justice was quickly becoming money.

However, while increasingly essential to justice in most jurisdictions in the 'West', the fine remained a regrettable anomaly in a criminal justice system focused on penal modernism. In the United States, its anomalous status was regarded as so problematic that it never gained more than a toehold. Criminology, wedded to the penal modernist project of reform, followed suit and confirmed the almost pariah status of this sanction by virtually ignoring it except occasionally to point to its shortcomings. It was (and still is) like the proverbial elephant in the (court) room. In this respect, the penal fine shares much in common with compensatory monetary damages. However much Bentham and his economist successors may have regarded money as the ideal currency of justice, both penal fines and compensatory damages – for the most part the main sanctions deployed in twentieth-century law – were regarded apologetically as 'the best that the court can do'.

About the same time these developments were occurring, regulatory fines were making their appearance too. Of course, at first there was no clear distinction between regulatory and penal sanctions: this had to be invented, and this proved a piecemeal process linked to many considerations. One set of issues was class linked. In different ways over the twentieth century the courts and the legislators were forced to recognize that the targets of much law enforcement were either wealthy, or at least did not fit the socioeconomic profile of those who usually made up the customers of justice. Often this stimulated partial or total decriminalization, the streamlining or virtual abandonment of hearings, the recognition that fines would not require complex and expensive default mechanisms, and the disarticulation of fines from the threat of imprisonment. Partly because these new offenders were the rapidly growing new consuming classes, the volume of infringements and violations grew exponentially, requiring even more streamlined procedures and even less in the way of formal stigmatization. Under similar pressures, new enforcement technologies were invented, ranging from the parking meter to the on-the-spot fine that magnified enforcement manpower, driving up the number of cases processed and creating yet further pressure for administrative acceleration. And underlying all this expansion, the fine (and 'fees' and all the other attachments) not only funded its own substructure but also invited more enforcement by offering itself as a form of revenue-raising taxation.

By World War II, legal innovation had generated a vicious or virtual circle of growth largely made possible by fines. The procedural streamlining they facilitated, their low stigma and impact on everyday life, and the revenues they generated made possible more regulation and prosecution than had ever before been possible. As it became normal to govern more and more problems of (especially) urban life through money, so money fines came almost to be taken for granted. The dislocation of regulatory fines from imprisonment by default meant that, even in America, where penal fines had been shunned – whether for their lack of reformism or because of the sense of injustice to the poor – fines now outnumbered other sanctions many times.

Such is the power of the 'only money' effect, that few have ever commented on the fact that within the space of about 50 years, money had moved from the margins to become by far and away the principal currency of justice.

While regulatory and penal fines vastly outnumber awards of damages, this should not lead to the conclusion that nothing in civil law was going to have much more of an affect on the centrality of money sanctions. All the more so because money damages were already the default sanction by the late 1800s when the expansion of fines begins. But, as mentioned, damages were very small beer even toward the end of the nineteenth century. Over the next half century, and beyond, damages were to become a matter of far greater importance, not only because of their rapid growth in number and scale – although this did occur – but because of the way in which they were articulated with insurance. Insurance and damages both turn harms and risks into amounts of money and provide compensation for loss. Unlike damages, insurance spreads risks across time and space through the instrument of insurance premiums and deploys actuarial techniques to calculate predicted losses. Unlike damages, it thus renders risk calculable and governable on a large scale. By articulating the 'incalculable' domain of damages with the calculable domain of insurance, a financial assemblage was created whereby damages could shift from being marginal to being part of a major circuit of financial governance. However, in order for this assemblage to be brought into being, tort had to undergo a significant transformation, and insurance imaginaries and technologies played no small role in this.

The emergence of social insurance generally, and workers' compensation as one variant of this, redefined security not as a matter of disciplined prudence that was the responsibility of individuals, but as an effect of social forces that could be governed better through regulatory techniques. These included the characteristics of industries and the characteristics of classes that gave them constant rates of injury and exposure to accidents. They also included those factors associated with the uneven distribution of social power and that thereby were held to reveal the social 'injustice' of a system of compensation that made workers bear disproportionate risks. In the domain of consumption, a parallel but distinct process was set in motion. If power differentials were seen to have slanted damages in favour of employers, much the same was being envisaged with respect to the relationship between consumers and manufacturers. The punitive and disciplinary orientation of damages, and particularly its effective protection of employers and manufacturers, was thereby struck a double blow. Through the model of insurance, and particularly social insurance, compensation became a feasible and just alternative – whether by changing tort law or by abandoning it in favour of insurance – while the punitive orientation of damages was rendered unjust, unnecessary and inefficient.

In the United States, perhaps to compensate for the relatively late and partial development of the welfare state, this process of tort reform went farthest. From the early 1900s through to the 1970s, manufacturers and suppliers increasingly had the burden of risk placed upon their shoulders through strict liability and (later) enterprise liability doctrines. As compensation became the focus, and insurance the model technique, then distributions became all. Fault receded to the margins as key questions instead became who was best placed to bear or spread risks. Compensatory damages had become regulatory or distributive. Especially with no-fault tort doctrines such as enterprise liability, and no-fault liability insurance, the identity of the tortfeasor was almost incidental, except for the administrative purpose of assigning a conduit to the distributive circuits of insurance. In this way, enterprises had become dividuals. In England, Australia and elsewhere, while the same trends toward enterprise liability were somewhat weaker, possibly because of the stronger welfare state, much the same distributive effect was achieved to a greater degree through widening the duty of care.

However this widening of liability was effected, its principal impact was to make it essential for enterprises to take out liability insurance against tort damages. As these businesses passed on to consumers the cost of liability insurance, effectively a parallel social insurance system was established, working entirely through the private sector. The scale of this assemblage is partially concealed by the fact that most tort actions in this domains are settled before ever going to court, and many of those that do end in court are settled before an award is made. Even so, Cane (1993: 193) is no doubt right to argue that tort damages should be put into perspective, for 'it is more accurate to view insurance as the primary medium for the payment of compensation, and tort law as a subsidiary part of the process'.

While it can now be recognized just how far the currency of justice has become money, and how this currency integrates 'justice' with the wider financial governance of a consumer society, it is equally clear that this is not a process generated solely by some form of technocratic or fiscal determinism. No matter how striking Deleuze' imagery of the control society may be, his account stands curiously above politics, and is available to an interpretation that foregrounds a movement toward regulation as driven by a logic of power. Yet, as a species of regulation, it will be completely transparent that politics is never absent from the nature and development of this diagram of control. Insofar as this book has provided a genealogy of the monetary currency of justice, then a strong case could be made that this has been characterized precisely by struggles in which the virtues of regulation – often pitted against discipline – are the focal points of contention. Not least among these, of course, were the various developments surrounding the formation of 'the social', especially social insurance, and the impact this had on the law of damages. Regulation was promoted not simply because it was self-evidently a more 'effective' form of government, although clearly it meshes well with key characteristics of a consumer society. We should, therefore, not simply take for granted that the future will be played out in terms of the continued and uniform development of justice in the direction of a set of modulated and distributive financial circuits.

Most obviously, the impact of critiques stemming from neoliberal politics (and in the USA the law and economics movement) have been effective in restoring to the law of damages what many regard as a lost focus on individual responsibility, on the moral weight of wrongdoing and on the just distribution of punishment and rewards. By restoring or strengthening fault-based concepts and doctrines, especially negligence, contributory negligence and volenti, law reformers have recreated a liberal vision in which individuals exercising responsible and reasonable foresight would not be subject to the financial burden of tort liability. In this new light, no-fault distributive principles were regarded as unjust, because they inflicted on the careful and the careless alike the same burden of risk. They were seen to make consumers dependent on a paternalistic law and manufacturers less careful of public safety, because they accrued no advantage by diligence. It was also argued the reassertion of a fault-based tort law would prove to be socially efficient, because whatever the additional costs of tort over insurance, tort law would act to prevent injuries through market pressures – by inflicting costs on negligent producers. In this vision, the roll-on effect of increases in insurance premiums inflicted on harmful enterprises – rather than on the entire risk pool of businesses – would be to drive up their costs of production, give them incentives to improve safety or ultimately price them out of the market. In such ways, a critique of distributive monetary justice was opened up from within the politics of the consumer society.

However, even were it the case that penal damages of this sort were restored to their nineteenth-century glory, things would never be quite the same. In the first place, at the broader governmental level, neoliberals and their allies have never sought to wind back insurance as a distributive technique of security. Quite to the contrary, in areas such as health and property security it is clear that insurance has been promoted as a resource for the responsible. It was argued that the forms of insurance needed to change. In the health sector, for example, the emphasis has been on winding back social insurances and promoting private insurance (O'Malley 1992). This shift was argued to be necessary on many grounds, but of greatest relevance here have been the claims that this provides a consumer-led market reform. In place of one-size fits all, private insurance provides for the level of risk-protection that suits individuals. In place of coverage, regardless of the care individuals take of themselves, their health, property or finances, insurance premiums would reflect the responsibility and capability of the consumer. What the neoliberal reforms have sought in the domain of monetary sanctions is not the destruction of insurance nor even the disarticulation of insurance and tort law. Rather, the ideal is the responsibilization of consumers and suppliers through reform of the way in which tort and insurance are articulated. Tort reform is one part of this move, pressure to shift from third party and no-fault insurance to first party insurance is the other. Suppliers would have to insure themselves against tort liability, and would be policed by the insurance industry through insurance premium pricing and the threat of loss of insurance coverage. Consumers would insure themselves against injury at the level of coverage that fits their preferences and situation.

What is envisaged, in short, is a reshaping of this aspect of monetary justice in line with a desocialized imaginary of consumption, in which the state no longer regards consumers as in need of paternalistic state protection but as subjects active on their own behalf. Such is the neoliberal dream of the consumer society. Insofar as this project were to be successful, its basic effect would be to restore contract to centre stage. However, it has to be said that in many respects the project so far has failed. Tort law reform has occurred, but insurance reform aimed at displacing third party insurance with first party insurance has been no more successful than has the parallel economist's vision of fines becoming the universal sanction. At this point, only speculative reasons for this can be put forward. For example, it is likely that the reforms to tort law, and especially the widespread caps placed on damages, have rendered this sector of the insurance industry sufficiently profitable that the institutional motivation to effect widespread restructuring is simply not there. In this sense, the future depends on the political and economic uncertainties of a society increasingly governed through the 'free market'.

However, what is rendered invisible by this development is that sector of the population that is not 'in' the insurance market. To a degree, the 'socialized' circuits of tort law provided security by protecting those who purchased consumer goods, a kind of private welfare state based on the subject as consumer. To the extent that this is wound back in favour of responsibilized consumers and increasing limits on recovery through tort law, the more reliance will be placed on private – and especially first party – insurance. For those who cannot afford such coverage, risk exposure is increased greatly. In short, existing 'contractual' trends in the monetization of civil justice will not simply exclude the risky in the name of security. It will, in the name of the responsible consumer, exclude from the shelter of market-based security those most at risk.

Of course, the responsible consumer is also the subject at the base of much regulatory fining. While changes have been wrought throughout monetary justice by the advent of neoliberal governance, very little of this is registered in the nature of use of regulatory fines. Perhaps this is simply because these fines are now relatively hard-wired into governance at all levels: so much governance depends on this and on the revenue generated, that such fines are immune to most political change. However, it should not be overlooked that like penal fines and penal damages, the regulatory fine is imagined to responsibilise. While working on distributions through dividuals, nevertheless the dividual is frequently, perhaps even normally, imagined as a rational choice actor. It is, after all, through this construct that pecuniary deterrence is imagined to be effected and the 'friction' introduced into distributive circulations. As well, while the regulatory fines are distributive, overwhelmingly they are not – unlike distributive damages – socially redistributive. Regulatory fines conform much more closely to the economist's preferred model of returning such externalities as the costs of speeding, parking and pollution to their producers. The persistence and expansion of regulatory fines in the 'post-social era', the era of consumer-led market liberalism, perhaps is due not to their 'technical' nature alone, but also to their conformity with neoliberal political ideals.

At the periphery of this 'system' of monetized control remains the penal fine. It merges with the circuits of regulatory money by all manner of relays, hybrids and overlappings that are the legacy of the uneven processes, whereby regulatory fines were developed by trial and error. Partly by accident, partly by design, the penal fine is a conduit between the money sanctions geared to governance of consumer society and a domain of governance whose targets are largely outside the charmed circle of the consumer society and its fiscal circuits of regulation and freedom. Those sentenced to the penal fine and who can stay afloat financially, who can demonstrate their eligibility to be consumers, pay their fee for continued liberty. Those who fail this test, despite all the consumerist bail-outs that seek to give credit to offenders in the form of time to pay and other forms of lay-by justice, are consigned to prison. Indeed, in many jurisdictions, such fiscal failures make up a very substantial proportion of prison intakes. At this point, the monetized circuits through which dividuals, harms and risks are distributed through the economy of consumption, transfers the offender to a moneyless domain in which bodies are incapacitated, liberty destroyed.

Despite the complexity of this genealogy and the diversity of monetary sanctions that have emerged from it, all is premised on the existence of a consumer society. It is a society of surplus income in which money can appear to have no meaning – to be 'only money' – because of its ubiquity and because that money (in the governmental imaginary at least) can be sacrificed without significant hardship. Things could have been different. If the main course of late twentieth century capitalist history had been toward the development of the leisure society, then the same opportunities for the almost limitless expansion of money sanctions would not have existed. Money would not have been so ubiquitous, surplus income not so available, the conduits of consumer pricing not so pervasive. Perhaps with respect to regulatory and even penal sanctions, it is conceivable that fines would not have been so central. Time, in the form of community service, could have become more central rather than the peripheral sanctions they now are – with sanctions eating into the 'surplus time' of those subject to penalties. It is even possible to imagine how time, in this fashion, could be digitized, as those who commit minor infringements work out so many hours of community service through virtual labour on the internet. This did not happen, because the leisure society was buried by consumption.

Rusche and Kirchheimer's maxim concerning the economic condition of the poor and the conditions of existence of fines now appears in distorted form. As far as the vast bulk of fines – regulatory fines – is concerned, and as far as the provision of security through the law of damages is concerned, it is the economic standing of consumers that is the vital condition of the existence and operation of monetary justice. Meanwhile, those who do not consume cannot be governed through their freedom of choice. To these millions, imprisoned or at risk of imprisonment Deleuze's (1995: 181) insightful but distorted claim that 'a man is no longer a man confined but a man in debt' must seem like a bad joke.

# Bibliography

Abel, R. (1982) 'Torts'. In D. Kairys (ed.) *The Politics of Law*. New York: Pantheon Books, pp. 85–200.

Abraham, K. and L. Liebman (1993) 'Private insurance, social insurance and tort reform: toward a new vision of compensation for illness and injury'. *Columbia Law Review*, 83: 75–118.

American Bar Association (1971) *Standards Relating to Sentencing Alternatives and Procedures*. Chicago: American Bar Foundation.

American Bar Association (1995) 'Report of the American Bar Association Action Commission to improve the tort liability system'. Appendix A in L. Schlueter, and K. Redden (1995) *Punitive Damages* (Third Edition). Charlottesville, VA: Michie Butterworth, pp. 669–673.

Atiyah, P. (1979) *The Rise and Fall of Freedom of Contract*. Oxford: Clarendon Press.

Atiyah, P. (1997) *The Damages Lottery*. Oxford: Hart.

Atiyah, P. (1999) 'Personal injuries in the twenty-first century: Thinking the unthinkable' In P. Birks (ed.) *Wrongs and Remedies in the Twenty First Century*. Oxford: Clarendon Press, pp. 1–46.

Australian Law Reform Commission (1980) *The Sentencing of Federal Offenders (Interim Report)*. Canberra: Australian Government.

Australian Law Reform Commission (2005) *Sentencing of Federal Offenders*. Canberra: Australian Government.

Balbus, I. (1977) 'Commodity form and legal form: An essay on the ' "relative autonomy" of law'. *Law and Society Review*, 11: 570–588.

Barton, J. (1987) 'Contractual damages and the rise of industry'. *Oxford Journal of Legal Studies*, 7: 40–59.

Baudrillard, J. (1984) *The Mirror of Production*. New York: Telos Press.

Baumann, Z. (2000) 'Social Issues of Law and Order'. *British Journal of Criminology*. 40: 205–221.

Beatty, D., S. Howley and D. Kilpatrick (1996) *Summary and Constitutional Protection for Victim's Rights*. Arlington, VA: National Center for Victims of Crime.

Becker, G. (1974) Crime and punishment: An economic approach'. In G. Becker, and W. Landes (eds) *Essays in the Economics of Crime and Punishment*. New York: Columbia University Press, pp. 27–36.

Beever, A. (2003) 'The structure of aggravated and exemplary damages'. *Oxford Journal of Legal Studies*, 23: 87–110.

Bein, D. (1974) 'Payment of a fine by a person other than the defendant'. *Israeli Law Review*, 9: 332–338.

Bentham, J. (1962) *The Works of Jeremy Bentham*, Vol. 1. J. Bowring (ed.), New York: Russell and Russell.

Bentham, J. (1982) *An Introduction to the Principles of Morals and Legislation* (ed. J. Burns and H.L.A. Hart). London: Methuen.

Berlin, I. (1969) 'Two concepts of liberty'. In I. Berlin, (ed.) *Four Essays on Liberty*. Oxford: Oxford University Press, pp. 118–172.

Beveridge, W. (1942) *Social Insurance and Allied Services* (Cmd. 6404). London: Her Majesty's Stationery Office.

Birks, P. (2003) 'Editor's preface'. In P. Birks (ed.) *Wrongs and Remedies in the Twenty-first Century*. Oxford: Clarendon Press, pp. i–x.

Bottoms, A. (1983) 'Some neglected features of contemporary penal systems'. In D. Garland and P. Young (eds) *The Power to Punish*. London: Heinemann.

Braithwaite, J. and G. Geiss (1982) 'On theory and action for crime control'. *Crime and Delinquency* 1982: 292–314.

Brent Fisse, W. (1981) 'Community Service as a Sanction Against Corporations'. *Wisconsin Law Review*, 1981: 970–1017.

Briggs, J., C. Harrison., A. McInnes and D. Vincent (1996) *Crime and Punishment in England*. London: UCL Press.

Bureau of Justice Statistics (2004a) *Compendium of Federal Justice Statistics 2004*. Washington, DC: US Department of Justice.

Bureau of Justice Statistics (2004b) *State Court sentencing of Convicted Felons 2004*. Washington, DC: US Department of Justice.

Cahill S. and P. Cahill (1999) 'Scarlet letters: Punishing the corporate citizen'. *International Journal of the Sociology of Law*, 27: 153–165.

Campbell, C. (1987) *The Romantic Ethic and the Spirit of Modern Consumerism*. Oxford: Basil Blackwell.

Cane, P. (1993) *Atiyah's Accidents, Compensation and the Law*, 5th edn. London: Butterworths.

Carson, W. (1974) 'Symbolic and instrumental dimensions of early factory legislation'. In W. Carson and P. Wiles (eds) *Crime, Criminology, and Public Policy*. London: Heinemann.

Carter, J. and G. Cole (1979) 'The use of fines in England: could the idea work here?'. *Judicature*, 63: 155–161.

Coffee, J. (1981) ' "No soul to damn: No body to kick": An unscandalized inquiry into the problem of corporate punishment'. *Michigan Law Review*, 79: 386–399.

Coffee, J. (1992) 'Paradigms lost: the blurring of the criminal and civil models – and what can be done about it'. *Yale Law Journal*, 101: 1875–1893.

Cohen, S. (1979) 'The Punitive City: Notes on the Dispersal of Social Control'. *Contemporary Crises*, 3: 339–363.

Cohen, S. (1985) *Visions of Social Control*. London: Polity Press.

Conaghan, J. and W. Mansell (1993) *The Wrongs of Tort*. London: Pluto Press.

Cross, G. (1993) *Time and Money. The Making of Consumer Culture*. London: Routledge.

de Certeau, M. (1984) *The Practice of Everyday Life*. Berkeley: University of California Press.

Deleuze, G. (1995) *Negotiations 1972–1990*. New York: Columbia University Press.

Departmental Committee (1934) *Imprisonment by Courts of Summary Jurisdiction in default of Payment of Fines and other Sums of Money*. London: His Majesty's Stationery Office (Command 4649).

Dinsdale, W. (1955) *History of Accident Insurance in Great Britain*. London: Stone and Cox.

Donaldson, Lord (2002) 'Forward' in Judicial Studies Board. *Guidelines for the Assessment of General Damages in Personal Injury Cases*. Oxford: Oxford University Press, pp. i–ii.

Dubber, M. (2002) *Victims in the War on Crime*. New York: New York University Press.

Dubber, M. and M. Kelman (2005) *American Civil Law: Cases, Materials and Comments*. New York: Foundation Press.

Duff, P. (1993) 'The prosecutor fine and social control'. *British Journal of Criminology*, 33: 481–503.

Elzinger, K. and W. Breit (1976) *The Antitrust Penalties: A Study in Law and Economics*. New Haven: Yale University Press.

Emsley, C. (1993) 'Mother, what did the police do before there were cars? The law, the police and the regulation of motor transport in England 1891–1939'. *Historical Journal*, 36: 357–381.

Ericson, R. and A. Doyle (2004) *Uncertain Business*. Toronto: Toronto University Press.

Featherstone, M. (1984) 'The body in consumer culture'. In M. Featherstone, M. Hepworth and B. Turner (eds) *The Body. Social Process and Cultural Theory*. London: Sage.

Feeley, M. and J. Simon (1992) 'The New Penology: Notes on the Emerging Strategy of Corrections and Its Implications'. *Criminology*, 30: 449–474.

Feeley, M. and J. Simon (1994) 'Actuarial Justice. The Emerging New Criminal Law'. In D. Nelken (ed.) *The Futures of Criminology*. New York: Sage.

Ferguson, A. (1995) *An Essay on the History of Human Society*. Cambridge: Cambridge University Press.

Fisse, B. (1973). 'Responsibility, prevention, and corporate crime'. *New Zealand Universities Law Review*, 5: 250–79.

Fisse, B. (1990) 'Sentencing options against corporations'. *Criminal Law Forum*, 1: 211–258.

Fogelson, R. (2001) *Downtown, its Rise and Fall 1880–1950*. London: Yale University Press.

Foucault, M. (1977) *Discipline and Punish*. London: Peregrine Books.

Foucault, M. (1984) *The History of Sexuality*, Vol 1. London: Peregrine Books.

Foucault, M. (2007) *Security, Territory, Population*. London: Palgrave MacMillan.

Fox, R. (1995) On the Spot Fines in Victoria. Melbourne: Faculty of Law, Monash University.

Fox, R. (1996) *Criminal Justice on the Spot. Infringement Penalties in Victoria*. Canberra: Australian Institute of Criminology.

Fox, R. (1999) 'Criminal sanctions at the other end' Paper presented to the 3rd National Outlook Symposium on Crime in Australia. Australian Institute of Criminology Canberra.

Frankowski, S. and E. Zielinska (1983) 'Non-custodial penal measures in European socialist countries'. *International Review of Criminal Policy*, 36: 38–46.

Freiberg, A. and P. O'Malley (1984) 'State intervention and the civil offense'. *Law and Society Review*, 18: 373–394.

Friedman, L. (1973) *A History of American Law*. New York: Simon and Schuster.

Friedman, L. and J. Ladinsky (1967) 'Social Change and the Law of Industrial Accidents'. *Columbia Law Review*, 67: 50–82.

Garland, D. (1991) *Punishment and Modern Society*. Oxford: Oxford University Press.

Garland, D. (2001) *The Culture of Control. Crime and Social order in Contemporary Society*. Oxford: Oxford University Press.

Garland, D. and P. Young (1983) Towards a social analysis of penality'. In D. Garland and P. Young (eds) *The Power to Punish. Contemporary Penality and Social Analysis*. London: Heinemann.

Garofalo, R. (1885[1968]) *Criminology*. Montclair, NJ: Patterson Smith.

Gartman, D. (1986) *Auto Slavery. The Labor Process in the American Automobile Industry 1897–1950*. London: Rutgers University Press.

Garton, S. (1982) 'Bad or mad? Developments in incarceration in NSW 1880–1920'. In Sydney Labour History Group (ed.) *What Rough Beast? The State and Social Order in Australian History*. Sydney: Allen and Unwin, pp. 89–1110.

Gillespie, R. (1981) 'Sanctioning traditional crimes with fines: A comparative analysis'. *International Journal of Comparative and Applied Criminal Justice*, 5: 195–204.

Gilmore, G. (1974) *The Death of Contract*. Columbus: The Ohio State University Press.

Gobert, J. and M. Punch (2003) *Rethinking Corporate Crime*. London: Butterworths.

Grebing, G. (1982) *The Fine in Comparative law: A Survey of 21 Countries.* Cambridge: Institute of Criminology Occasional Papers No. 9.

Gregory, C. (1951) 'Trespass to negligence to absolute liability'. *Virginia Law Review*, 37: 359–370.

Gurner, R. (1997) 'Structural sanctions: corporate sentences beyond fines'. In W. Lofquist, M. Cohen and G. Rabe (eds) *Debating Corporate Crime.* Cincinnati: Anderson Publishing, pp. 143–167.

Haggerty, K. and R. Ericson (2000) 'The surveillant assemblage'. *British Journal of Criminology*, 51: 605–622.

Harvey, D. (1989) *The Condition of Postmodernity.* Oxford: Blackwell.

Heine, G. (1999) 'Sanctions in the field of corporate criminal liability'. In A. Eser (ed.) *Criminal responsibility of Legal and Collective Entities.* Freiberg: Max Planck Institute, pp. 237–254.

Hillsman, S. (1990) 'Fines and day fines'. *Crime and Justice. A Review of Research*, 12: 50–98.

Hillsman, S., J. Sichel and B. Mahoney (1984) *Fines in Sentencing. A Study of the Use of the Fines as a Criminal Sanction.* Washington, DC: U.S. Department of Justice.

Himmelfarb, G. (1968) *Victorian Minds.* New York: Alfred Knopf.

Home Office (1988) *Road Traffic Law Review Report.* London: HMSO.

Home Office (2001) *Criminal Statistics England and Wales 2001.* London: Home Office.

Home Office (2002) *Criminal Statistics England and Wales 2002.* London: Home Office.

Horwitz, M. (1977) *The Transformation of American Law.* Harvard: Harvard University Press.

Hunt, A. (2006) 'Police and the regulation of traffic. Policing as a civilizing process?' In M. Dubber and M. Valverde (eds) *The New Police Science. The Police Power in Domestic and International Governance.* New York: Yale University Press, pp. 168–184.

Jefferson, M. (2001) 'Corporate criminal liability: The problem of sanctions'. *Journal of Criminal Law*, 65: 235–261.

Judicial Studies Board (2002) *Guidelines for the Assessment of General Damages in Personal Injury Cases.* Oxford: Oxford University Press.

Kann, M. (forthcoming) 'Limited liberty, durable patriarchy'. In M. Dubber and M. Valverde (eds) *Police and the Liberal State.* Stanford: Stanford University Press.

Keeler, J. (1994) 'Social insurance, disability injury: a retrospective view'. *University of Toronto Law Journal*, 44: 275–352.

Kercher, B. and Noone, M. (1990) *Remedies.* Sydney: Law Book Company.

King, P. (1996) 'Punishing assault: The transformation of attitudes in the English courts'. *Journal of Interdisciplinary History*, 27: 43–74.

Kirchengast, T. (2006) *The Victim in Criminal Law and Justice.* London: Macmillan.

Landes, W. and R. Posner (1994) 'The Economics of Anticipatory Adjudication'. *Journal of Legal Studies*, 223: 683–719.

Laster, K. and P. O'Malley (1996) 'Sensitive New Age Laws? The Rediscovery of Emotionality in Law'. *International Journal of the Sociology of Law*, 24: 21–40.

Law Reform Commission (New South Wales) (2003) *Sentencing Corporate Offenders (Report 102)*. Sydney: Lawlink NSW.

Law Reform Commission of Canada (1974) *Working papers 5 and 6. Restitution and Compensation. Fines*. Ottawa: Law Reform Commission of Canada.

Lebegott, S. (1993) *Pursuing Happiness. American Consumers in the Twentieth Century*. Princeton, NJ: Princeton University Press.

Levi, R. (2000) 'The mutuality of risk and community: the adjudication of community notification statutes'. *Economy and Society*, 29: 578–601.

Levitt, S. (1997) 'Incentive compatibility constraints as an explanation for the use of prison sentences instead of fines'. *International Review of Law and Economics*, 17: 179–192.

Lukes, S. and A. Scull (eds) (1983) *Durkheim and the Law*. Oxford: Oxford University Press.

Luntz, H. (1990) *Assessment of Damages for Personal Injury and Death* (Third Edition). Sydney: Butterworths.

Macaulay, S. (1985) 'An empirical view of contract'. *Wisconsin Law Review*, 465–482.

Mann, K. (1993) 'Punitive civil sanctions: The middle ground between civil and criminal law'. *Yale Law Journal*, 101: 1795–1874.

Marx. K. (1976) *Capital* (Vol 1). London: Pelican Books.

McDonald, T. and C. Moody (1992) *Day Fines in American courts. The Staten Island and Milwaukee Experiments*. Washington, DC: National Institute of Justice.

McGregor, H. (1997) *McGregor on Damages* (Sixteenth Edition). London: Sweet and Maxwell.

Melossi, D. (1981) 'Addendum'. In D. Melossi and M. Pavariani (eds) *The Prison and the Factory. Origins of the Penitentiary System*. London: MacMillan, pp. 189–196.

Melossi, D. and M. Pavariani (1981) *The Prison and the Factory. Origins of the Penitentiary System*. London: MacMillan.

Mitchell-Banks, T. (1983) *The Fine: An Enigma*. Simon Fraser University: Unpublished Masters Thesis.

Morris, C. (1931) 'Punitive damages in tort cases'. *Harvard Law Review*, 44: 1173–1194.

Morris, N. and M. Tonry (1990) *Between Prison and Probation. Intermediate Punishments in a Rational Sentencing System*. New York: Oxford University Press.

Nagel, I. and W. Swenson (1993) 'The Federal Sentencing Guidelines for corporations: their development, theoretical underpinnings and some thoughts about their future'. *Washington University Law Quarterly*, 71: 205–252.

National Commission on Reform of Federal Criminal Laws (1971) Final Report. Washington, DC.

Nolan, V. and E. Ursin (1999) 'The de-academification of tort theory'. *University of Kansas Law Review*, 48: 59–67.

O'Connell, J. and T. Bailey (1972) 'The history of payment for pain and suffering' *University of Illinois Law Forum* 1972: 82–120.

O'Connell, J. and R. Simon (1972) 'Payment for pain and suffering: Who wants what, when and why?' *University of Illinois Law Forum* 1972: 1–82.

O'Driscoll, G. (1980) 'Justice, efficiency, and the economic analysis of law: A comment on Fried'. *Journal of Legal Studies*, 9: 355–366.

Ogus, A. (1973) *The Law of Damages*. London: Butterworths.

O'Malley, P. (1981) 'From feudal honour to bourgeois reputation. Ideology, law and the rise of industrial capitalism'. *Sociology*, 15: 79–93.

O'Malley, P. (1992) 'Risk, power and crime prevention'. *Economy and Society*, 21: 252–275.

O'Malley, P. (1994) 'Neo-liberal crime control. Political agendas and the future of crime prevention in Australia'. In D. Chappell and P. Wilson (eds) *The Australian Criminal Justice System. The Mid 1990s* (4th edition). Sydney: Butterworths.

O'Malley, P. (1999). Volatile and contradictory punishment. *Theoretical Criminology*, 3: 175–196.

O'Malley, P. (2004) *Risk, Uncertainty and Government*. London: Glasshouse Press.

O'Malley, P. and D. Palmer (1996) 'Post-Keynesian policing'. *Economy and Society*, 25: 137–155.

Palmer, G. (1994) 'New Zealand's Accident Compensation Scheme. Twenty Years On'. *University of Toronto Law Journal*, 44: 223–273.

Pashukanis, E. (1978) *Law and Marxism*. London: Ink Links.

Paulus, I. (1974) *The Search for Pure Food*. London: Martin Roberston.

Plowden, W. (1971) *The Motor Car and Politics 1986–1970*. London: The Bodley Head.

Posner, R. (1979) 'Utilitarianism, economics and legal theory'. *Journal of Legal Studies*, 8: 103–140.

Posner, R. (1986) *Economic Analysis of Law*. Boston: Little Brown.

Poulantzas, N. (1978) *State, Power, Socialism*. London: NLB.

Pratt, J. (2007) *Penal Populism*. London: Routledge.

Priest, G. (1985) 'The invention of enterprise liability: a critical history of the intellectual foundations of modern tort law'. *Journal of Legal Studies*, 14: 461–527.

Priest, G. (1987) 'The current insurance crisis and modern tort law'. *The Yale Law Journal*, 96: 1521–1590.

Priest, G. (1990) 'The new legal structure of risk control' *Daedalus* 119: 207–220.

Quick, J. (1915) *The Annotated Workers Compensation Act 1914*. Melbourne: Maxwell.

Rabin, R. (1981) 'The historical development of the fault principle: a reinterpretation'. *Georgia Law Review*, 15: 925–961.

Reichman, N. (1986) 'Managing crime risks: toward an insurance based model of social control'. *Research in Law and Social Control*, 8: 151–172.

Rose, N. (1999) *Powers of Freedom: Reframing Political Thought*. Cambridge: Cambridge University Press.

Royal Commission (1978) *Royal Commission on Civil Liability and Compensation for Personal Injury* (The Pearson Report). London: HMSO.

Rusche, G and O. Kirchheimer (1939) *Punishment and Social Structure*. New York: Columbia University Press.

Schleuter, L and K. Redden (1995) *Punitive Damages* (Third Edition). Charlottesville, VA: Michie Butterworth.

Seagle, W. (1948) 'Fines'. In E. Seligman and A. Johnson (eds) *Encyclopaedia of the Social Science*. New York: MacMillan.

Sharpe, J. (1990) *Judicial Punishment in England*. London: Faber and Faber.

Shearing, C. and P. Stenning (1985) 'From Panopticon to Disneyland: The Development of Discipline'. In A. Doob and E. Greenspan (eds) *Perspectives in Criminal Law*. Toronto: Canada Law Book Co.

Sideman, J. and D. Bancroft (2004) 'Multinational cooperation with the investigation of international cartels'. International Law Office. http://www.google.com.au/search?source=ig&hl=en&rlz=&q=antitrust+fines+USA&meta=

Simmel, G. (1990) *The Philosophy of Money* (Enlarged edition). New York: Routledge.

Simon, J. (1998) 'Driving governmentality, Automobile accidents. Insurance and the challenge to social order in the inter-war years 1919–1941'. *Connecticut Insurance Law Journal*, 4: 522–588.

Simon, J. (2007) *Governing Through Crime: How the War on Crime Transformed American Democracy and Created a Culture of Fear*. New York: Oxford University Press.

Simpson, S. (2002) *Corporate Crime, Law and Social Control*. Cambridge: Cambridge University Press.

Sison, A. (2000) 'Integrated risk management and global business ethics'. *Business Ethics: A European Review*, 9: 288–295.

Spitzer, S. (1975) 'Punishment and social organization. A study of Durkheim's theory of penal evolution'. *Law and Society Review*, 9: 613–639.

Stapleton, J. (1995) 'Tort, insurance and ideology'. *Modern Law Review*, 58: 820–845.

Stevens, E. and B. Payne (2002) 'Applying deterrence theory in the context of corporate wrongdoing: Limitations on punitive damages'. *Journal of Criminal Justice*, 27: 195–207.

Stewart, P. and A. Stuhmcke (2005) *Australian principles of Tort Law*. Sydney: Cavendish.

Sugarman, D. (1985) 'Doing away with tort law'. *California Law Review*, 73: 553–599.

Thatcher, M. (1994) *The Downing Street Years*. London: Harper Collins.

Ulen, T. (1997) 'The economic case for corporate criminal sanctioning'. In W. Lofquist, M. Cohen and G. Rabe (eds) *Debating Corporate Crime*. Cincinnati: Anderson Publishing, pp. 119–141.

United States Sentencing Commission (2007) *Guidelines Manual*. http://www.ussc.gov/guidelin.htm

University of Pennsylvania Law Review (1953) 'Fines and fining—an evaluation'. *University of Pennsylvania Law Review*, 101: 1013–1030.

Weber, M. (1954) *Max Weber on Law in Economy and Society*, (ed. M. Reinhardt) Harvard: Harvard University Press.

Wells, C. (2001) *Corporations and Criminal Responsibility*. Oxford: Oxford University Press.

White, G. (2003) *Tort Law in America. An Intellectual History* (Expanded edition). Oxford: Oxford University Press.

White, P. (2002) 'The practical effects of split-recovery statutes and their validity as a tool of modern day "tort reform"'. *Drake Law Review*, 50: 593–607.

Wightman, J. (1996) *Contract: A Critical Commentary*. London: Pluto Press.

Young, P. (1989) 'Punishment, money and a sense of justice'. In P. Carlen and D. Cook (eds) *Paying for Crime*. Milton Keynes: Open University Press.

Zaloom, C. (2006) *Out of the Pits. Traders and Technology from Chicago to London*. Chicago: University of Chicago Press.

Zelizer, V. (1994) *The Social Meaning of Money*. New York: Basic Books.

Zelizer, V. (2000) 'Fine tuning the Zelizer view'. *Economy and Society*, 29: 383–89.

Zelizer, V. (2005) *The Purchase of Intimacy*. Princeton, NJ: Princeton University Press.

# Index